# Marx and Modern Economics

Most of the creations of the intellect or fancy pass away for good after a time that varies between an after-dinner hour and a generation. Some, however, do not. They suffer eclipses but they come back again, and they come back not as unrecognizable elements of a cultural inheritance, but in their individual garb and with their personal scars which people may see and touch. These we may well call the great ones – it is no disadvantage of this definition that it links greatness to vitality. Taken in this sense, this is undoubtedly the word to apply to the message of Marx ... We need not believe that a great achievement must necessarily be a source of light or faultless in either fundamental design or details ... In the case of the Marxian system, such adverse judgment or even exact disproof, by its very failure to injure fatally, only serves to bring out the power of the structure.

SCHUMPETER

# Marx and Modern Economics

Edited by David Horowitz

**MODERN READER PAPERBACKS**
NEW YORK AND LONDON

Library of Congress Catalog Card Number: 68-24053
Standard Book Number: 85345-072-2

First Modern Reader Paperback Edition 1968
Fifth Printing

Published by Monthly Review Press
62 West 14th Street, New York, N.Y. 10011

Manufactured in the United States of America

# Contents

## 4. NEO-MARXISM

# Acknowledgements

Grateful acknowledgement is made to the following journals and publishers for permission to reprint the essays in this volume.

Routledge and Kegan Paul for 'Classical Political Economy and Marx', by Maurice Dobb.

*The Review of Economic Studies* (Cambridge) for 'Marxian Economics and Modern Economic Theory', by Oskar Lange.

The *American Economic Review* and the American Economic Association for 'The Significance of Marxian Economics for Present Day Economic Theory', by Wassily Leontief.

Basil Blackwell for 'Marx and Keynes', by Joan Robinson, and 'Karl Marx and the Accumulation of Capital', by J. Steindl.

*The Journal of Political Economy* and the University of Chicago Press for 'Theories of Effective Demand and Employment', by L. R. Klein.

Rutgers University Press for 'Keynes v. Marx': The Methodology of Aggregates', by S. Tsuru.

*Science and Society* for "*Das Kapital* for the Modern Man", by Martin Bronfenbrenner.

*Kyklos* for 'Technical Change and Marxian Economics', by Mark Blaug, and 'Social Imbalance and the Marxian System', by James F. Becker.

PWN – Polish Scientific Publishers for 'Economics of Two Worlds', by Paul Baran and Paul Sweezy.

Monthly Review Press for 'A Crucial Difference between Capitalism and Socialism', by Paul Sweezy, and 'The Concept of the Economic Surplus', by Paul Baran.

I would also like to thank Mark Blaug, Anthony Brewer, Daniel Coleman, Alfred Evenitsky and Paul Sweezy for their help in the preparation of this volume.

# List of Contributors

PAUL BARAN was Professor of Economics at Stanford University and is the author of *The Policital Economy of Growth* and co-author of *Monopoly Capital* with Paul Sweezy.

JAMES F. BECKER is Associate Professor of Economics at New York University.

MARK BLAUG is a Senior Lecturer and Head of the Research Unit in the Economics of Education at the University of London Institute of Education. He is the author of *Ricardian Economics* and *Economic Theory in Retrospect*.

MARTIN BRONFENBRENNER is Professor of Economics at the Carnegie Institute of Technology.

MAURICE DOBB is Reader in Economics at Cambridge University and the author of *Political Economy and Capitalism, Studies in the Development of Capitalism, On Economic Theory and Socialism, Economic Growth and Planning* and other works.

L. R. KLEIN is Professor of Economics, Wharton School of Business, University of Pennsylvania and is the author of *The Keynesian Revolution, Economic Fluctuations in the US 1921–41, A Textbook of Econometrics* and co-author of *An Econometric Model of the United States, 1929–53*.

OSKAR LANGE was Chairman of the Economic Council of Poland, and a member of the Polish Academy of Sciences. He is author of *Price Flexibility and Employment, The Working Principles of the Soviet Economy, Introduction to Econometrics, Political Economy*, Vol. 1, *Wholes and Parts: A General Theory of System Behaviour*, and other works. He is co-author of *On the Economic Theory of Socialism*.

WASSILY LOENTIEF is Littauer Professor of Economics at Harvard University. He is the author of *Studies in the Structure of the American Economy*.

JOAN ROBINSON is Professor of Economics at Cambridge University and the author of *The Economics of Imperfect Competition*, *An Essay on Marxian Economics*, *The Accumulation of Capital*, *Essays in the Theory of Economic Growth*, and other works.

J. STEINDL is the author of *Big Business and Small*, *Maturity and Stagnation in the American Economy*, and *Random Processes and the Growth of Firms*.

PAUL SWEEZY is co-editor of *Monthly Review* and author of *Monopoly and Competition in the English Coal Trade, 1550–1850* *The Theory of Capitalist Development*, and *The Present as History*. He is co-author of *Cuba: Anatomy of a Revolution*, and *Monopoly Capital*.

S. TSURU is Professor of Economics, and Director, Institute of Economic Research, Hitotsubashi University, Japan, author of *National Income and Economic Reproduction*, *Postwar Inflation in Japan*, and editor of *Has Capitalism Changed?*

# Introduction

IN THE hundred years since the publication of *Das Kapital*, few generations can have been as well situated as the present one to appreciate Marx's real place in the history of economic thought. What has only recently become generally apparent in professional academic circles, and what the present volume of essays makes amply clear, is that Marx was a major figure in the economic tradition in precisely the sense in which Smith, Ricardo and Marshall were all major figures. Such recognition of Marx's imposing stature in the field of economic theory has not always been forthcoming, however. Indeed, in the heyday of neo-classical (Marshallian) economics, there was 'an impassable gulf' dividing the Marxian from the orthodox schools, and Marx himself was generally treated in academic circles 'with contemptuous silence, broken only by an occasional mocking footnote'.[1]

This attitude towards Marx, however, did not survive the 'Keynesian revolution', and the attendant changes in orthodox theory induced by the Great Depression. Indeed, the striking similarities between the Keynesian and Marxian analyses of the economic *modus operandi* of the system (see the essays by Joan Robinson, Fan-Hung and L. R. Klein in the present volume) compelled the more candid academic economists to thoroughly revise their former patronizing appraisals of Marx.

In fact, as the Polish Marxist Oskar Lange had pointed out just prior to the publication of Keynes' *General Theory*, in so far as a great gap existed between orthodox and Marxian economics, it stemmed mainly from the fact that the two theories belonged to different economic 'ranges' (see Lange's essay in the present volume). The one concentrated on questions of micro-economics and the general theory of static equilibrium; the other was primarily a macro-dynamic theory of specifically capitalist development. When the post-Keynesian shift took place in

[1] Joan Robinson, *An Essay on Marxian Economics*, Macmillan, 1942, p. v.

orthodox economics, first to macro-static concerns, and then to the macro-dynamic questions of economic development and growth, Lange's observation was confirmed in a striking way. For it soon became apparent that wherever orthodox and Marxian economists confronted similar *economic* questions, they '[did] not really differ in results'.[1]

Orthodox economists studying the problems of macro-economic fluctuations and trends, in the post-Keynes period, moreover, were no longer in a position to ignore their nineteenth-century predecessors. Accordingly, a revival of interest took place in what Professor Baumol has called the 'magnificent dynamics' of classical political economy, which necessarily included the dynamics of Marx. The extent to which Marx was soon discovered to have been a precursor of modern orthodox growth theory, may be suggested by the following passage from a recent textbook on the Keynesian theory of economic development: '[The] Marxian theory of capitalist development', writes the author, Professor Kurihara, 'anticipates many modern long-run theories, namely, the stagnation theories of Keynes and Hansen, the dynamic theories of Harrod and Domar, and "cyclical growth" theories of Schumpeter, Kalecki, Kaldor, and Goodwin, and Mrs Joan Robinson's theory of structural under-employment.'[2] Indeed, Professor L. R. Klein (in the essay reprinted in this volume) has gone so far as to describe Marx's theory as 'probably the origin of macro-economics'.

In the light of Marx's anticipation of later growth theories, it is not surprising that his disciples should have been able to develop, albeit incompletely, a dynamic economics well in advance of their orthodox rivals. In the words of Professor Domar, one of the pioneers of orthodox growth theory, 'Of all the several schools of economics the Marxists have, I think, come closest to developing a substantial theory of economic growth, and they might have succeeded had they given less time and effort to defending their master's virtue.'[3]

[1] M. Blaug, *Economic Theory in Retrospect*, 1962, p. 246.

[2] K. K. Kurihara. *The Keynesian Theory of Economic Development*, 1959, pp. 17–18.

[3] *Essays in Economic Growth*, OUP, 1957, p. 17. The essay in which this statement appears was written in 1951.

The heroic period of Marxist growth theory occurred in the Soviet Union in the middle twenties. A recent chronicler of the Soviet debates on the question of industrialization, concludes that both, the problems raised and answers given anticipate to an astonishing degree the work done in the same field at a much higher level of sophistication, within a different conceptual framework, by economists outside the Soviet orbit during the last two decades'.[1] (The chief theorists and participants in the debate all perished subsequently in Stalin's purges.)

An estimate of Marx's relation to the modern theory of business cycles very similar to that of his relation to modern growth theory was given by the late Joseph Schumpeter, whose own two-volume *Business Cycles* is generally recognized as a monumental work in the field: in Marx, writes Schumpeter, 'we find practically all the elements that ever entered into any serious analysis of business cycles, and on the whole very little error. Moreover, it must not be forgotten that the mere perception of the existence of cyclical movements was a great achievement at the time.'[2]

However, while it is certainly true that with the 'Keynesian revolution', the Marxian and at least some of the orthodox schools of economics came to occupy much of the same ground, and in consequence to yield similar results when facing similar problems, it is by no means the case that the range of problems considered by each of them, ceased to reflect serious differences in approach between them. In other words, despite the closing of the gap which attended the 'Keynesian revolution', it is by no means the case, that the distinction between the Marxian and orthodox viewpoints in the field of economic theory ceased to have any meaning.

The nature of this distinction, moreover, is still that outlined by Marx, himself, with respect to the similarly closely related orthodox tradition of his own day. Perhaps the best exposition of it is to be found in a generally neglected introduction which Marx wrote (and which is reprinted in this volume) to his uncompleted *Critique of Political Economy*, of which the four

[1] Alexander Erlich, *The Soviet Industrialization Debate, 1924–1928*, Harvard: 1960.
[2] Schumpeter, *Capitalism, Socialism and Democracy*, 1942, p. 40.

volumes of *Capital* were to be but the first part. In this introduction, Marx noted that while economic categories possess characteristics which are general and therefore applicable to common types of human activity in all historical epochs, they also have characteristics which are historically specific and socially conditioned. From the point of view of a theory of development, it is these characteristics that provide the key to the operation of the economic mechanism in an historically given social formation.

The error committed by orthodox economists, according to Marx, lies in not being aware of the socially conditioned character of general economic categories and relationships, and hence in taking the given social arrangement as natural, harmonious and eternal. Or, rather, it is precisely because orthodox economists desire to see the present social arrangement as natural and eternal, that they abstract from the historically specific character of economic categories and relationships and treat only their universal characteristics. 'But', writes Marx, 'political economy is not technology': its subject matter is, rather, the social determination of economic categories and relationships and their development.[1]

Another way of formulating this distinction is to say that Marxist and non-Marxist economists disagree as to the scope of economics, i.e., the level of abstraction appropriate to economic theory.[2] For the orthodox economist takes as given, precisely that institutional data which, in Professor Lange's words, is 'the very corner-stone of [the Marxian] analysis' (see his essay in this volume). Marx begins his analysis with the division of capitalist society into owners of means of production and subsistence and propertyless wage-labourers, i.e. with the existence of a *class monopoly* of the conditions of labour and of life itself, a fact which impinges on all major economic relationships, and shapes the general development of the capitalist system (see the essays by Lange and Dobb in the present volume).

[1] This distinction is an important theme of Oskar Lange's *Political Economy, Volume One*, Pergamon, 1963.

[2] Cf. Blaug, *op. cit.*, Sweezy; *The Theory of Capitalist Development*, Monthly Reveiw (NY) and Dobson (London), 1962, pp. 3–8 and Dobb, 'Some Tendencies in Modern Economic Theory' in *Political Economy and Capitalism*, 1937.

This placing of a primary sociological datum at the centre of his analysis is certainly an important part of what has led some to speak of Marx's 'sense of reality' as being stronger than that of orthodox economists, who tend to abstract their analyses from the real conditions of existence in capitalist society.[1] It is certainly, therefore, an important part of the impressive durability of his vision. But, whether one ascribes this sense of reality to a methodological approach or to greater 'empirical knowledge', it remains undeniable, in the light of the historical data, that Marx was, in Professor Leontief's formulation, 'the great character reader of the capitalist system' (see his essay in this volume).

Of course, as need hardly be pointed out, many of the important features of capitalism have changed radically since Marx's day, particularly the role of government in the economic process, and less recently, the predominance of monopoly forms in the market. Moreover, some of the key tendencies of the system postulated by Marx, such as a rising organic composition of capital (underpinning the general law of capitalist accumulation and the tendency of the rate of profit to fall) have failed to materialize, so that from both angles Marx's analytic structure requires significant modification if it is to maintain its relevance to a rapidly evolving system (e.g. see the essays by Blaug, Bronfenbrenner and Steindl in the present volume).

However, the essential characteristic of the system in the

[1] Robinson, op. cit., p. 2. The comment occurs in connection with a discussion of the theory of wages, the orthodox theory equating the wage with the *marginal disutility of labour*, a concept 'which has its origin in the picture of a peasant farmer leaning on his hoe in the evening and deciding whether the extra product of another hour's work will repay the extra backache', whereas in the modern labour market 'the individual worker has no opportunity to decide anything except whether it is better to work or to starve'. Professor Robinson continues: 'the orthodox economists have been much preoccupied with elegant elaborations of minor problems, which distract the attention of their pupils from the uncongenial realities of the modern world, and the development of abstract argument has run far ahead of any possibility of empirical verification. Marx's intellectual tools are far cruder, but his sense of reality is far stronger, and his argument towers above their intricate constructions in rough and gloomy grandeur.'

Marxian vision – that its ends are dominated by the needs of capital rather than by social needs – has, if anything, become more apparent with increasing material wealth, i.e. with the increasing power of the productive framework alongside the increasing poverty of its human content. Contemporary capitalism, like that of Marx's original model, remains a system dominated by the drive to accumulate wealth in its abstract money form, a feature which it shares, significantly, with Keynes' 'monetary economy'[1]: 'production is only production for *capital* and not vice versa, the means of production ... mere means for a constant expansion of the living process of the society of producers.'[2] The means (the expansion of capital wealth) dominate the ends (the expansion of real wealth),[3] so that just 'as in religion man is governed by the products of his own brain, so in capitalistic production, he is governed by the products of his own hand'.[4] This domination of society and its real needs, by the needs of the capitalist market, has been well expressed by a contemporary British Marxist:

> How many business men resolutely decide that they must leave schools and hospitals to rot, and press on with doubling their TV commercials and lacquering their reception rooms with the money saved? Do any at all? On the contrary, how many mightn't even feel a stealthy susurrus of dismay if they learnt that this was the end outcome of their harmless, familiar routines? ... What finally defines the whole system is that it utterly expunges men from the place of its essential working. These decisions are not taken in the board room or the bank manager's suite or even the exclusive club or the pleasure yacht. They are taken *nowhere*. They are *not taken*,

[1] 'Unemployment develops ... because people want the moon;— men cannot be employed when the object of desire (i.e. money) is something which cannot be produced and the demand for which cannot be readily choked off.' Keynes, *The General Theory*, p. 235, cf. D. Dillard, 'The Theory of a Monetary Economy' in Kurihara (ed.), *Post-Keynesian Economics* NY and London: 1954 and 1955.

[2] *Capital*, Vol. III, FLPH ed., 1962, p. 245.

[3] The same point is made with the same distinction, albeit between real and 'paper' values in D. Bazelon; *The Paper Economy* 1963.

[4] *Capital*, Vol. I, p. 618.

they are not decisions: fatalities. Nobody calculates them and enacts them, they happen unmeant.[1]

Moreover, as Baran and Sweezy point out in their essay in the present volume, this basic irrationality of capitalism applies not only to the composition of output, but to its volume as well, and therefore to the whole fundamental question of the system's adjustment to abundance, and the attempt to construct a humane post-industrial social order (see also Sweezy's essay in this volume).

In addition to being the 'great character reader' of the capitalist system, however, Marx was also the great prophet of its doom, and it is in this and related features of his analysis, that it becomes possible to see why a gulf should still separate a 'Marxian' from an 'orthodox' analytic school. For whether the prophecy is regarded as a deterministic foreshadowing, or simply a revolutionary call,[2] whether the Marxian tendencies are regarded as being flatly falsified by subsequent history or merely counteracted, the fact remains that to base an analysis of capitalism and capitalist development on the fundamental institutional (class) relations of capitalist production, and to lay bare its glaring irrationalities in the Marxian manner, is to call into question the very existence of the social system, and to pose, albeit even implicitly, a 'Marxian' socialist alternative. This is something, however, that orthodox economists are not, by nature, ready to do. Thus, while Professor Robinson concluded her path-breaking attempt to reconcile the Keynesian and Marxian schools with the thought that 'if there is any hope of progress in economics at all, it must be in using academic methods to solve the problems posed by Marx', it is the Marxists, alone, who have been ready to take up her challenge.[3]

[1] Perry Anderson; 'Sweden: a study in Social Democracy', *New Left Review*, No. 8.

[2] Both Marx and Engels seem to have rejected a deterministic reading of the famous, deterministic-sounding passage on the 'Historical Tendency of Capitalist Accumulation'. See Engels, *Anti-Duhring*, Part One, Ch. 13, and Marx, *Selected Correspondence*, p. 376.

[3] E.g., see Paul Baran and Paul Sweezy; *Monopoly Capital; An Essay On the American Economic and Social Order*, Monthly Review, 1966.

# 1. Marx and the Classics

# Introduction to the Critique of Political Economy

*Karl Marx*

## I. PRODUCTION IN GENERAL

THE subject of our discussion is first of all *material* production by individuals as determined by society, which naturally constitutes the starting point. The individual and isolated hunter or fisher

[1] This introduction was first published in the *Neue Zeit* of March 7, 14 and 21, 1903, by Karl Kautsky, with the following explanation:

'This article has been found among the posthumous papers of Karl Marx. It is a fragmentary sketch of a treatise that was to have served as an introduction to his main work, which he had been writing for many years and whose outline was clearly formed in his mind. The manuscript is dated August 23, 1857. . . . As the idea is very often indicated only in fragmentary sentences, I have taken the liberty of introducing here and there changes in style, insertions of words, etc. . . . A mere reprint of the original would have made it unintelligible. . . . Not all the words in the manuscript are legible. . . .

'Wherever there could be no doubt as to the necessity of corrections, I did so without indicating them in the text; in other cases I put all insertions in brackets. Wherever I am not certain as to whether I have deciphered a word correctly, I have put an interrogation point after it; other changes are specially noted. In all other respects this is an exact reprint of the original, whose fragmentary and incomplete passages serve to remind us only too painfully of the many treasures of thought which went down to the grave with Marx, treasures which would have sufficed for generations if Marx had not so anxiously avoided giving to the world any of his ideas until he had tested them repeatedly from every conceivable point of view and had given them a wording that would be incontrovertible. In spite of its fragmentary character it opens before us a wealth of new points of view.'

Originally appeared as an appendix to *A Contribution to the Critique of Political Economy*: Chicago: Kerr & Co., 1904. A final, extremely fragmentary section has been omitted from the present version.

who forms the starting point with Smith and Ricardo, belongs to the insipid illusions of the eighteenth century. They are Robinsonades which do not by any means represent, as students of the history of civilization imagine, a reaction against over-refinement and a return to a misunderstood natural life. They are no more based on such a naturalism than is Rousseau's 'contrat social', which makes naturally independent individuals come in contact and have mutual intercourse by contract. They are the fiction and only the aesthetic fiction of the small and great Robinsonades. They are, moreover, the anticipation of 'bourgeois society', which had been in course of development since the sixteenth century and made gigantic strides towards maturity in the eighteenth. In this society of free competition the individual appears free from the bonds of nature, etc., which in former epochs of history made him a part of a definite, limited human conglomeration. To the prophets of the eighteenth century, on whose shoulders Smith and Ricardo are still standing, this eighteenth-century individual, constituting the joint product of the dissolution of the feudal form of society and of the new forces of production which had developed since the sixteenth century, appears as an ideal whose existence belongs to the past; not as a result of history, but as its starting point.

Since that individual appeared to be in conformity with nature and [corresponded] to their conception of human nature, [he was regarded] not as a product of history, but of nature. This illusion has been characteristic of every new epoch in the past. Steuart, who, as an aristocrat, stood more firmly on historical ground, contrary to the spirit of the eighteenth century, escaped this simplicity of view. The further back we go into history, the more the individual and, therefore, the producing individual seems to depend on and constitute a part of a larger whole: at first it is, quite naturally, the family and the clan, which is but an enlarged family; later on, it is the community growing up in its different forms out of the clash and the amalgamation of clans. It is but in the eighteenth century, in 'bourgeois society', that the different forms of social union confront the individual as a mere means to his private ends, as an outward necessity. But the period in which this view of the isolated individual be-comes prevalent, is the very one in which the interrelations of society (general from this point of view) have reached the highest state of development. Man is in the most literal sense of the word a *zoon politikon*, not only a social animal, but an animal which can develop into an individual only in society. Production by isolated individuals outside of society – something which might happen as an exception to a civilized man who by accident got into the wilderness and already dynamically possessed within himself the forces of society – is as great an absurdity as the idea of the development of language without individuals living together and talking to one another. We need not dwell on this any longer. It would not be necessary to touch upon this point at all, were not the vagary which had its justification and sense with the people of the eighteenth century transplanted in all earnest into the field of political economy by Bastiat, Carey, Proudhon and others. Proudhon and others naturally find it very pleasant, when they do not know the historical origin of a certain economic phenomenon, to give it a quasi historico-philosophical explanation by going into mythology. Adam or Prometheus hit upon the scheme cut and dried, whereupon it was adopted, etc. Nothing is more tediously dry than the dreaming *locus communis*.

Whenever we speak, therefore, of production, we always have in mind production at a certain stage of social development, or production by social individuals. Hence, it might seem that in order to speak of production at all, we must either trace the historical process of development through its various phases, or declare at the outset that we are dealing with a certain historical period, as, for example, with modern capitalistic production which, as a matter of fact, constitutes the subject proper of this work. But all stages of production have certain landmarks in common, common purposes. *Production in general* is an abstraction, but it is a rational abstraction, in so far as it singles out and fixes the common features, thereby saving us repetition. Yet these general or common features discovered by comparison constitute something very complex, whose constituent elements have different destinations. Some of these elements belong to all epochs, others are common to a few. Some of them are common to the most modern as well as to the most ancient epochs. No production is conceivable without them; but while even the most completely developed languages have laws and conditions in common with the least developed ones, what is characteristic of their development are the points of departure from the general and common. The conditions which generally govern production must be differentiated in order that the essential points of difference be not lost sight of in view of the general uniformity which is due to the fact that the subject, mankind, and the object, nature, remain the same. The failure to remember this one fact is the source of all the wisdom of modern economists who are trying to prove the eternal nature and harmony of existing social conditions. Thus they say, for example, that no production is possible without some instrument of production, let that instrument be only the hand; that none is possible without past accumulated labour, even if that labour consist of mere skill which has been accumulated and concentrated in the hand of the savage by repeated exercise. Capital is, among other things, also an instrument of production, also past impersonal labour. Hence capital is a universal, eternal natural phenomenon; which is true if we disregard the specific properties which turn an 'instrument of production' and 'stored up labour' into capital. The entire history of production appears to a man like Carey, for example, as a malicious perversion on the part of governments.

If there is no production in general, there is also no general production. Production is always some special branch of production or an aggregate, as, for example, agriculture, stock raising, manufactures, etc. But political economy is not technology. The connection between the general destinations of production at a given stage of social development and the particular forms of production, is to be developed elsewhere (later on).

Finally, production is not only of a special kind. It is always a certain body politic, a social personality that is engaged on a larger or smaller aggregate of branches of production. The connection between the real process and its scientific presentation also falls outside of the scope of this treatise. [We must thus distinguish between] production in general, special branches of production and production as a whole.

It is the fashion with economists to open their works with a general introduction, which is entitled 'production' (see, for example, John Stuart Mill) and deals with the general 'requisites of production'.

This general introductory part treats or is supposed to treat:

1. Of the conditions without which production is impossible, i.e., of the most essential conditions of production. As a matter of fact, however, it dwindles down, as we shall see, to a few very simple definitions, which flatten out into shallow tautologies;

2. Of conditions which further production more or less, as, for example Adam Smith's [discussion of] a progressive and stagnant state of society.

In order to give scientific value to what serves with him as a mere summary, it would be necessary to study the *degree of productivity* by periods in the development of individual nations; such a study falls outside of the scope of the present subject, and in so far as it does belong here is to be brought out in connection with the discussion of competition, accumulation, etc. The commonly accepted view of the matter gives a general answer to the effect that an industrial nation is at the height of its production at the moment when it reaches its historical climax in all respects. Or, that certain races, climates, natural conditions, such as distance from the sea, fertility of the soil, etc., are more favourable to production than others. That again comes down to the tautology that the facility of creating wealth depends on the extent to which its elements are present both subjectively and objectively. As a matter of fact a nation is at its industrial height so long as its main object is not gain, but the process of gaining. In that respect the Yankees stand above the English.

But all that is not what the economists are really after in the general introductory part. Their object is rather to represent production in contradistinction to distribution – see Mill, for example – as subject to eternal laws independent of history, and then to substitute bourgeois relations, in an underhand way, as immutable natural laws of society *in abstracto*. This is the more or less conscious aim of the entire proceeding. On the contrary, when it comes to distribution, mankind is supposed to have indulged in all sorts of arbitrary action. Quite apart from the fact that they violently break the ties which bind production and distribution together, so much must be clear from the outset: that, no matter how greatly the systems of distribution may vary at different stages of society, it should be possible here, as in the case of production, to discover the common features and to confound and eliminate all historical differences in formulating *general human* laws. For example, the slave, the serf, the wage-worker – all receive a quantity of food, which enables them to exist as slave, serf, and wage-worker. The conqueror, the official, the landlord, the monk, or the levite, who respectively live on tribute, taxes, rent, alms and the tithe – all receive [a part] of the social product which is determined by laws different from those which determine the part received by the slave, etc. The two main points which all economists place under this head, are: first, property; second, the protection of the latter by the administration of justice, police, etc. The objections to these two points can be stated very briefly.

1. All production is appropriation of nature by the individual within and through a definite form of society. In that sense it is a tautology to say that property (appropriation) is a condition of production. But it becomes ridiculous, when from that one jumps at once to a definite form of property, e.g. private property (which implies, besides, as a prerequisite the existence of an opposite form, viz. absence of property). History points rather to common property (e.g. among the Hindus, Slavs, ancient Celts, etc.) as the primitive form, which still plays an important part at a much later period as communal property. The question as to whether wealth grows more rapidly under this or that form of property, is not even raised here as yet. But that there can be no such a thing as production, nor, consequently, society, where property does not exist in any form, is a tautology. Appropriation which does not appropriate is a *contradictio in subjecto*.

2. Protection of property, etc. Reduced to their real meaning, these commonplaces express more than what their preachers know, namely, that every form of production creates its own legal relations, forms of government, etc. The crudity and the short-comings of the conception lie in the tendency to see but an accidental reflective connection in what constitutes an organic union. The bourgeois economists have a vague notion that it is better to carry on production under the modern police, than it was, for example, under club law. They forget that club law is also law, and that the right of the stronger continues to exist in other forms even under their 'government of law'.

When the social conditions corresponding to a certain stage of production are in a state of formation or disappearance, disturbances of production naturally arise, although differing in extent and effect.

To sum up: all the stages of production have certain destinations in common, which we generalize in thought; but the so-called general conditions of all production are nothing but abstract conceptions which do not go to make up any real stage in the history of production.

## 2. THE GENERAL RELATION OF PRODUCTION TO DISTRIBUTION, EXCHANGE, AND CONSUMPTION

Before going into a further analysis of production, it is necessary to look at the various divisions which economists put side by side with it. The most shallow conception is as follows: By production, the members of society appropriate (produce and shape) the products of nature to human wants; distribution determines the proportion in which the individual participates in this production; exchange brings him the particular products into which he wishes to turn the quantity secured by him through distribution; finally, through consumption the products become objects of use and enjoyment, of individual appropriation. Production yields goods adopted to our needs; distribution distributes them according to social laws; exchange distributes further what has already been distributed, according to individual wants; finally, in consumption the product drops out of the social movement, becoming the direct object of the individual want which it serves and satisfies in use. Production thus appears as the starting point; consumption as the final end; and distribution and exchange as the middle; the latter has a double aspect, distribution being defined as a process carried on by society, while exchange, as one proceeding from the individual. In production the person is embodied in things, in [consumption[1]] things are embodied in persons; in distribution, society assumes the part of go-between of production and consumption in the form of generally prevailing rules; in exchange this is accomplished by the accidental make-up of the individual.

Distribution determines what proportion (quantity) of the products the individual is to receive; exchange determines the

[1] The original reads 'person'.

products in which the individual desires to receive his share allotted to him by distribution.

Production, distribution, exchange, and consumption thus form a perfect connection, production standing for the general, distribution and exchange for the special, and consumption for the individual, in which all are joined together. To be sure this is a connection, but it does not go very deep. Production is determined [according to the economists] by universal natural laws, while distribution depends on social chance: distribution can, therefore, have a more or less stimulating effect on production: exchange lies between the two as a formal (?) social movement, and the final act of consumption which is considered not only as a final purpose, but also as a final aim, falls, properly outside of the scope of economics, except in so far as it reacts on the starting point and causes the entire process to begin all over again.

The opponents of the economists – whether economists themselves or not – who reproach them with tearing apart, like barbarians, what is an organic whole, either stand on common ground with them or are *below* them. Nothing is more common than the charge that the economists have been considering production as an end in itself, too much to the exclusion of everything else. The same has been said with regard to distribution. This accusation is itself based on the economic conception that distribution exists side by side with production as a self-contained, independent sphere. Or [they are accused] that the various factors are not treated by them in their connection as a whole. As though it were the text books that impress this separation upon life and not life upon the text books; and the subject at issue were a dialectic balancing of conceptions and not an analysis of real conditions.

(*a*) *Production is at the same time also consumption.* Twofold consumption, subjective and objective. The individual who develops his faculties in production, is also expending them, consuming them in the act of production, just as procreation is in its way a consumption of vital powers. In the second place, production is consumption of means of production which are used and used up and partly (as for example in burning) reduced to their natural elements. The same is true of the consumption of raw materials which do not remain in their natural form and state, being greatly absorbed in the process. The act of production is, therefore, in all its aspects an act of consumption as well. But this is admitted by economists. Production as directly identical with consumption, consumption as directly coincident with production, they call productive consumption. This identity of production and consumption finds its expression in Spinoza's proposition, *Determinatio est negatio*. But this definition of productive consumption is resorted to just for the purpose of distinguishing between consumption as identical with production and consumption proper, which is defined as its destructive counterpart. Let us then consider consumption proper.

Consumption is directly also production, just as in nature the consumption of the elements and of chemical matter constitutes production of plants. It is clear that in nutrition, for example, which is but one form of consumption, man produces his own body; but it is equally true of every kind of consumption, which goes to produce the human being in one way or another. [It is] consumptive production. But, say the economists, this production which is identical with consumption, is a second production resulting from the destruction of the product of the first. In the first, the producer transforms himself into things; in the second, things are transformed into human beings. Consequently, this consumptive production – although constituting a direct unity of production and consumption – differs essentially from production proper. The direct unity in which production coincides with consumption and consumption with production, does not interfere with their direct duality.

Production is thus at the same time consumption, and consumption is at the same time production. Each is directly its own counterpart. But at the same time an intermediary movement goes on between the two. Production furthers consumption by creating material for the latter which otherwise would lack its object. But consumption in its turn furthers production, by providing for the products the individual for whom they are products. The product receives its last finishing touches in consumption. A railroad on which no one rides, which is, consequently not used up, not consumed, is but a potential railroad, and not a real one. Without production, no consumption; but, on the other hand, without consumption, no production; since production would then be without a purpose. Consumption produces production in two ways.

In the first place, in that the product first becomes a real product in consumption; e.g. a garment becomes a real garment only through the act of being worn; a dwelling which is not inhabited, is really no dwelling; consequently, a product as distinguished from a mere natural object, proves to be such, first *becomes* a product in consumption. Consumption gives the product the finishing touch by annihilating it, since a product is the [result] of production not only as the material embodiment of activity, but also as a mere object for the active subject.

In the second place, consumption produces production by creating the necessity for new production, i.e. by providing the ideal, inward, impelling cause which constitutes the prerequisite of production. Consumption furnishes the impulse for production as well as its object, which plays in production the part of its guiding aim. It is clear that while production furnishes the material object of consumption, consumption provides the ideal object of production, as its image, its want, its impulse and its purpose. It furnishes the object of production in its subjective form. No wants, no production. But consumption reproduces the want.

In its turn, production

First, furnishes consumption[1] with its material, its object. Consumption without an object is no consumption, hence production works in this direction by producing consumption.

Second. But it is not only the object that production provides for consumption. It gives consumption its definite outline, its character, its finish. Just as consumption gives the product its finishing touch as a product, production puts the finishing touch on consumption. For the object is not simply an object in general, but a definite object, which is consumed in a certain definite manner prescribed in its turn by production. Hunger is hunger; but the hunger that is satisfied with cooked meat eaten with fork and knife is a different kind of hunger from the one that devours raw meat with the aid of hands, nails, and teeth. Not only the object of consumption, but also the manner of consumption is produced by production; that is to say, consumption is created by production not only objectively, but also subjectively. Production thus creates the consumers.

[1] The manuscript reads 'production'.

Third. Production not only supplies the want with material, but supplies the material with a want. When consumption emerges from its first stage of natural crudeness and directness – and its continuation in that state would in itself be the result of a production still remaining in a state of natural crudeness – it is itself furthered by its object as a moving spring. The want of it which consumption experiences is created by its appreciation of the product. The object of art, as well as any other product, creates an artistic and beauty-enjoying public. Production thus produces not only an object for the individual, but also an individual for the object.

Production thus produces consumption: first, by furnishing the latter with material; second, by determining the manner of consumption; third, by creating in consumers a want for its products as objects of consumption. It thus produces the object, the manner, and the moving spring of consumption. In the same manner, consumption [creates] the *disposition* of the producer by setting (?) him up as an aim and by stimulating wants. The identity of consumption and production thus appears to be a threefold one.

First, direct identity: production is consumption; consumption is production. Consumptive production. Productive consumption. Economists call both productive consumption, but make one distinction by calling the former reproduction, and the latter productive consumption. All inquiries into the former deal with productive and unproductive labour; those into the latter treat of productive and unproductive consumption.

Second. Each appears as the means of the other and as being brought about by the other, which is expressed as their mutual interdependence; a relation, by virtue of which they appear as mutually connected and indispensable, yet remaining outside of each other.

Production creates the material as the outward object of consumption; consumption creates the want as the inward object, the purpose of production. Without production, no consumption; without consumption, no production; this maxim figures (?) in political economy in many forms.

Third. Production is not only directly consumption and consumption directly production; nor is production merely a means of consumption and consumption the purpose of production.

In other words, not only does each furnish the other with its object; production, the material object of consumption; consumption, the ideal object of production. On the contrary, either one is not only directly the other, not (?) only a means of furthering the other, but while it is taking place, creates the other as such for itself (?). Consumption completes the act of production by giving the finishing touch to the product as such, by destroying the latter, by breaking up its independent material form; by bringing to a state of readiness, through the necessity of repetition, the disposition to produce developed in the first act of production; that is to say, it is not only the concluding act through which the product becomes a product, but also [the one] through which the producer becomes a producer. On the other hand, production produces consumption, by determining the manner of consumption, and further, by creating the incentive for consumption, the very ability to consume, in the form of want. This latter identity mentioned under point 3, is much discussed in political economy in connection with the treatment of the relations of demand and supply, of objects and wants, of natural wants and those created by society.

Hence, it is the simplest matter with a Hegelian to treat production and consumption as identical. And this has been done not only by socialist writers of fiction but even by economists, e.g. Say; the latter maintained that if we consider a nation as a whole, or mankind *in abstracto* – her production is at the same time her consumption. Storch pointed out Say's error by calling attention to the fact that a nation does not entirely consume her product, but also creates means of production, fixed capital, etc. To consider society as a single individual is moreover a false mode of speculative reasoning. With an individual, production and consumption appear as different aspects of one act. The important point to be emphasized here is that if production and consumption be considered as activities of one individual or of separate individuals, they appear at any rate as aspects of one process in which production forms the actual starting point and is, therefore, the predominating factor. Consumption, as a natural necessity, as a want, constitutes an internal factor of productive activity, but the latter is the starting point of realization and, therefore, its predominating factor, the act into which the entire process resolves itself in the end. The individual produces a certain article and turns again into himself by consuming it; but he returns as a productive and a self-reproducing individual. Consumption thus appears as a factor of production.

In society, however, the relation of the producer to his product, as soon as it is completed, is an outward one, and the return of the product to the individual depends on his relations to other individuals. He does not take immediate possession of it. Nor does the direct appropriation of the product constitute his purpose, when he produces in society. Between the producer and the product distribution steps in, which determines by social laws his share in the world of products; that is to say, distribution steps in between production and consumption.

Does distribution form an independent sphere standing side by side with and outside of production?

(b) *Production and Distribution.* In perusing the common treatises on economics one can not help being struck with the fact that everything is treated there twice; e.g. under distribution there figure rent, wages, interest, and profit; while under production we find land, labour, and capital as agents of production. As regards capital, it is at once clear that it is counted twice: first, as an agent of production; second, as a source of income; as determining factors and definite forms of distribution, interest and profit figure as such also in production, since they are forms, in which capital increases and grows, and are consequently factors of its own production. Interest and profit, as forms of distribution, imply the existence of capital as an agent of production. They are forms of distribution which have for their pre-requisite capital as an agent of production. They are also forms of reproduction of capital.

In the same manner, wages is wage-labour when considered under another head; the definite character which labour has in one case as an agent of production, appears in the other as a form of distribution. If labour were not fixed as wage-labour, its manner of participation in distribution[1] would not appear as wages, as is the case for example under slavery. Finally, rent – to take at once the most developed form of distribution – by means of which landed property receives its share of the

[1] The manuscript reads 'production'.

products, implies the existence of large landed property (properly speaking, agriculture on a large scale) as an agent of production, and not simply land, no more than wages represents simply labour. The relations and methods of distribution appear, therefore, merely as the reverse sides of the agents of production. An individual who participates in production as a wage labourer, receives his share of the products, i.e., of the results of production, in the form of wages. The subdivisions and organization of distribution are determined by the subdivisions and organization of production. Distribution is itself a product of production, not only in so far as the material goods are concerned, since only the results of production can be distributed; but also as regards its form, since the definite manner of participation in production determines the particular form of distribution, the form under which participation in distribution takes place. It is quite an illusion to place land under production, rent under distribution, etc.

Economists, like Ricardo, who are accused above all of having paid exclusive attention to production, define distribution, therefore, as the exclusive subject of political economy, because they instinctively[1] regard the forms of distribution as the clearest forms in which the agents of production find expression in a given society.

To the single individual distribution naturally appears as a law established by society determining his position in the sphere of production, within which he produces, and thus antedating production. At the outset the individual has no capital, no landed property. From his birth he is assigned to wage-labour by the social process of distribution. But this very condition of being assigned to wage-labour is the result of the existence of capital and landed property as independent agents of production.

From the point of view of society as a whole, distribution seems to antedate and to determine production in another way as well, as a pre-economic fact, so to say. A conquering people divides the land among the conquerors establishing thereby a certain division and form of landed property and determining the character of production; or, it turns the conquered people

[1] The German text reads 'instruktiv', which I take to be a misprint of 'instinktiv'. *Translator.*

into slaves and thus makes slave labour the basis of production. Or, a nation, by revolution, breaks up large estates into small parcels of land and by this new distribution imparts to production a new character. Or, legislation perpetuates land ownership in large families or distributes labour as an hereditary privilege and thus fixes it in castes.

In all of these cases, and they are all historic, it is not distribution that seems to be organized and determined by production, but on the contrary, production by distribution.

In the most shallow conception of distribution, the latter appears as a distribution of products and to that extent as further removed from and quasi-independent of production. But before distribution means distribution of products, it is first, a distribution of the means of production, and second, what is practically another wording of the same fact, it is a distribution of the members of society among the various kinds of production (the subjection of individuals to certain conditions of production). The distribution of products is manifestly a result of this distribution, which is bound up with the process of production and determines the very organization of the latter. To treat of production apart from the distribution which is comprised in it, is plainly an idle abstraction. Conversely, we know the character of the distribution of products the moment we are given the nature of that other distribution which forms originally a factor of production. Ricardo, who was concerned with the analysis of production as it is organized in modern society and who was the economist of production *par excellence*, for that very reason declares *not* production but distribution as the subject proper of modern economics. We have here another evidence of the insipidity of the economists who treat production as an eternal truth, and banish history to the domain of distribution.

What relation to production this distribution, which has a determining influence on production itself, assumes, is plainly a question which falls within the province of production. Should it be maintained that at least to the extent that production depends on a certain distribution of the instruments of production, distribution in that sense precedes production and constitutes its prerequisite; it may be replied that production has in fact its prerequisite conditions, which form factors of it. These may appear at first to have a natural origin. By the very process of production they are changed from natural to historical, and if they appear during one period as a natural prerequisite of production, they formed at other periods its historical result. Within the sphere of production itself they are undergoing a constant change. For example, the application of machinery produces a change in the distribution of the instruments of production as well as in that of products, and modern land ownership on a large scale is as much the result of modern trade and modern industry, as that of the application of the latter to agriculture.

All of these questions resolve themselves in the last instance to this: How do general historical conditions affect production and what part does it play at all in the course of history? It is evident that this question can be taken up only in connection with the discussion and analysis of production.

Yet in the trivial form in which these questions are raised above, they can be answered just as briefly. In the case of all conquests three ways lie open. The conquering people may impose its own methods of production upon the conquered (e.g. the English in Ireland in the nineteenth century, partly also in India); or, it may allow everything to remain as it was contenting itself with tribute (e.g. the Turks and the Romans); or, the two systems by mutually modifying each other may result in something new, a synthesis (which partly resulted from the Germanic conquests). In all of these conquests the method of production, be it of the conquerors, the conquered, or the one resulting from a combination of both, determines the nature of the new distribution which comes into play. Although the latter appears now as the prerequisite condition of the new period of production, it is in itself but a product of production, not of production belonging to history in general, but of production relating to a definite historical period. The Mongols with their devastations in Russia for example acted in accordance with their system of production, for which sufficient pastures on large uninhabited stretches of country are the main prerequisite. The Germanic barbarians, with whom agriculture carried on with the aid of serfs was the traditional system of production and who were accustomed to lonely life in the country, could introduce the same conditions in the Roman provinces so much easier since the concentration of landed property which had taken place there, did away completely with the older systems of agriculture. There is a prevalent tradition that in certain periods robbery constituted the only source of living. But in order to be able to plunder, there must be something to plunder, i.e. there must be production.[1] And even the method of plunder is determined by the method of production. A stock-jobbing nation,[2] for example, cannot be robbed in the same manner as a nation of shepherds.

In the case of the slave the instrument of production is robbed directly. But then the production of the country in whose interest he is robbed, must be so organized as to admit of slave labour, or (as in South America, etc.) a system of production must be introduced adapted to slavery.

Laws may perpetuate an instrument of production, e.g. land, in certain families. These laws assume an economic importance if large landed property is in harmony with the system of production prevailing in society, as is the case for example in England. In France agriculture had been carried on on a small scale in spite of the large estates, and the latter were, therefore, broken up by the Revolution. But how about the legislative attempt to perpetuate the minute subdivision of the land? In spite of these laws land ownership is concentrating again. The effect of legislation on the maintenance of a system of distribution and its resultant influence on production are to be determined elsewhere.

(c) *Exchange and Circulation.* Circulation is but a certain aspect of exchange, or it may be defined as exchange considered as a whole. Since *exchange* is an intermediary factor between production and its dependent, distribution, on the one hand, and consumption, on the other; and since the latter appears but as a

---

[1] Compare this with footnote 1, on p. 34 of *Capital*, Humboldt edition, New York:

'Truly comical is M. Bastiat, who imagines that the ancient Greeks and Romans lived by plunder alone. But when people plunder for centuries, there must always be something at hand for them to seize; the objects of plunder must be continually reproduced.' K. Kautsky.

[2] The English expression is used by Marx in his German original. *Translator.*

constituent of production, exchange is manifestly also a constituent part of production.

In the first place, it is clear that the exchange of activities and abilities which takes place in the sphere of production falls directly within the latter and constitutes one of its essential elements. In the second place, the same is true of the exchange of products, in so far as it is a means of completing a certain product, designed for immediate consumption. To that extent exchange constitutes an act included in production. Thirdly, the so-called exchange between dealers and dealers[1] is by virtue of its organization determined by production, and is itself a species of productive activity. Exchange appears to be independent of and indifferent to production only in the last stage when products are exchanged directly for consumption. But in the first place, there is no exchange without a division of labour, whether natural or as a result of historical development; secondly, private exchange implies the existence of private production; thirdly, the intensity of exchange, as well as its extent and character are determined by the degree of development and organization of production, as for example exchange between city and country, exchange in the country, in the city, etc. Exchange thus appears in all its aspects to be directly included in or determined by production.

The result we arrive at is not that production, distribution, exchange, and consumption are identical, but that they are all members of one entity, different sides of one unit. Production predominates not only over production itself in the opposite sense of that term, but over the other elements as well. With it the process constantly starts over again. That exchange and consumption can not be the predominating elements is self-evident. The same is true of distribution in the narrow sense of distribution of products; as for distribution in the sense of distribution of the agents of production, it is itself but a factor of production. A definite [form of] production thus determines the

[1] Marx evidently has in mind here a passage in Adam Smith's *Wealth of Nations* (Vol. 2, Ch. 2) in which he speaks of the circulation of a country as consisting of two distinct parts: circulation between dealers and dealers, and that between dealers and consumers. The word dealer signifies here not only a merchant or shopkeeper, but also a producer. *K. Kautsky.*

[forms of] consumption, distribution, exchange, and *also the mutual relations between these various elements*. Of course, production *in its one-sided form* is in its turn influenced by other elements; e.g. with the expansion of the market, i.e. of the sphere of exchange, production grows in volume and is subdivided to a greater extent.

With a change in distribution, production undergoes a change; as for example in the case of concentration of capital, of a change in the distribution of population in city and country, etc. Finally, the demands of consumption also influence production. A mutual interaction takes place between the various elements. Such is the case with every organic body.

### 3. THE METHOD OF POLITICAL ECONOMY

When we consider a given country from a politico-economic standpoint, we begin with its population, then analyse the latter according to its subdivision into classes, location in city, country, or by the sea, occupation in different branches of production; then we study its exports and imports, annual production and consumption, prices of commodities, etc. It seems to be the correct procedure to commence with the real and concrete aspect of conditions as they are; in the case of political economy, to commence with population which is the basis and the author of the entire productive activity of society. Yet, on closer consideration it proves to be wrong. Population is an abstraction, if we leave out for example the classes of which it consists. These classes, again, are but an empty word, unless we know what are the elements on which they are based, such as wage-labour, capital, etc. These imply, in their turn, exchange, division of labour, prices, etc. Capital, for example does not mean anything without wage-labour, value, money, price, etc. If we start out, therefore, with population, we do so with a chaotic conception of the whole, and by closer analysis we will gradually arrive at simpler ideas; thus we shall proceed from the imaginary concrete to less and less complex abstractions, until we get at the simplest conception. This once attained, we might start on our return journey until we would finally come back to population, but this time not as a chaotic notion of an integral whole, but as a rich aggregate of many conceptions and relations. The former method is the one which political economy had adopted in the past at its inception. The economists of the seventeenth century, for example always started out with the living aggregate: population, nation, state, several states, etc., but in the end they invariably arrived, by means of analysis, at certain leading, abstract general principles, such as division of labour, money, value, etc. As soon as these separate elements had been more or less established by abstract reasoning, there arose the systems of political economy which start from simple conceptions, such as labour, division of labour, demand, exchange value, and conclude with state, international exchange and world market. The latter is manifestly the scientifically correct method. The concrete is concrete, because it is a combination of many objects with different destinations, i.e. a unity of diverse elements. In our thought, it therefore appears as a process of synthesis, as a result, and not as a starting point, although it is the real starting point and, therefore, also the starting point of observation and conception. By the former method the complete conception passes into an abstract definition; by the latter, the abstract definitions lead to the reproduction of the concrete subject in the course of reasoning. Hegel fell into the error, therefore, of considering the real as the result of self-co-ordinating, self-absorbed, and spontaneously operating thought, while the method of advancing from the abstract to the concrete is but a way of thinking by which the concrete is grasped and is reproduced in our mind as a concrete. It is by no means, however, the process which itself generates the concrete. The simplest economic category, say, exchange value, implies the existence of population, population that is engaged in production under certain conditions; it also implies the existence of certain types of family, clan, or state, etc. It can have no other existence except as an abstract one-sided relation of an already given concrete and living aggregate.

As a category, however, exchange value leads an antediluvian existence. And since our philosophic consciousness is so arranged that only the image of the man that it conceives appears to it as the real man and the world as it conceives it, as the real world; it mistakes the movement of categories for the real act of production (which unfortunately (?) receives only its impetus from outside) whose result is the world; that is true – here we have, however, again a tautology – in so far as the concrete aggregate is a thought aggregate, in so far as the concrete subject of our thought is in fact a product of thought, of comprehension; not, however, in the sense of a product of a self-emanating conception which works outside of and stands above observation and imagination, but of a mental consummation of observation and imagination. The whole, as it appears in our heads as a thought-aggregate, is the product of a thinking mind which grasps the world in the only way open to it, a way which differs from the one employed by the artistic, religious, or practical mind. The concrete subject continues to lead an independent existence after it has been grasped, as it did before, outside of the head, so long as the head contemplates it only speculatively, theoretically. So that in the employment of the theoretical method [in political economy], the subject, society, must constantly be kept in mind as the premise from which we start.

But have these simple categories no independent historical or natural existence antedating the more concrete ones? *Ça dépend.* For instance, in his Philosophy of Law Hegel rightly starts out with possession, as the simplest legal relation of individuals. But there is no such thing as possession before the family or the relations of lord and serf, which are a great deal more concrete relations, have come into existence. On the other hand, one would be right in saying that there are families and clans which only *possess*, but do not *own* things. The simpler category thus appears as a relation of simple family and clan communities with respect to property. In earlier society the category appears as a simple relation of a developed organism, but the concrete substratum from which springs the relation of possession, is always implied. One can imagine an isolated savage in possession of things. But in that case possession is no legal relation. It is not true that the family came as the result of the historical evolution of possession. On the contrary, the latter always implies the existence of this 'more concrete category of law'. Yet so much may be said, that the simple categories are the expression of relations in which the less developed concrete entity may have been realized without entering into the manifold relations and bearings which are mentally expressed in the concrete category; but when the concrete entity attains fuller development it will retain the same category as a subordinate relation.

Money may exist and actually had existed in history before

capital, or banks, or wage-labour came into existence. With that in mind, it may be said that the more simple category can serve as an expression of the predominant relations of an undeveloped whole or of the subordinate relations of a more developed whole [relations] which had historically existed before the whole developed in the direction expressed in the more concrete category. In so far, the laws of abstract reasoning which ascends from the most simple to the complex, correspond to the actual process of history.

On the other hand, it may be said that there are highly developed but historically unripe forms of society in which the highest economic forms are to be found, such as co-operation, advanced division of labour, etc., and yet there is no money in existence, e.g. Peru.

In Slavic communities also, money, as well as exchange to which it owes its existence, does not appear at all or very little within the separate communities, but it appears on their boundaries in their inter-communal traffic; in general, it is erroneous to consider exchange as a constituent element originating within the community. It appears at first more in the mutual relations between different communities, than in those between the members of the same community. Furthermore, although money begins to play its part everywhere at an early stage, it plays in antiquity the part of a predominant element only in one-sidedly developed nations, viz. trading nations, and even in most cultured antiquity, in Greece and Rome, it attains its full development, which constitutes the prerequisite of modern bourgeois society, only in the period of their decay. Thus, this quite simple category attained its culmination in the past only at the most advanced stages of society. Even then it did not pervade (?) all economic relations; in Rome e.g. at the time of its highest development taxes and payments in kind remained the basis. As a matter of fact, the money system was fully developed there only so far as the army was concerned; it never came to dominate the entire system of labour.

Thus, although the simple category may have existed historically before the more concrete one, it can attain its complete internal and external development only in complex (?) forms of society, while the more concrete category has reached its full development in a less advanced form of society.

Labour is quite a simple category. The idea of labour in that sense, as labour in general, is also very old. Yet, 'labour' thus simply defined by political economy is as much a modern category, as the conditions which have given rise to this simple abstraction. The monetary system, for example defines wealth quite objectively, as a thing (?)[1] in money. Compared with this point of view, it was a great step forward, when the industrial or commercial system came to see the source of wealth not in the object but in the activity of persons, viz. in commercial and industrial labour. But even the latter was thus considered only in the limited sense of a money producing activity. The physiocratic system [marks still further progress] in that it considers a certain form of labour, viz. agriculture, as the source of wealth, and wealth itself not in the disguise of money, but as a product in general, as the general result of labour. But corresponding to the limitations of the activity, this product is still only a natural product. Agriculture is productive, land is the source of production *par excellence*. It was a tremendous advance on the part of Adam Smith to throw aside all limitations which mark wealth-producing activity and [to define it] as labour in general, neither industrial, nor commercial, nor agricultural, or one as much as the other. Along with the universal character of wealth-creating activity we have now the universal character of the object defined as wealth, viz. product in general, or labour in general, but as past incorporated labour. How difficult and great was the transition, is evident from the way Adam Smith himself falls back from time to time into the physiocratic system. Now, it might seem as though this amounted simply to finding an abstract expression for the simplest relation into which men have been mutually entering as producers from times of yore, no matter under what form of society. In one sense this is true. In another it is not.

The indifference as to the particular kind of labour implies the existence of a highly developed aggregate of different species of concrete labour, none of which is any longer the predominant one. So do the most general abstractions commonly arise only where there is the highest concrete development, where one

---

[1] Here two words in the manuscript cannot be deciphered. They look like 'ausser sich' 'outside of itself'. K. Kautsky.

feature appears to be jointly possessed by many, and to be common to all. Then it can not be thought of any longer in one particular form. On the other hand, this abstraction of labour is but the result of a concrete aggregate of different kinds of labour. The indifference to the particular kind of labour corresponds to a form of society in which individuals pass with ease from one kind of work to another, which makes it immaterial to them what particular kind of work may fall to their share. Labour has become here, not only categorically but really, a means of creating wealth in general and is no longer grown together with the individual into one particular destination. This state of affairs has found its highest development in the most modern of bourgeois societies, the United States. It is only here that the abstraction of the category 'labour', 'labour in general', labour *sans phrase*, the starting point of modern political economy, becomes realized in practice. Thus, the simplest abstraction which modern political economy sets up as its starting point, and which expresses a relation dating back to antiquity and prevalent under all forms of society, appears in this abstraction truly realized only as a category of the most modern society. It might be said that what appears in the United States as an historical product, – viz. the indifference as to the particular kind of labour – appears among the Russians for example as a natural disposition. But it makes all the difference in the world whether barbarians have a natural predisposition which makes them applicable alike to everything, or whether civilized people apply themselves to everything. And, besides, this indifference of the Russians as to the kind of work they do, corresponds to their traditional practice of remaining in the rut of a quite definite occupation until they are thrown out of it by external influences.

This example of labour strikingly shows how even the most abstract categories, in spite of their applicability to all epochs – just because of their abstract character – are by the very definiteness of the abstraction a product of historical conditions as well, and are fully applicable only to and under those conditions.

The bourgeois society is the most highly developed and most highly differentiated historical organization of production. The categories which serve as the expression of its conditions and the comprehension of its own organization enable it at the same time to gain an insight into the organization and the conditions of production which had prevailed under all the past forms of society, on the ruins and constituent elements of which it has arisen, and of which it still drags along some unsurmounted remnants, while what had formerly been mere intimation has now developed to complete significance. The anatomy of the human being is the key to the anatomy of the ape. But the intimations of a higher animal in lower ones can be understood only if the animal of the higher order is already known. The bourgeois economy furnishes a key to ancient economy, etc. This is, however, by no means true of the method of those economists who blot out all historical differences and see the bourgeois form in all forms of society. One can understand the nature of tribute, tithes, etc., after one has learned the nature of rent. But they must not be considered identical.

Since, furthermore, bourgeois society is but a form resulting from the development of antagonistic elements, some relations belonging to earlier forms of society are frequently to be found in it but in a crippled state or as a travesty of their former self, as for example communal property. While it may be said, therefore, that the categories of bourgeois economy contain what is true of all other forms of society, the statement is to be taken *cum grano salis*. They may contain these in a developed, or crippled, or caricatured form, but always essentially different. The so-called historical development amounts in the last analysis to this, that the last form considers its predecessors as stages leading up to itself and perceives them always one-sidedly, since it is very seldom and only under certain conditions that it is capable of self-criticism; of course, we do not speak here of such historical periods which appear to their own contemporaries as periods of decay. The Christian religion became capable of assisting us to an objective view of past mythologies as soon as it was ready for self-criticism to a certain extent, *dynamei* so-to-say. In the same way bourgeois political economy first came to understand the feudal, the ancient, and the oriental societies as soon as the self-criticism of the bourgeois society had commenced. So far as bourgeois political economy has not gone into the mythology of purely (?) identifying the bourgeois system with the past, its criticism of the feudal system against which it still had to wage war resembled Christian criticism of the heathen religions or Protestant criticism of Catholicism.

In the study of economic categories, as in the case of every historical and social science, it must be borne in mind that as in reality so in our mind the subject, in this case modern bourgeois society, is given and that the categories are therefore but forms of expression, manifestations of existence, and frequently but one-sided aspects of this subject, this definite society; and that, therefore, the origin of [political economy] *as a science* does not by any means date from the time to which it is referred *as such*. This is to be firmly held in mind because it has an immediate and important bearing on the matter of the subdivisions of the science.

For instance, nothing seems more natural than to start with rent, with landed property, since it is bound up with land, the source of all production and all existence, and with the first form of production in all more or less settled communities, viz. agriculture. But nothing would be more erroneous. Under all forms of society there is a certain industry which predominates over all the rest and whose condition therefore determines the rank and influence of all the rest.

It is the universal light with which all the other colours are tinged and are modified through its peculiarity. It is a special ether which determines the specific gravity of everything that appears in it.

Let us take for example pastoral nations (mere hunting and fishing tribes are not as yet at the point from which real development commences). They engage in a certain form of agriculture, sporadically. The nature of land-ownership is determined thereby. It is held in common and retains this form more or less according to the extent to which these nations hold on to traditions; such for example is land-ownership among the Slavs. Among nations whose agriculture is carried on by a settled population – the settled state constituting a great advance – where agriculture is the predominant industry, such as in ancient and feudal societies, even the manufacturing industry and its organization, as well as the forms of property which pertain to it, have more or less the characteristic features of the prevailing system of land ownership; [society] is then either entirely dependent upon agriculture, as in the case of ancient Rome, or, as in the middle ages, it imitates in its city relations the forms of organization prevailing in the country. Even capital, with the exception of pure money capital, has, in the form of the traditional working tool, the characteristics of land ownership in the Middle Ages.

The reverse is true of bourgeois society. Agriculture comes to be more and more merely a branch of industry and is completely dominated by capital. The same is true of rent. In all the forms of society in which land ownership is the prevalent form, the influence of the natural element is the predominant one. In those where capital predominates the prevailing element is the one historically created by society. Rent can not be understood without capital, nor can capital, without rent. Capital is the all dominating economic power of bourgeois society. It must form the starting point as well as the end and be developed before land-ownership is. After each has been considered separately, their mutual relation must be analysed.

It would thus be impractical and wrong to arrange the economic categories in the order in which they were the determining factors in the course of history. Their order of sequence is rather determined by the relation which they bear to one another in modern bourgeois society, and which is the exact opposite of what seems to be their natural order or the order of their historical development. What we are interested in is not the place which economic relations occupy in the historical succession of different forms of society. Still less are we interested in the order of their succession 'in idea' (*Proudhon*), which is but a hazy (?) conception of the course of history. We are interested in their organic connection within modern bourgeois society.

The sharp line of demarkation (abstract precision) which so clearly distinguished the trading nations of antiquity, such as the Phoenicians and the Carthagenians, was due to that very predominance of agriculture. Capital as trading or money capital appears in that abstraction, where capital does not constitute as yet the predominating element of society. The Lombardians and the Jews occupied the same position among the agricultural nations of the Middle Ages.

As a further illustration of the fact that the same category plays different parts at different stages of society, we may mention the following: one of the latest forms of bourgeois society, viz., stock companies, appear also at its beginning in the form of the great chartered monopolistic trading companies.

The conception of national wealth which is imperceptibly formed in the minds of the economists of the seventeenth century, and which partly continues to be entertained by those of the eighteenth century, is that wealth is produced solely for the state, but that the power of the latter is proportional to that wealth. It was as yet an unconsciously hypocritical way in which wealth announced itself and its own production as the aim of modern states considering the latter merely as a means to the production of wealth.

The order of treatment must manifestly be as follows: first, the general abstract definitions which are more or less applicable to all forms of society, but in the sense indicated above. Second, the categories which go to make up the inner organization of bourgeois society and constitute the foundations of the principal classes; capital, wage-labour, landed property; their mutual relations; city and country; the three great social classes, the exchange between them; circulation, credit (private). Third, the organization of bourgeois society in the form of a state, considered in relation to itself; the 'unproductive' classes; taxes; public debts; public credit; population; colonies; emigration. Fourth, the international organization of production; international division of labour; international exchange; import and export; rate of exchange. Fifth, the world market and crises.


## SELECTED BIBLIOGRAPHY

BLAKE, W. J. *Elements of Marxian Economic Theory and its Criticism.* 1939.

HOOK, SIDNEY. *Towards the Understanding of Karl Marx: A Revolutionary Interpretation.* London: Gollancz, 1933.

KORSCH, KARL. *Karl Marx.* London: Chapman & Hall, 1938.

LANGE, OSKAR. *Political Economy:* Vol. 1. Pergamon Press, 1963.

MANDEL, ERNEST. *Traité d'Economie Marxiste.* English translation published in 1967; London: Merlin and New York: Monthly Review Press.

MEEK, R. L. 'Karl Marx's Economic Method' in *Economics and Ideology.* London: Chapman & Hall, 1967.

SWEEZY, P. M. *The Theory of Capitalist Development.* London: Dobson, and New York: Monthly Review, 1962.

# Classical Political Economy and Marx

*Maurice Dobb*

FOR MARX the analysis which the classical economists had conducted disclosed only half of the problem. As Engels put it in an important passage in his *Anti-Dühring*, they had shown the positive side of capitalism, in contrast to what had preceded it. In demonstrating the laws of *laissez-faire* they had provided a critique of previous orders of society; but they had not provided an historical critique of capitalism itself. This latter remained to be done, unless capitalism was to be regarded as a stable and permanent order of nature or an unchanging final term of social development. It remained to be done in order to give capitalism its proper place in historical evolution and to provide a key to the forecast of its future. Economic science to date, said Engels, 'begins with the critique of the survivals of feudal forms of production and exchange, shows the necessity of their replacement by capitalist forms, and develops the laws of the capitalist mode of production and its corresponding forms of exchange in their positive aspects; that is, the aspects in which they further the general aims of society'. Equally necessary was the dialectical completion of Political Economy by 'a socialist critique of the capitalist mode of production; that is, with the statement of its laws in their negative aspects, with the demonstration that this mode of production, through its own development, drives towards the point at which it makes itself impossible'.[1]

The crux of the matter was a precise interpretation of Profit as a category of income. The economists had postulated conditions which regulated the exchange-values of commodities. These they had explained in terms of a cost-theory; and they had also provided what was virtually a cost-theory of the value

[1] *Anti-Dühring*, Eng. trans., p. 171.

Originally appeared as Chapter III of *Political Economy and Capitalism*. London: Routledge, Kegan Paul, 1937.

of labour-power itself. Profit was then regarded as a residual quantity, the size of which was determined by these other given factors – the value of the product and the value of labour-power. So far the explanation might appear to be satisfactory enough. But, as it stood, it was seriously incomplete; since profit had been left as a mere residual element without being itself explained. The nature of profit, the why and wherefore of its existence as a category of income at all, remained a secret; and until this secret was revealed, not only were important practical questions left unanswered, but there could be no certainty that the terms of the relation which was said to determine profit (namely, wages and the value of the product) could properly be treated as independent. In the theory of rent, the limited supply and consequent scarcity of available land was adduced as the reason for the emergence of rent and its acquisition by the landowner. Classical theory had adduced no parallel reason for the emergence of profit and its acquisition by the capitalist. Its necessity had simply been assumed. There remained the question: Why, even though there might exist a difference between the expenses of production and the value of the product, should this difference accrue to the capitalist and his partners rather than to anyone else? Why in a régime of economic freedom and competition did not such a surplus tend to disappear either into rent or into wages? If its persistence was to be explained in terms of a cost-theory, how was this consistent with the labour-theory of value? Or was it to be interpreted in terms analogous to the theory of rent? That this was no superfluous inquiry can be seen from the importance of the type of practical question which depended on it: for instance, what would be the effect if profit were taxed or otherwise appropriated, or if wages rose and encroached upon profit, or if the rate of profit for any reason tended to fall? Was the maintenance of a capitalist class as much the fostering of an unproductive burden on industry as the Ricardians had alleged the existence of a landed class to be? Would the interest of this class in protecting profit become as much a fetter on the productive forces as was the interest of landlords in the protection of rents?

Sensing this *lacuna* in their argument, the economists, particularly the successors of Ricardo, sought to develop an explanation of profit along two lines – on the one hand, by inventing a new category of 'real cost', for which profit was the exchange-equivalent; on the other hand, in terms of an alleged special 'productivity' of capital (and hence, by imputation, of its creator the capitalist). It is these shallow and inconsistent theories which afford the principal evidence of that decline of Political Economy after Ricardo which so many commentators have refused to recognize, and which elicited from Marx the title of 'vulgar economics'. It was against these concepts that Marx directed his fiercest polemics – in particular what Böhm-Bawerk termed[1] his 'weighty attacks' against the productivity theory of capital. To Marx the explanation of Profit lay, not in any inherent property of capital as such, not in any real cost or productive activity contributed by the capitalist (no more than land-rent was to be explained in terms of the properties of nature or any activity of the landowner), but in the class structure of existing society – that class division into propertyless and dispossessed which lay behind the appearance of equality and free contract and 'natural values' in terms of which the laws of Political Economy had been framed.

According to Marx's view of history, progress had seen the march of various class systems, each generating and in turn conditioned by the technical conditions and their associated modes of production at the time. Class antagonisms, rooted in the relationships of different sections of society to the prevailing means of production, had been the basic motive-force of the process – of the passage from one form to the next. As became clear from an examination of its origins, capitalism was also a class system: different in significant respects from preceding ones, yet nevertheless a system rooted in a dichotomy between possessing masters and subject dispossessed. It was natural that Marx should look to the peculiarities of this class relation to find a key to the essential rhythm of capitalist society – to find the disequilibria, the tendencies to movement, and to movement *in* its base and not merely *on* its base, behind the veil of economic harmonies which an analysis merely of exchange relations in a free market seemed to reveal. As contrasted with equality of rights, here was revealed inequality of economic status; as contrasted with contractual freedom, economic dependence and compulsion.

[1] *Capital and Interest*, p. 173.

Clearly, the essence of this relation between capitalist and labourer, on which the emergence of profit hinged, must bear a major analogy to the relation between owner and labourer in earlier forms of class society – for instance, between master and slave or between lord and serf. In these earlier forms of society there was no doubt about the character of the relationship as one of force and exploitation, or about the nature and origin of the income of the owning class. The latter annexed the surplus product, over and above the subsistence of their labourers, by virtue of law or custom. The relationship was openly written as what it was. But in capitalist society this was not so. Relations assumed exclusively a value-form. There was no surplus product, but only a surplus-value, which was presumably controlled by the law of value operating in a competitive market where normal exchange was a transfer of equivalent against equivalent. How under such circumstances could one explain the emergence of a surplus-value at all? How was it to be made consistent with the theory of value, which was itself an abstract expression of the operation of a free competitive market? The formula of exchange on a free market was $C - M - C$. No one, it seemed, could acquire a money-income without first offering C, some equivalent commodity-value, in exchange. The possibility of buyers and sellers moving freely from one side of a market to another and between markets ensured that in neither half of this exchange-cycle, neither $C - M$ nor $M - C$, did any surplus-value emerge. How then could one class start with M, a sum of money-capital, and by introducing it into the cycle of exchange draw out a larger value than the value originally put in: $M - C - M'$? 'To explain the general nature of profit,' said Marx, 'you must start from the theorem that on an average commodities are sold at their real values, and that profits are derived from selling them at their real values. If you cannot explain profit upon this supposition, you cannot explain it at all.'[1] Tudor monopolies or

[1] In *Value Price and Profit*. Here he also said of the comparison between slavery and a wage-system: 'On the basis of the wages system even the *unpaid* labour seems to be *paid* labour. With the slave, on the contrary, even that part of his labour which is paid appears to be unpaid.' In the former 'the nature of the whole transaction is completely masked by the intervention of the contract and the pay received at the end of the week'.

feudal liens on the labour of others could no longer be used to explain how a class drew income without contributing any productive activity. Gains of chance or of individual 'sharp practice' could exert no permanent influence in a régime of 'normal values'. Universal and persistent cheating of the productive by the unproductive seemed impossible in an order of free contract. At most this could explain individual gains and losses among the class of capitalists – what one gained another losing: it could not account for the income of a whole class. Therefore, to explain Profit as had Sismondi simply as 'spoliation of the worker', acquired by the entrepreneur 'not because the enterprise produces more than it cost him, but because he does not pay all that it costs him, because he does not give to the worker a sufficient compensation for his work',[1] or, in Bray's description of it, as product of 'a system of unequal exchanges',[2] was not a sufficient explanation: it afforded no answer to the central difficulty and still left the contradiction unresolved.

James Mill had actually drawn attention to the analogy between a wage-system and slave-labour. 'What is the difference,' he asked, 'in the case of the man who operates by means of labourers receiving wages (instead of owning slaves)? ... He is equally the owner of the labour with the manufacturer who operates with slaves. The only difference is the mode of purchasing. The owner of the slave purchases at once the whole of the labour which the man can ever perform: he who pays wages purchases only so much of a man's labour as he can perform in a day, or any other stipulated time. Being equally, however, the owner of the labour so purchased, as the owner of the slave is of that of the slave, the product which is the result of this labour, combined with his capital, is all equally his own.'[3] But here Mill

---

[1] *Nouveaux Principles*, Vol. I, p. 92.

[2] *Labour's Wrongs and Labour's Remedy*, p. 50.

[3] *Elements of Pol. Econ.*, pp. 21–2. Cf. also Richard Jones, *Introductory Lectures on Pol. Econ.* (1833), pp. 58–9. This 'only difference' may, however, make the position of the wage-earner economically inferior to that of the slave, as well as enabling it to be better, since if the labourer is not the property of the master, the latter has no long-period interest in the former's upkeep (the wear and tear of labour and its depreciation through destitution is not a cost to the employer as is the wear and tear of his machinery). Hence it may

left the matter. For Marx it was the beginning of what was essential. The solution which he reached for this central problem turned on that distinction which he regarded as so crucial between labour and labour-power. Capitalist production had its historical root precisely in the transformation of human productive activity itself into a commodity. Labour-power became alienated as something to be bought and sold, and as itself acquiring a value. Since the proletarian was devoid of land or instruments of production, no alternative livelihood existed for him; and while the legal coercion to work for another was gone, the coercion of class circumstance remained. Since the individual labourer (at least in the absence of organization and association) was devoid alike of alternative or of a 'reserve price', the commodity he sold, like other commodities, acquired a value equal to the labour which its creation cost; and this consisted in the labour required to produce the subsistence of the human labourer. Hence the emergence of profit was to be attributed, not to any procreative quality of capital *per se*, but to the historically conditioned fact that labour in action was able to realize a product of greater value (depending on the quantum of labour involved) than the labour-power itself as a commodity was valued at. Hence the transaction between labourer and capitalist both was and was not an exchange of equivalents. Given the social basis which constituted labour-power as a commodity, an exchange of equivalents took place which satisfied the requirements of the law of value – the capitalist advanced subsistence to the labourer and acquired labour-power of equivalent market-value in return. The capitalist acquired the labour-power of the worker; the worker obtained in exchange sufficient to replace in his own person the physical wear and tear that working for the capitalist involved. Economic justice was satisfied. But without the historical circumstance that a class existed which had the sale of its labour-power as a commodity for its only livelihood to confront the capitalist with the possibility of this remunerative transaction, the capitalist would not have been in a position to annex this surplus-value to himself.

---

well be in the employer's interest to treat a free labourer less well than he would a horse or a slave.

The rival interpretation which Lauderdale and Malthus had advanced in terms of the productivity of capital involved a relapse either into mysticism or into the superficialities of mere 'supply and demand' explanations, which Marx in common with Ricardo condemned. Marx never wished to deny that capital, or rather the concrete instruments in which stored-up labour was embodied, were creative of wealth or 'riches': to have done so would have been patently absurd. In fact, he explicitly states that 'it is wrong to speak of labour as the only source of wealth'.[1] No more did Ricardo deny that land even uncultivated might yield utilities. But this was not to say that land or capital were productive of *value*. In fact, the more lavish was nature with the fruits of the earth, the *less* value were the latter likely to have and the *less* chance was there that land would yield a rent. Value, Marx emphasized, was not a mysterious intrinsic attribute of *things*: it was merely an expression of a social relation between *men*. It was an attribute with which objects were endowed by virtue of the form and manner in which the disposition of human labour took place between various lines of production in the course of the division of labour throughout society; and this disposition of the social labour-force was not arbitrary, but followed a determinate law of cost by virtue of Adam Smith's 'unseen hand' of competitive forces. To explain surplus-value, therefore, in terms of some property of an object (capital) was to relapse into what Marx termed the Fetishism of Commodities – a species of animism in which post-Ricardian 'vulgar economy' became increasingly enmeshed. This consisted in attributing animistically to things *in abstracto* the cause of exchange-relationships, when actually the latter were merely the resultant of the social relationships between *men*. It was to explain the course of a puppet-show exclusively in terms of the qualities and behaviour of the puppets. 'A definite social relation between men assumes in their eyes the fantastic form of a relation between things.'[2] 'The existence of the revenue, as it appears on the surface, is separated from its inner relations and from all connections. Thus land becomes the source of rent, capital the

---

[1] *Critique of Political Economy*, p. 33.
[2] Marx, *Capital*, Vol. I, p. 43.

source of profit, and labour the source of wages.'[1] A Political Economy which spoke in these terms, which used as its constants properties of objects abstracted both from individuals and the class circumstances of these individuals, could deal only with surface appearance, could afford only a partial analysis of phenomena, and hence postulate laws and tendencies which were not merely incomplete, but also contradictory and false. At such a level of abstraction there could be no *differentia* because none of the essential differentiating qualities were included in the assumptions. Factors of production were treated solely in their technical aspect as indispensable each to the whole and hence each to the other: an abstraction which yielded an *ex hypothesi* demonstration of an essential harmony between them. It was not surprising that on this plane of reasoning no concept of rent or surplus could appear, and that equivalents should always exchange against equivalents because the situation was so defined that this must be so.

A more recent example may perhaps be cited of the lack of meaning attaching to certain fundamental concepts when exchange relations are treated in abstraction from men as producers and from their relation to a background of social institutions. Pareto has pointed to the significant distinction between 'activities of men directed to the production or transformation of economic goods', and 'to the appropriation of goods produced by others'. Clearly, if one views the economic problem simply as a pattern of exchange relations, separated from the social relations of the individuals concerned – treating the individuals who enter into exchange simply as so many x's and y's, performing certain 'services', but abstracted from their concrete relation to the means of production (e.g. whether propertied or unpropertied, whether passive *rentiers* or active labourers) – then Pareto's distinction can have no meaning in a free competitive market. 'Appropriation of goods produced by others' can only result from the incursion of monopoly or of extra-economic fraud or force. From the régime of 'normal' exchange-values it is excluded by the very definition of a free market. This is, in fact, the answer which is given by Professor Pigou. Citing

[1] Marx, *Theorien über den Mehrwert* (Ed. 1923), Vol. III, pp. 521-2.

Pareto's distinction, he proceeds to suggest that 'acts of mere appropriation' can be excluded by the assumption that 'when one man obtains goods from another man, he is conceived to obtain them by the process, not of seizure, but of exchange in an open market, where the bargainers are reasonably competent and reasonably cognizant of the conditions'.[1] It may be said that this conclusion is perfectly consistent with the scope of the inquiry. But does not the very answer which this scope demands suggest the unreality of such limits and the barrenness, at least on matters fundamental to problems of *Political* Economy, of so limited an analysis? Yet the whole tendency of economics since the days of the post-Ricardians has been to narrow the scope of economic inquiry in this way: moreover, while doing so, at the same time to persist in rendering pronouncements on fundamental issues similar to those with which the classical economists were concerned.

Suppose that toll-gates were a general institution, rooted in custom or ancient legal right. Could it reasonably be denied that there would be an important sense in which the income of the toll-owning class represented 'an appropriation of goods produced by others' and not payment for an 'activity directed to the production or transformation of economic goods?' Yet toll-charges would be fixed in competition with alternative road-ways, and hence would, presumably, represent prices fixed 'in an open market, where the bargainers on both sides are reasonably competent and cognizant of the conditions'. Would not the opening and shutting of toll-gates become an essential factor of production, according to most current definitions of a factor of production, with as much reason at any rate as many of the functions of the capitalist entrepreneur are so classed today? This factor, like others, could then be said to have a 'marginal productivity' and its price be regarded as the measure and equivalent of the service it rendered. At any rate, where is a logical line to be drawn between toll-gates and property-rights over scarce resources in general? Perhaps it will be said that the distinction depends on whether the toll-gate owner himself constructed the road. If so, it is precisely to break through the restricted circle of abstract exchange-relations to seek a

[1] *Economics of Welfare*, p. 130.

definition in terms of the productive activity of the person in question, as separate from and more fundamental than the opening and shutting of toll-gates. But notions which confine themselves to the circle of pure exchange-relations are clearly unfitted to rise above the wisdom of a contemporary critic of Ricardo, who, in attacking Quesnay and Smith, roundly declared that, since none could charge a price who did no service, all classes which drew an income must *ipso facto* be 'productive', and their income the measure of their value to society.[1] Perhaps it will be said that such distinctions are not the province of economics. But this injunction, if it were obeyed, would both render economics barren of most of its practical fruit and make it something radically different from what the founders of the subject designed and intended.

It must not be thought that, in criticizing this type of abstraction, Marx was tilting at all abstractions from the standpoint of a crude empiricism. He was criticizing a particular method of abstraction on the ground that it ignored the essential and mistook shadow for substance and appearance for reality. Any generalization, from its very nature, must, of course, make abstraction of certain elements in a situation; and to this extent 'theory' and 'fact' must necessarily be at variance. Indeed, the method of Marx, as we have seen, was an abstract method as much as that of the classical economists. The theory of value which Marx took over from classical Political Economy, and developed in important particulars, was an abstraction which based itself not simply on certain features general to any exchange economy, but on essential characteristics of capitalism as a system of commodity-production. It seems to be generally forgotten, when Marx is criticized for giving no adequate 'proof' of his theory of value in *Das Kapital*, that he was not propounding a novel and unfamiliar doctrine, but was adopting a principle which was part of the settled tradition of classical Political Economy and without which he considered any determinate statement to be impossible. Clearly in these circumstances he

[1] George Purves, *All Classes Productive of National Wealth* (1817). This gentleman had commenced by declaring that 'the grand fundamental question, on which the whole science of statistics must more or less depend' is 'whether all classes are productive of wealth or whether some are unproductive'.

had no intention of prefacing his analysis of capitalist production with more than a definition and contrast of certain basic concepts such as value, exchange-value and use-value. These and kindred concepts were admittedly abstractions which had only a more or less imperfect representation in the real world. But here his method was no more and no less abstract than that of his predecessors. Competition itself was an abstraction, and so was the 'perfect market' in which 'normal values' emerged. 'Normal values', like Euclidean points and straight lines, were to be found in the real world only as 'limiting cases'.

The two abstractions which have caused most clamour among Marx's critics – the concept of homogeneous 'simple labour' and the assumption in volume I of *Capital* of equal 'organic compositions of capital' in all lines of production – were also common to preceding and contemporary economists, and the ground of many of their most signal corollaries. The latter assumption figured prominently, as we have seen, with Ricardo. In the theory of international trade, for instance, it was the basis of the proposition that a high or low wage-level in a country did not affect the terms of trade, but only caused an equivalent and opposite change in the level of profits.[1] As we have also seen, it underlay John Stuart Mill's dictum that 'demand for commodities does not constitute demand for labour'. The assumption of homogeneity of units of a factor of production is common to economic method up to the present day. Without it the conception of a 'normal' return has no meaning: tacit or explicit, it is part of any discussion of the 'general level of wages' or of a theory of 'normal profit'. When Marx in the third volume of *Capital* admitted that the assumption of equal 'compositions of capital', which formed the basis of his value-principle in the first volume, was only a first approximation, Böhm-Bawerk made great play with the 'great contradiction' between the first approximation of the first volume and the later approximation of the third. On this great contradiction, he triumphantly

[1] Since, if the 'composition of capital' is equal in all industries, a change in wages will not affect the ratio of comparative costs. But if this assumption does not hold, a change in wages will affect the industries with a high proportion of labour to machinery more than those with a low proportion, and hence will alter the comparative cost-ratios.

declared, the whole Marxian system foundered. A recent writer has
said that 'nowhere is there in print such a miracle of confusion'
as the Marxian system.[1] Yet all deductive reasoning proceeds by
a process of approximation; and similar 'contradictions' could
be demonstrated in all such cases between successive approxi-
mations, or between *any* approximation and the facts. It is a
question of the *uses* to which an approximation is put. What is
important is whether or not the corollaries, held to be deducible
from the approximation, are invalidated by the qualifications which
the closer approximation requires – whether the alterations introduced in Volume III make any substantial difference to the conclusions developed from the assumptions made in Volume I.

Like Ricardo, Marx attached chief importance to an analysis
of the movements of the class revenues. So much, indeed, had
Ricardo's interest lain in the distribution of wealth as to evoke
the anger of a writer such as Carey, who declared that 'the system of Ricardo is a system of discord . . . it creates hostility
between classes . . . his book is a manual for demagogues who
seek to gain power by the distribution of the soil, by war and by
pillage'.[2] Similarly, a recent writer has said of Marx that, weaving
'a tissue of economic fallacy' on 'a prophetic note of righteous
indignation', he made it his purpose 'to demonstrate that class-
hatred is justified'.[3] Such tortured verdicts may ring strangely.
But what they emphasize is to this extent true: that Marx
focused attention on the class relation, expressed in class incomes, as the relation which defined the major rhythm of
capitalist society and was crucial for any forecast of the future.
At the same time, it would be wrong to say that his interest was
confined to the sphere of distribution, and to treat his analysis
as essentially a theory of distribution. Production, Exchange,
Distribution, while they might be separate facets, could not be
treated as separate categories of economic relations; and, as he
insisted in his *Critique of Political Economy*, they had an essential
unity.[4]

The law of value was a principle of exchange relations be-

[1] A. Gray, *Development of Economic Doctrine*, p. 301.
[2] Carey, *Past, Present and The Future* (1848), p. 74, *cit.* in
*Theorien über den Mehrwert*, Vol. II, p. 4.
[3] E. Hallett Carr, *Karl Marx*, p. 277.
[4] *Critique* (Ed. Kerr), p. 291, etc. (See p.27 of this volume et seq).

tween commodities, including labour-power. It was simultaneously a determinant of the mode in which labour was allocated
between different industries in the general social division of
labour and of the distribution of the product between classes.
To say that commodities had certain exchange-values was an
alternative way of saying that the labour-force of society was
divided between occupations in a certain way, and (included in
the latter statement) that the social product was divided between
subsistence for labourers and income for capitalists in certain
proportions. (For instance, a statement concerning the values of
corn and silk is at the same time a statement about the proportions in which labour is divided between the production of corn
and of silk. If corn and silk were the only two commodities
produced, the former being consumed by workers and the latter
by capitalists, the statement that labour was divided between
silk-manufacture and corn-culture in a certain ratio would be
equivalent to saying that the social income was distributed
between workers and capitalists in a corresponding way.) In his
first volume Marx adopted the simplifying assumption of a
'pure' capitalist economy: an economy of 'pure competition', as
did the classical economists, and a mode of production based on
a simple relationship between capitalists and workers; the latter
performing the sum-total of essential productive activities, the
former figuring simply *qua* capitalist, as owners of property-
rights and hirers of labour-power.[1] This was competent to
provide the generalized type-form of all existent capitalist societies
(to which admittedly the concept of 'pure' capitalism was only
an approximation) as Euclidean lines and points and circles and
cubes could represent the essential characteristics of all actual
three-dimensional spatial relations. The guiding motive of this volume was to analyse the relation between the revenues of these two
classes and to explain the origin and character of capitalist profit.

[1] In a letter to Engels in 1858 Marx stated the assumptions made
for the purpose of Volume I as follows: It is 'assumed that the wages
of labour are constantly equal to their lowest level. ... Further
landed property is taken as = 0. ... This is the only possible way to
avoid having to deal with everything under each particular relation.'
On these assumptions value is 'an abstraction', which figures in
'this abstract undeveloped form' as distinct from its 'more concrete
economic determinations'. '*Marx-Engels Correspondence*, p. 106.'

In the third volume Marx pointed out that, when account was taken of the fact that the ratio between labour and machinery (or, more precisely, between variable and constant capital) was different in different industries, it was seen that commodities exchanged, not according to the principle as enunciated in the first volume, but according to what he termed their Prices of Production (i.e. wages *plus* an average or 'normal' profit). Nevertheless, he declared that the principle of the first volume was still the determinant of what the value of commodities was in the *aggregate*, and hence the determinant of the rate of profit and in turn of the Prices of Production themselves. In making this statement he was not guilty of the stupidity of asserting merely that a total equals a total, as Böhm-Bawerk charges.[1] Clearly what he had in mind was the relation between the value of finished commodities, treated as an aggregate, and the value of labour-power – the crucial relation on which, in common with Ricardo, he conceived profit to depend. He was stating that it still remained true that the distribution of the total product between workers and capitalists (and hence the volume and rate of profit) depended on the relation between these two quantities; and that (provided one could assume the 'composition of capital' in the group of industries producing subsistence to be not very different from the average of industry as a whole) this crucial relation could still be treated as determined according to the simple manner of volume I. If this was so, the analysis of surplus-value and of the influences which determined it was not invalidated by the qualifications introduced in Volume III. The revenue of the capitalist class, and movements in it, were still ruled by the same causes, even if this revenue was differently distributed between various industries from what had been envisaged in the 'first approximation'.[2] To use an analogy, let us

---

[1] *Karl Marx and the Close of his System*, pp. 68–75.

[2] It is perfectly clear that Marx was fully aware of the nature and significance of these qualifications introduced in Volume III and in what measure they affected the corollaries to be drawn from the assumptions of Volume I. Engels, in his Preface to the 1891 Edition of *Wage-Labour and Capital*, says: 'If therefore we say today with economists like Ricardo that the value of a commodity is determined by the labour necessary to its production, we always imply

suppose that one were to enunciate the theory of rent on the assumption that all land was of homogeneous quality, stating that rent would be equal to the difference between the cost of production and the selling-price of corn (the latter being determined by the cost of production at the intensive margin). To introduce the fact of heterogeneity of land (and hence of *different* costs of production on each farm and each acre) as a later approximation would then make no essential difference to the corollaries based on the simpler assumption, provided that the cost of production of corn on the average remained the same and bore the same relation to the price of corn. Moreover, the corollaries of the earlier approximation would embody certain essential truths about the nature and determination of rent (those connected with what one may term the scarcity aspect of rent, as distinct from its differential aspect), which no formulation of the theory of rent could imply without some reference to this relation between the average cost and the average selling-price.[1]

_____

the reservations and restrictions made by Marx.' Much earlier than this Marx had taken Proudhon to task for saying that a rise of wages would lead to a general rise of prices. 'If all the industries employ the same number of workers in relation to the fixed capital or the instruments which they use, a general rise of wages will produce a general lowering of profits and the current price of goods will not undergo any alteration.' 'But as the relation of manual labour to fixed capital is not the same in different industries, all the industries which employ a relatively greater amount of fixed capital and less workers will be forced, sooner or later, to lower the price of their goods', and conversely in industries employing 'a relatively smaller amount of fixed capital and more workers. . . . Thus a rise in the wage-level will lead, not as M. Proudhon declares, to a general increase of prices, but to an actual fall of some prices, namely; to a fall in the price of those goods which are largely manufactured with the aid of machinery.' (*Misère de la Philosophie* [Ed. 1847], pp. 167–8.)

[1] Curiously enough Böhm-Bawerk, in constructing his own theory of capital, makes use as a first approximation of what amounts to the same assumption as that which he condemns in Marx, namely, that 'an equally long production-period would prevail simultaneously over all employments'. (*Positive Theory of Capital*, pp. 382 and 405.)

The corollaries which remained unaffected by these later qualifications were various and were among the most important for the main purpose which he had in hand: namely, to discover 'the law of motion of capitalist society'. Ricardo's doctrine that 'if wages rise, profits fall', and with it the conclusion that a rise in wages will encourage capitalists to substitute machinery for labour, remained undisturbed. So also did the influences which caused the rate of profit to alter, including Marx's explanation of the 'tendency of the rate of profit to fall', which will later be considered, and to which it is clear that Marx attached considerable significance in defining the long-term trend of capitalist society. But there is also a less familiar corollary, which today has more central importance than when it was written; namely, that concerning the effect of monopoly. Marx had pointed out that monopoly cannot increase the rate of profit *in general* (as distinct from raising it for some sections and lowering it for others), except in so far as it has the effect of lowering wages. Unless monopoly affected the relation between the value of labour-power and the value of commodities (i.e. altered 'the rate of exploitation'), it was powerless to raise the rate of profit as a whole. Apart from such an effect of monopoly in depressing real wages below their normal level, the growth of monopoly 'would merely transfer a portion of the profit of other producers of commodities to the commodities with a monopoly-price. A local disturbance in the distribution of the surplus-value among the various spheres of production would take place indirectly, but they would leave the boundaries of the surplus-value itself unaltered.'[1]

The essential difference between Marx and classical Political Economy lay, therefore, in the theory of surplus-value. If its significance was not an ethical one, wherein then lay its practical importance? Clearly, its importance as basis for a critique of capitalism was in many respects parallel to that of the theory of rent for a critique of the landed interest in the hands of the Ricardian School. The theory of rent had formed the ground for maintaining that the very policies which would tend to the lowering of the rate of profit and the consequent retardation of capital accumulation and industrial progress would at the same

[1] *Capital*, Vol. III, p. 1003.

time augment the revenue of the landed class and swell the burden of unproductive consumption on the national wealth.[1] The theory of surplus-value implied that, since the two class-incomes of profits and wages were so contrasted in their essential character and in the manner of their determination, the relation between them was necessarily one of antagonism in a sense which made it qualitatively distinct from the relation between ordinary buyers and sellers on a free market. The capitalist class would have an interest in perpetuating and extending the institutions of a class society, which maintained the proletariat in a dependent position and created surplus-value as a category of income, as powerfully as the landed interest had formerly had in maintaining the Corn Laws; while the proletariat would have a corresponding interest in weakening and destroying these basic property-rights. Any change in profit, as the income of the class upon whose decisions and expectations the operation of industry depended, would have an effect on the economic system altogether different from a change in any other price or revenue – a difference which had particular relevance, as we shall see, to Marx's theory of crises. Moreover, it might well be in the interest of capital to retard the development of the productive forces and to promote policies which were detrimental to the production of wealth, provided that these policies tended to extend the opportunities of exploitation and augment its revenue. This possibility was converted into a probability by the very nature of the technical basis on which industrial capitalism had been built. Founded on power-machinery and large-scale technique, the process of progressive capital accumulation tended continually to extend and to enlarge this basis: a process which, by encouraging a progressive concentration and centralization of capital, increasingly prepared the ground for monopoly. The picture which Marx drew of these developments is a familiar one. With the growth of monopoly, class antagonism was rendered

[1] The Ricardian argument was that the fact of diminishing returns on land would, in the course of progress, cause rents to rise and by increasing the cost of subsistence for the workers cause profits to fall. The only way to avert this, and so to maintain the possibilities of capital accumulation and industrial expansion, was to throw open foreign trade and allow the competition of imported raw produce.

more acute, and not less; the income of the propertied class became with increasing openness the fruit of monopoly-policies and of little else. But the same process which established the growing 'social character' of the productive process itself forged the instrument which was to break the fetters of 'individual appropriation'. 'The productive forces developing within the framework of bourgeois society create at the same time the material conditions for the liquidation of this antagonism.' It created also the homogeneity, the discipline and the organization of the factory proletariat as a class; until this class, finding itself in ever sharper antagonism to a system of property-relations which had grown so patently a fetter on production, should demand and enforce the emancipation of itself and of society by the expropriation of its exploiters. Since a régime of large-scale technique and complex productive relations could not revert to petty property and the small-scale production which this entailed, the negative act of expropriation must necessarily take the positive form of socialization, in the sense of the transference of land and capital into the collective ownership of the workers' State. This revolutionary act of the organized workers which established collective property would in fact be the charter both of equality and of individual rights of which nineteenth-century liberalism had dreamed, but which it had been impotent to attain. It would be the only real charter of individual rights precisely because (in the words of the *Communist Manifesto*) 'in bourgeois society capital is independent and has individuality, whereas the living person is dependent and lacks individuality'; because only by the suppression of the power of one class to exploit another through the suppression of private property in land and capital, which endowed this power, could the substance of liberty for the mass of the people appear.

## SELECTED BIBLIOGRAPHY

DOBB, M. 'On Some Tendencies in Modern Economic Theory' in *On Economic Theory and Socialism*. London: Routledge, Kegan Paul, 1955.

GOTTLEIB, M. 'Marx's Mehrwert Concept and the Theory of Pure Capitalism': *Review of Economic Studies*, XVIII, 3, No. 47: 1950–51, and R. L. Meek: 'Mr Gottleib on Marx; A Comment' in *Review of Economic Studies*, XIX, No. 2, 1951–2.

JOHANSEN, L. 'Some Observations on the Labour Theory of Value and Marginal Utilities', *Economics of Planning* (Oslo), No. 2, 1963.

MARX, KARL. *Theories of Surplus Value.*

MEEK, R. L. 'Piero Sraffa's Rehabilitation of Classical Economics', *Science and Society*, XXV, No. 2, 1961.

# Marxian Economics and Modern Economic Theory

*Oskar Lange*

1. IN A recent issue of the *Kyoto University Economic Review*[1] Professor Shibata brought up the question of the relative merits of Marxian economics and the modern theory of economic equilibrium. He contends that the theory of general economic equilibrium, which has received its most precise and complete formulation in the works of the School of Lausanne, 'is ineffectual in making clear systematically either the organization of present-day capitalistic society or the laws of its development',[2] while the Marxian political economy, 'though it is now shown to contain many defects, sets forth theories which are either intended to enunciate systematically the organization of present-day capitalistic society and the laws governing its development, or have inseparable and necessary bearings on them'.[3] And Professor Shibata asks what it is that makes Marxian economics so powerful a tool for understanding the basic phenomena of Capitalism while the mathematical theory of economic equilibrium is quite powerless.

This superiority of Marxian economics seems strange, indeed, in view of the fact that it works with concepts which are long since outdated and which ignore the whole development of economic theory since the time of Ricardo. Professor Shibata thinks that the sterility of the theory of general economic equilibrium is due to its complexity and the high degree of abstraction which make its application to actual problems impossible.

[1] Kei Shibata, 'Marx's Analysis of Capitalism and the General Equilibrium Theory of the Lausanne School', *The Kyoto University Economic Review*, July 1933.

[2] *loc. cit.*, p. 107.

[3] *Ibid.*, p. 108.

Reprinted from *The Review of Economic Studies*, June 1935.

Marxian economics instead, being concerned rather with aggregates and averages than with the mental structure of the individuals taking part in the organization of capitalist production, is more amenable to direct practical application. Professor Shibata tries, therefore, to restate and simplify the Lausanne system of equations so as to make it possible to apply them practically. In this Professor Shibata has performed an exceedingly fine piece of analysis for which any serious economist should be grateful. It seems to me, however, that Professor Shibata has not touched the very essential point which accounts for the (real or alleged) superiority of Marxian over 'bourgeois' economics. It is, therefore, my purpose to discuss: (1) in what the real or alleged superiority of Marxian economics consists, and (2) whether this superiority is due to the economic concepts used by Marx, or to an exact specification of the institutional (or, if the reader prefers the expression, sociological) data which form the framework in which the economic process works in Capitalist society.[1]

2. The Marxist's claim to superiority for his economics is that 'bourgeois' economics has utterly failed to explain the fundamental tendencies of the development of the Capitalist system. These tendencies are: (i) the constant increase of the scale of production which by substituting large-scale for small-scale production has led to the transition from the free-competitive Capitalism of the nineteenth century to the present monopolistic (or rather oligopolistic) Capitalism; (ii) the substitution of interventionism and 'planning' for *laisser-faire*; (iii) the transition from free trade to high protectionism and economic nationalism in international relations; (iv) the constant expansion of the capitalist method of production in non-capitalist

---

[1] As the word Capitalism is used frequently very ambiguously it should be mentioned here that it is used in this paper in its Marxian sense, i.e. Capitalism means an exchange-economy with private ownership of the means of production, to which the further sociological datum is added that the population is divided into two parts, one of which owns the means of production while the other part, owning no means of production, is compelled to work as wage-earners with the means of production belonging to the other part. Only because of this sociological datum do profit and interest appear as personal income separate from wages.

countries, which as long as competition was free led to a relatively peaceful permeation of capitalist economy and Western civilization through the whole world, but which with oligopolistic and interventionist Capitalism leads to imperialist rivalry among the principal capitalist powers; (v) the increase of economic instability in the capitalist system, which by destroying the economic and social security of the population of capitalist countries, causes them to rebel against the existing economic system, whatever the ideology and programme underlying this rebellion (Socialism or Fascism).

The claim that 'bourgeois' economists have failed to explain these tendencies in the development of Capitalism, and to formulate them into a theory of economic evolution seems to be justified indeed. How utterly they failed to do so is conspicuous from the fact that many of them denied this development until the phenomena apparently became so overwhelming as to be familiar to anybody but the professional economist who was always the last to recognize their existence. Thus the tendency towards the concentration of production was denied, or, if admitted, was regarded as of minor significance for the nature of the economic system, until the monopolistic (or oligopolistic) character of the basic industries became so obvious that a special theory of limited competition had to be developed to supplement orthodox economic theory. The transition from free trade to protectionism was mainly interpreted as an act of economic folly; its close connection with the transition from free competition to monopolistic control has as yet scarcely been realized by 'bourgeois' economists. The imperialist rivalry of capitalist powers has mainly been explained in purely political terms, the connection between imperialist rivalry and the fight for monopolistic control scarcely being realized. It was very generally held among 'bourgeois' economists both at the beginning of the twentieth century and in the years preceding 1929, that the economic stability of Capitalism was increasing and that business fluctuations were becoming less and less intense. Thus the Marxian claim that 'bourgeois' economists failed to grasp the fundamental tendencies of the evolution of the Capitalist system proves to be true. They either denied the existence of these tendencies or if they took account of them they never succeeded in explaining them by a consistent theory of economic evolution, but effectively offered no more than a historical description. On the other hand, Marxian economics must be admitted to have anticipated these tendencies correctly, and to have developed a theory which investigates the causal mechanism of this evolution and thus shows its inevitability.

It may be contended, however, that the lack of understanding of the basic phenomena of the evolution of Capitalism by the professional economists was not a failure of their science, but rather a personal failure due to their middle-class social allegiance. They certainly could not be expected to look with favour on a theory of evolution which draws the conclusion that the middle-class will be wiped out in the process of evolution. If this were the case, it would have been an 'error artificis' rather than an 'error artis', the psychological grounds of which are easily explained. There are, however, reasons which seem to suggest that the failure is more than a purely personal one and that some 'error artis' is involved. In order to display this let us imagine two persons: one who has learned his economics only from the Austrian School, Pareto and Marshall, without ever having seen or even heard a sentence of Marx or his disciples; the other one who, on the contrary, knows his economics exclusively from Marx and the Marxists and does not even suspect that there may have been economists outside the Marxist School. Which of the two will be able to account better for the fundamental tendencies of the evolution of Capitalism? To put the question is to answer it.

But this superiority of Marxian economics is only a partial one. There are some problems before which Marxian economics is quite powerless, while 'bourgeois' economics solves them easily. What can Marxian economics say about monopoly prices? What has it to say on the fundamental problems of monetary and credit theory? What apparatus has it to offer for analysing the incidence of a tax, or the effect of a certain technical innovation on wages? And (irony of Fate!) what can Marxian economics contribute to the problem of the optimum distribution of productive resources in a socialist economy?

Clearly the relative merits of Marxian economics and of modern 'bourgeois' economic theory belong to different 'ranges'. Marxian economics can work the economic evolution of capitalist society into a consistent theory from which its necessity is deduced, while 'bourgeois' economists get no further than mere historical description. On the other hand, 'bourgeois' economics is able to grasp the phenomena of the everyday life of a capitalist economy in a manner that is far superior to anything the Marxists can produce.[1] Further, the anticipations which can be deduced from the two types of economic theory refer to a different range of time. If people want to anticipate the development of Capitalism over a long period a knowledge of Marx is a much more effective starting point than a knowledge of Wieser, Böhm-Bawerk, Pareto or even Marshall (though the last-named is in this respect much superior). But Marxian economics would be a poor basis for running a central bank or anticipating the effects of a change in the rate of discount.

3. The difference between the explanatory value of Marxian and 'bourgeois' economics respectively is easily accounted for if the essential features of modern economic theory are recalled. Economic theory as developed by the Austrian, Marshallian and Lausanne schools is essentially a *static* theory of economic equilibrium analysing the economic process under a system of constant *data* and the mechanism by which prices and quantities produced adjust themselves to changes in these data. The data themselves, which are psychological (the preference scales of the consumers), technical (the production functions), and insti-

---

[1] This difference is connected, of course, with the respective social functions of 'bourgeois' and Marxian economics. The first has to provide a scientific basis for rational measures to be taken in the current administration of the capitalist economy 'monetary and credit policy, tariffs, localization, monopoly prices, etc.', the social function of the latter has been to provide a scientific basis for long range anticipations guiding the rational activity of a revolutionary movement directed against the very institutional foundations of the capitalist system. But in providing a scientific basis for the current administration of the capitalist economy 'bourgeois' economics has developed a theory of equilibrium which can also serve as a basis for the current administration of a socialist economy. It is obvious that Marshallian economics offers more for the current administration of the economic system of Soviet Russia than Marxian economics does, though the latter is surely the more effective basis for anticipating the future of Capitalism. In so far, modern economic theory, in spite of its undoubted 'bourgeois' origin, has a universal significance.

tutional (the forms and distribution of property of the factors of production, the monetary and banking system, etc.) are regarded as outside the scope of economic theory. The study of the data is a matter of descriptive and statistical investigation, the study of changes in the data is the province of economic history. If there are any 'laws' discoverable in the change of data, their study is outside the range of economic theory. Further, the institutional data of the theory are not specified. In so far as the theory of economic equilibrium is merely a theory of distribution of scarce resources between different uses it does not need any institutional data at all, for the relevant considerations can be deduced from the example of Robinson Crusoe. In so far economics is not even a social science. When economic theory is concerned with the pricing process, the specification of institutional data is very general. All that is assumed is the existence of the institutions necessary for the functioning of an exchange economy. But the consequences of the additional institutional[1] datum which distinguishes Capitalism from other forms of exchange economy, i.e. the existence of a class of people who do not possess any means of production, is scarcely examined.

Now, Marxian economics is distinguished by making the specification of this additional institutional datum the very corner-stone of its analysis, thus discovering the clue to the peculiarity of the Capitalist system by which it differs from other forms of exchange-economy. Another characteristic feature of Marxian economics (which will be shown to be closely connected with the former one), is that it provides not only a theory of economic equilibrium, but also a theory of economic evolution. For modern 'bourgeois' economics the problem of economic evolution belongs not to economic theory but to economic history. The study of changes in the data of the economic system is regarded as being beyond the scope of economic

---

[1] By calling the fact of division of society into proletarians and owners of means of production an institutional datum I do not mean to imply that it is imposed by law. It might be better, perhaps, to distinguish between institutional data, resulting from legal institutions, and other types of sociological data which are not expressed in the form of legal institutions, but as the term 'institutional' is used generally in a very broad sense there is no need to make such distinction for the purpose of this paper.

theory: for these changes are considered to be from the economists' point of view accidental, not results of the economic
process.[1] In opposition to this point of view, Marxian economics
provides further a *theory* of economic evolution.[2]

The Marxian theory of economic evolution is based on the
contention that it is possible, in certain circumstances, to deduce
the necessity for, and also the direction of a certain change of
economic data, and that such a change follows, in a particular
sense, from the very mechanism of the economic process in
capitalist society. What this mechanism is and what the term
'necessity' means in this connection will be seen later; here it is
sufficient to mention that the fundamental change in data occurs
in production (a change of the production function) and that
the 'necessity' of such change can be deduced only under the
institutional set-up specific to Capitalism. Thus a 'law of development' of the Capitalist system is established. Hence the anticipation of the future course of events deduced from the Marxian
theory is not a mechanical extrapolation of a purely empirical
trend, but an anticipation based on the recognition of a law of
development and is, with certain reservations, not less stringent
than an anticipation based on the static theory of economic
equilibrium such as, for instance, the anticipation that a rise in
price leads, under certain circumstances, to a decline of the
amount of a commodity demanded.

[1] Also H. L. Moore's theory of moving equilibrium explains only
the reaction of the economic system to a given continuous change of
data. The change of data itself is determined statistically but is not
an object of theoretical analysis. The same is true of the 'dynamic'
theories which deduce the necessity of fluctuations from time-lags
in adjusting supply to changes in price. These theories deduce the
impossibility of an equilibrium in certain cases from the very nature
of the adjustment mechanism, but they cannot deduce theoretically
the changes of data responsible for the trend on which the fluctuations due to the process of adjustment are superimposed.

[2] The difference between a *theory* of economic evolution and a
mere historical account of it is excellently explained in Chapter II of
Schumpeter's *Theory of Economic Development* (English translation.
Cambridge, Mass., 1934). Schumpeter is the only economist outside
the Marxist camp who has formulated a theory of economic evolution. However, the close connection of his theory with Marxian ideas
is obvious.

4. The economist whose horizon does not extend beyond the limits of a purely static theory of equilibrium usually denies the possibility of a theory of economic evolution. He is too much accustomed to see in the evolution of what he regards as the pure data of his science a certain kind of 'accident' which may be described by the historian and statistician but which cannot be accounted for causally, at any rate not by economic theory. His argument is in general that the phenomena are too complicated to be capable of theoretical formulation, i.e. to be accounted for by one single principle (or a few principles). He contends that in the study of economic evolution so many factors must be taken into account that economic evolution can virtually only be described historically and cannot be forced into the pattern of an over-simplified (and therefore wrong) theory.[1] However, this argument is scarcely convincing, it is too much like that put forward by the historical school against the possibility of even static economic theory. The pricing problem, so the historical and purely institutionalist economist argues, is much too complicated to be explained by one single principle (marginal utility), but should rather be described historically and statistically so as to take due account of all the factors influencing the price of a commodity. And such factors are, besides utility, the cost of production, relative scarcity, the cost of transportation, the extent to which the commodity is imported or exported, its quality, the climate if the commodity is an article of clothing, etc., etc.[2] How crazy, one might conclude on this type of argument, to explain the complicated result of so many causes by one single principle such as marginal utility.

[1] The same type of argument is generally raised against the theory of historical materialism which explains social evolution in terms of a few definite principles.

[2] I know, for instance, of an institutionalist economist who actually maintained that the price level depends on exactly twelve factors. From his enumeration of these factors I happen to remember: the confidence people have in the national currency, whether the national budget is balanced or not, the balance of foreign trade, the size of agricultural crops (and thus indirectly rainfall). The ratio of the volume of monetary and credit circulation to the volume of trade he recognized as *one* of the factors, of course, but how wrong, he argued, to think of it as *the* principle explaining the price level.

Another argument is that even if a theory of economic evolution is in principle possible it does not belong to the field of economics. If by this it is meant that the theory of economic evolution requires *additional* assumptions beyond those contained in the theory of economic equilibrium this is obvious, for if the theory of economic equilibrium already contained these assumptions it would deduce a process of evolution instead of a state of equilibrium. Whether, however, the deduction of the necessity for a change of certain data from certain principles is called *economic* theory or not is merely a matter of terminology. It should be noted, however, that in Marxian theory this change of data is deduced from the principle of profit maximization which is at the basis of the theory of economic equilibrium and that the phenomena connected with it were regarded by the classical economists as belonging to the traditionally established body of economic theory. Hence a theory of economic evolution explaining certain changes of data as resulting from 'within' the economic process in capitalist society may duly be included in the science of economics.

5. I have pointed out that the real source of the superiority of Marxian economics is in the field of explaining and anticipating a process of economic evolution. It is not the specific economic concepts used by Marx, but the definite specification of the institutional framework in which the economic process goes on in capitalist society that makes it possible to establish a theory of economic evolution different from mere historical description. Most orthodox Marxists, however, believe that their superiority in understanding the evolution of Capitalism is due to the economic concepts with which Marx worked, i.e. to his using the labour theory of value. They think that the abandonment of the classical labour theory of value in favour of the theory of marginal utility is responsible for the failure of 'bourgeois' economics to explain the fundamental phenomena of capitalist evolution. That they are wrong can be easily shown by considering the economic meaning of the labour theory of value. It is nothing but a static theory of general economic equilibrium. In an individualistic exchange economy, based on division of labour, in which there is no central authority to direct which commodities, and in what quantities, are to be produced, the problem is solved automatically by the fact that competition

enforces such a distribution of productive resources between the various industries that prices are proportional to the amount of labour necessary for producing the respective commodities (these being the 'natural prices' of classical economics). In essence this is as static as the modern theory of economic equilibrium, for it explains price and production equilibrium only under the assumption of certain data (i.e. a given amount of labour such as is necessary to produce a commodity – an amount determined by the technique of production). Nor is this theory based on more specialized institutional assumptions than the modern theory of economic equilibrium; it holds not only in a capitalist economy, but in any exchange economy in which there is free competition.[1] To be exact, however, it really holds precisely only in a non-capitalistic exchange-economy of small producers each of whom owns his own means of production (an exchange economy composed of small self-working artisans and peasant farmers, for instance; Marx calls it 'einfache Warenproduktion').[2] In a capitalist economy it requires, as Marx has shown himself in the third volume of *Das Kapital*, certain modifications due to differences in the organic composition of capital (i.e. the ratio of the capital invested in capital *goods* to the capital invested in payment of wages) in different industries. Thus the labour theory of value has no qualities which would make it, from the Marxist point of view, superior to the modern more elaborate theory of economic equilibrium.[3] It is only a more

[1] Cf. for instance, *Das Kapital*, Vol. I, p. 132 (7th ed. Hamburg, Meissner, 1914).

[2] Cf. *Das Kapital*, Vol. III, 1, p. 154 *seq.* (4th ed. Hamburg, Meissner, 1919).

[3] In the Marxian system the labour theory of value serves also to demonstrate the exploitation of the working class under Capitalism, i.e. the difference between the personal distribution of income in a capitalist economy and in an 'einfache Warenproduktion'. It is this deduction from the labour theory of value which makes the orthodox Marxist stick to it. But the same fact of exploitation can also be deduced without the help of the labour theory of value. Also without it, it is obvious that the personal distribution of income in a capitalist economy is different from that in an 'einfache Warenproduktion' (or in a socialist economy based on equalitarian principles, in which the distribution of income would be substantially the same as in an

primitive form of the latter, restricted to the narrow field of
pure competition and even not without its limitations in this
field.[1] Further, its most relevant statement (i.e., the equality of

'e'nfache Warenproduktion'), for profit, interest and rent can obviously be the personal income of a separate class of people only in a
capitalist economy. If interest is explained by the marginal productivity of capital, it is only because the workers do not own the
capital they work with that interest is the personal income of a
separate class of people. If interest is regarded as due to a higher
valuation of present than future goods it is only because the workers
do not possess the subsistence fund enabling them to wait until the
commodities they produce are ready that the capitalist advancing it
to the workers gets the interest as his personal income. Just as in
Marx's case it is because the workers do not possess the means of
production that the surplus value is pocketed by the capitalist. To
make the Marxian concept of exploitation clearer by contrast it may
be noticed that Pigou (*The Economics of Welfare*, 3rd ed., 1929,
p. 556) and Mrs Robinson (*The Economics of Imperfect Competition*,
p. 281 *seq.*) define exploitation of the worker as occurring when he
gets less than the value of the marginal physical product of his
labour. This means that exploitation is defined by contrasting the
distribution of income in monopolistic Capitalism and in competitive
Capitalism. The middle-class character of this idea of social justice
is obvious. For the Socialist the worker is exploited even if he gets
the full value of the marginal product of his labour, for from the
fact that interest or rent is determined by the marginal productivity
of capital or land it does not follow, from the socialist point of view,
that the capital- or land-owner ought to get it as his personal
income. The Marxian definition of exploitation is derived from
contrasting the personal distribution of income in a capitalist
economy (irrespective of whether monopolistic or competitive) with
that in an 'einfache Warenproduktion' in which the worker owns
his means of production.

[1] It is limited to the assumption that the ratio of capital goods to
labour in each industry is determined by technical considerations
alone, i.e. is a datum and not a variable depending on wages and the
prices of capital goods. The very moment substitution between
capital goods and labour is assumed to be possible the theory of
marginal productivity must be introduced to determine the organic
composition of capital, the knowledge of which is necessary in the
Marxian system to determine the deviation of 'production prices'
from the respective labour values.

price to average cost plus 'normal' profit) is included in the modern theory of economic equilibrium. Thus the labour theory of value cannot possibly be the source of the superiority of Marxian over 'bourgeois' economics in explaining the phenomena of economic *evolution*. In fact, the adherence to an antiquated form of the theory of economic equilibrium is the cause of the inferiority of Marxian economics in many fields. The superiority of Marxian economics on the problem of the evolution of Capitalism is due to the exact specification of the institutional datum which distinguishes Capitalism from 'einfache Warenproduktion'. It was thus that Marx was able to discover the peculiarities of the capitalist system and to establish a theory of economic evolution.

6. The short-comings of Marxian economics due to its antiquated theory of economic equilibrium and its merits due to its possession of a theory of economic evolution both become conspicuous if the contribution of Marxian and of 'bourgeois' economics to the theory of the business cycle are considered. Neither of them can give a complete solution of the problem.

That Marxian economics fails is due to the labour theory of value, which can explain prices only as equilibrium prices (i.e. 'natural prices' in the terminology of Ricardo). Deviations of actual from 'natural prices' are more or less accidental and the labour theory has nothing definite to say about them. But the central problem of business cycle theory is one of deviation from equilibrium – of the causes, the course and the effect of such deviation. Here the labour theory of value inevitably fails. The inability of Marxian economics to solve the problem of the business cycle is demonstrated by the considerable Marxist literature concerned with the famous reproduction schemes of the second volume of *Das Kapital*. This whole literature tries to solve the fundamental problems of economic equilibrium and disequilibrium without even attempting to make use of the mathematical concept of functional relationship.

But on the other hand, 'bourgeois' economics has also failed to establish a consistent theory of business cycles. It has done an exceedingly good job in working out a number of details of the greatest importance for a theory of business cycles, such as studying the effects of the different elasticities of the legamina in our economic system. And it has elucidated in a manner hitherto unprecedented the role of money and credit in the business cycle. But it has not been able to formulate a complete theory of business cycles. This inability is a direct consequence of its being only a static theory of equilibrium and of adjustment processes. Such a theory can analyse why, if a disturbance of equilibrium has occurred, certain adjustment processes necessarily follow. It can also analyse the nature of the adjustment processes following a given change of data. But it cannot explain why such disturbances recur regularly, for this is only possible with a theory of economic evolution. Thus the modern theory of economic equilibrium can show that a boom started by an inflationary credit expansion must lead to a breakdown and a process of liquidation. But the real problem is to explain why such credit inflations occur again and again, being inherent in the very nature of the capitalist system. Similarly with the case of technical innovations as a cause of the business cycle. In a theory of economic evolution the business cycle would prove to be the form in which economic evolution takes place in capitalist society.[1]

Only by a theory of economic evolution can the 'necessary' recurrence of a constellation of data leading to a constantly recurring business cycle be explained. A mere theory of economic equilibrium which considers the problem of change of data to be outside its scope can tackle the problem of the business cycle only in two ways: (i) either by seeking the regularity of the recurrence of business cycles in a regularity of changes of data resulting from forces outside the economic process as, for instance, meteorological cycles or successive waves of optimism or pessimism, or (ii) by denying the existence of a regularly recurrent business cycle and regarding business fluctuations as due to changes of data which are, from the economic theorist's point of view, 'accidental' and hence the concern rather of the economic historian. In the latter case the scope of economic theory would be limited to explaining each business fluctuation separately, as a unique historical phenomenon, by applying the

---

[1] This character of the business cycle as the specific form of economic development under Capitalism has been stated very clearly by Schumpeter.

principles of the theory of economic equilibrium to the factual material collected by the economic historian.[1]

7. I have stressed the point that the distinguishing feature of Marxian economics is the precise specification of an institutional datum by which Marx defines Capitalism as opposed to an 'einfache Warenproduktion', i.e. an exchange economy consisting of small independent producers each of whom possesses his own means of production. The institutional datum, which is the corner-stone of the Marxian analysis of Capitalism, is the division of the population into two parts, one of which owns the means of production while the other owns only labour power. It is obvious that only through this institutional datum can profit and interest appear as a form of income separate from wages. I believe that nobody denies the important sociological bearing of this institutional datum. However, the question arises whether this institutional datum which is the basis of the Marxian definition of Capitalism has any bearing on economic theory. Most of modern economic theory is based on the tacit assumption or even flat denial that any such bearing exists. It is generally assumed that, however important the concept of Capitalism (as distinct from a mere exchange economy), may be for sociology and economic history, it is unnecessary for economic theory, because the nature of the economic process in the capitalist system is not substantially different from the nature of the economic process in any type of exchange economy.

This argument is perfectly right in so far as the theory of economic equilibrium is concerned. The formal principles of the theory of economic equilibrium are the same for any type of exchange economy. The system of Walrasian equations is applicable indiscriminately to a capitalist economy or to an 'einfache Warenproduktion'. Whether the persons who own the productive services of labour and capital (labour power and the means of production in the Marxian terminology) are the same or not affects, of course, the concrete results of the economic equilibrium process, but not its formal theoretical aspect. But the same is true of the formulation of the theory of economic

---

[1] This point of view has been argued very ably by Friedrich Lutz, *Das Konjunkturproblem in der Nationaloekonomie*, Jena 1932.

equilibrium which was used by Marx, i.e. of the labour theory of value. This theory, too, applies indiscriminately to any type of exchange economy, provided only that there is pure competition. It was argued repeatedly by Marx himself that the 'law of value' by which equilibrium asserts itself in an exchange economy based on the division of labour holds for any type of exchange economy, whether capitalistic or an 'einfache Warenproduktion'. Even more, Marx develops his theory of value first for an 'einfache Warenproduktion' later showing the (unessential from his point of view) slight modification it must undergo if applied to a capitalist economy. Thus the institutional basis of capitalist society has no essential significance for the general theory of economic equilibrium. In so far, the prevailing opinion of economists is right. The whole significance of this datum is in terms of a sociological interpretation of the economic equilibrium process.

However, the institutional datum underlying the Marxian analysis of capitalism becomes of fundamental significance where the theory of economic evolution is concerned. A theory of economic evolution can be established only on very definite assumptions concerning the institutional framework in which the economic process goes on. The instability of the technique of production which is the basis of the Marxian[1] theory of economic evolution can be shown to be inevitable only under very specific institutional data. It is clear that it could not be shown to exist in a feudal society, or even in an 'einfache Warenproduktion'. Of course, a certain amount of technical progress exists in any type of human society, but only under Capitalism can it be shown to be the necessary condition for the maintenance of the system.

8. The necessity of technical progress[2] for the maintenance of the capitalist system is deduced in Marxian economics by showing that only in a progressive economy can capitalist profit and interest exist.

---

[1] And also of Schumpeter's.

[2] By technical progress I mean here not only technical improvements in the narrow meaning of the word, but also improvements in organization, etc., i.e. any innovation increasing the efficiency of the optimum combination of factors of production.

The profit of the capitalist entrepreneur, from which also interest on capital is derived, is explained by Marx to be due to the difference between the value of the worker's labour power and the value of the product created by the worker. Now, according to the labour theory of value, the value of labour power is determined by its cost of reproduction. As in any civilized society a worker is able to produce more than he needs for his subsistence he creates a surplus which is the basis of his employer's profit. However, the crucial point in the Marxian theory is the application of the labour theory of value to the determination of wages. If the market price of cotton cloth exceeds its 'natural price' capital and labour flow into the cotton cloth industry until, through increase of the supply of cotton cloth, its market price conforms to the 'natural price'. But this equilibrating mechanism, which is the foundation of labour theory of value, cannot be applied to the labour market. If wages rise above the 'natural price' of labour power so as to threaten to annihilate the employers' profits, there is no possibility of transferring capital and labour from other industries to the production of a larger supply of labour power. In this respect labour power differs fundamentally from other commodities. Therefore, in order to show that wages cannot exceed a certain maximum and thus annihilate profits a principle different from the ordinary mechanism making market prices tend towards 'natural prices' must be introduced.

The classical economists found such a principle in the theory of population. They taught that the pressure of the reproductive instincts of the population on the means of subsistence reacts on any increase of wages above the 'natural price' of labour power to such an extent as to counteract effectively the increase of wages. Ricardo says explicitly[1]: 'However much the market price of labour may deviate from its natural price, it has, like commodities, a tendency to conform to it. . . . When the market price of labour exceeds its natural price, . . . by the encouragement which high wages give to the increase of population, the number of labourers is increased, wages again fall to their natural price.' Thus the working class is assumed to be in a vicious circle which it cannot transcend. Marx rejected the Malthusian

[1] *Principles*, Ch. V, p. 71 (of Gonner's ed. 1929).

theory of population,[1] contending that even without such re-productive facilities wages could not rise so as to annihilate profits. For Capitalism creates, according to Marx, its own surplus population (industrial reserve army) through technical progress, replacing workers by machines. The existence of the surplus population created by technical progress prevents wages from rising so as to swallow profits. Thus technical progress is necessary to maintain the capitalist system[2] and the dynamic nature of the capitalist system, which explains the constant increase of the organic composition of capital, is established.

That the labour theory of value is not necessary for this argument is easily seen, for its application to the labour market is a purely formal one, since the equilibrating mechanism which is at the basis of this theory does not work on the labour market. It is technical progress (or the 'law of population' in the case of the classical economists) which prevents wages from swallowing profits.

We can now see in what sense Marxian economics deduces from theoretical considerations the 'necessity' of economic evolution. Of course, the necessity of the fact that labour-saving technical innovations are always available at the right moment cannot be deduced by economic theory and in this sense the

---

[1] *Das Kapital*, I, Ch. XXIII.

[2] Marx himself did not see clearly that in his theoretical system the virtual existence of a surplus population created by technical progress is necessary for the maintenance of the capitalist system. He applied the labour theory of value to the labour market without being aware that the equilibrating mechanism at the basis of this theory does not work in respect to labour power. But his theory of surplus population which he opposed to the Malthusian theory allows us to complete Marx's argument so as to bridge the gap in his system. It may be mentioned that a proletarian surplus population can also be created through driving out of small independent producers (for instance, artisans and peasants) from the market through the competition of capitalist industry. This source of surplus population was very important in the early history of Capitalism. So long as such a source of surplus population exists the capitalist system might exist, in theory, even without technical progress other than the dynamic process inherent in the destruction of pre-capitalist systems.

'necessity' of economic evolution cannot be proved. But Marxian economics does not attempt to prove this. All it establishes is that the capitalist system cannot maintain itself without such innovations. And this proof is given by an economic theory which shows that profit and interest on capital can exist only on account of the instability of a certain datum, i.e., the technique of production, and that it would necessarily disappear the moment further technical progress proved impossible. The economic theory presented here is, of course, but a mere sketch of how Marx explains the evolution of Capitalism and a suggestion as to how his theory can be completed so as to bridge over the gaps he left. The modern development of economic theory, however, makes it possible to construct a far more satisfactory theory of economic evolution.

It is obvious that the necessity of economic evolution under Capitalism is entirely due to the institutional datum distinguishing Capitalism from an 'einfache Warenproduktion' and that it would not exist in the latter form of exchange economy. Therefore, 'bourgeois' economics, omitting to specify exactly the institutional datum of Capitalism, is unable to establish a theory of economic evolution, for such a theory cannot be evolved from the very broad assumptions of exchange economy in general. From our account of the Marxian theory of economic evolution, it becomes evident that the necessity of economic evolution does not result from the exchange and pricing process as such, but from the special institutional set-up under which this process goes on in a Capitalist system.[1] The specification of institutional data by 'bourgeois' economic theory is too broad, since it gives no more than the institutional data common to any type of exchange economy. But since this very broad specification gives results which are too general to be applicable to special problems, it usually superimposes a very narrow specification of institutional data concerning the monetary and banking system (e.g. the existence or non-existence of the gold standard, whether the banking system makes an inflationary credit expansion possible or not, etc.). But between the first specification

---

[1] Similarly Schumpeter's theory of economic evolution is based on very definite institutional data and does not hold for any type of exchange economy.

of institutional data which is very broad and the second specification which is very narrow there is a gap: the institutional datum distinguishing Capitalism from an 'einfache Warenproduktion'. And this is precisely the datum which is of fundamental significance for the theory of economic evolution.

9. Through the exact specification of the institutional framework of capitalist economy, Marxian economics is able to establish a theory of economic evolution in which certain data evolve 'from within' the economic system. But not all changes of data are explained in this way by the Marxian theory. The evolution of certain data resulting from the very mechanism of the economic system influences certain extra-economic factors such as the policy of the state, political and social ideas, etc., which, reacting back on the economic system, change other of its data. This consideration supplies the explanation of the transition from *laissez-faire* to state interventionism and from free trade to protectionism and economic nationalism, the emergence of imperialist rivalries, etc. The causal chain through which the evolution of certain economic data influences certain extra-economic factors and the reaction of these factors back on the data of the economic system is, however, not within the subject-matter of economics. It belongs to the theory of historical materialism the object of which is to elucidate the causal chains connecting economic evolution with social evolution as a whole. Therefore, the full evolution of Capitalism in all its concreteness cannot be explained by a theory of economic evolution alone. It can be explained only by a joint use of both economic theory and the theory of historical materialism. The latter is an inseparable part of the Marxian analysis of Capitalism.

10. Our results may be summarized as follows:

(1) The superiority of Marxian economics in analysing Capitalism is not due to the economic concepts used by Marx (the labour theory of value), but to the exact specification of the institutional datum distinguishing Capitalism from the concept of an exchange economy in general.

(2) The specification of this institutional datum allows of the establishment of a theory of economic evolution from which a 'necessary' trend of certain data in the capitalist system can be deduced.

(3) Jointly with the theory of historical materialism this theory of economic evolution accounts for the actual changes occurring in the capitalist system and forms a basis for anticipating the future.

## SELECTED BIBLIOGRAPHY

DOBB, MAURICE. 'Requirements of a Theory of Value' in *Political Economy and Capitalism*. London: Routledge, Kegan Paul, 1937.

LERNER, ABBA. 'From Vulgar Economics to Vulgar Marxism' and Maurice Dobb: 'A Reply' in *Journal of Political Economy*, August 1939 and August 1940.

MEEK, R. L. *Studies in the Labour Theory of Value*. London: Lawrence and Wishart, 1956.

ROBINSON, J. 'A Reconsideration of the Theory of Value' in *Collected Economic Papers*, III. Oxford: Blackwell, 1965.

SCHLESINGER, R. J. *Marx: His Time and Ours*. London, Routledge, Kegan Paul, 1950.

WOLFSON, MURRAY. *A Reappraisal of Marxian Economics*. New York: Columbia University Press, 1966.

# The Significance of Marxian Economics for Present-day Economic Theory

*Wassily Leontief*

THE SUBJECT of this discussion can be conveniently approached under three separate headings. First, I will say a few words about the significance of Marxian economics for the modern theory of value. Next, I propose to advance towards the frontier line of contemporary theoretical discussion – the problems of business cycles and of progressive economy in general. I shall conclude this survey by raising certain issues connected with the methodological aspect of Marxian economics.

The modern theory of prices does not owe anything to the Marxian version of the classical labour theory of value nor can it in my opinion profit from any attempts towards reconciliation or mediation between the two types of approach. A number of economists who consider themselves as belonging to the Marxist school of thought have taken a similar stand, so that in stressing this point further I could be rightfully accused of trying to break into an open door.

There exists, however, in the value controversy one point which apparently did not attract sufficient attention. In the very first pages of the first volume of *Capital*, Marx raised against the 'vulgar' (I guess he would call them today 'orthodox' or 'neo-classical') economists the accusation of 'fetishism'. Instead of looking for the ultimate deep-lying price-determinants, they operate, according to Marx, with superficial, imaginary concepts of supply and demand, money costs, etc., all of which refer to purely fictitious relations. Although these subjective concepts acquire in the mind of acting economic individuals the quality of independent, tyrannically dominating forces, actually they

Reprinted from 'Proceedings of the 50th Annual Meeting of the American Economic Association, 1937': *American Economic Review Supplement*, March 1938.

are nothing but the products of deliberate actions of the same individuals.

This typically Hegelian observation is strikingly correct. Is, however, the theoretical conclusion which Marx seems to draw from it actually justified? If it were, his criticism would indict modern price theory even in a greater degree than any of the theories of his contemporaries, John Stuart Mill, Senior, or Malthus.

Is not it a pure and simple fetishism to construct a theory of duopoly in terms of evaluation by Mr Jones of Mr Smith's expectations concerning Mr Robinson's probable actions?

The procedure of the modern value theory comprises two clearly separable and fundamentally different types of analysis. First, it considers the behaviour of individual entrepreneurs and householders in terms of their own economic motivations and explains this behaviour in terms of their own notions – in terms of individual demand schedules as they appear to them, of the monetary cost curves as they appear to them, and so on. Next, the modern theory shows how the actions of these individuals determine independently of their rational will and, using the famous Marxian expression, 'behind their consciousness', the shape and position of the very same imaginary demand and cost curve.

In the first stage of his analysis, the modern theorist simply reproduces the rational considerations of entrepreneurs engaged in the business of maximizing their profits, and describes the reactions of consumers seeking the best possible satisfactions of their wants. In principle, at least, each individual knows this part of economic theory and acts accordingly. For the theorist, it would be inadmissible to introduce at this stage of his analysis any other concepts but those which dominate the mind of actual producers and consumers. He explains their actions in terms of their own beliefs and fetishes.

The opposite is true of the second part of economic theory, which could be called the theory of external interdependence. Here we analyse certain objective repercussions of individual economic activities entirely independently of the subjective attitude of the individual actors. As a matter of fact, and this has been repeatedly pointed out, a large part of theoretical analysis at this stage of argument is based on the assumption that the economic individuals concerned are ignorant of any such objective repercussions of their own activities. If they were to taste the apple of knowledge their behaviour would become fundamentally different and our theoretical system would turn false the very moment it became the property of manufacturers, workers, or consumers.

At this level of the argument, the theorist actually removes the veil of subjective appearances and, instead of interpreting actions of economic individuals in terms of subjective motivations and beliefs, he explains these very beliefs and motivations in terms of objective actions and reactions.

What did Marx mean exactly in accusing the bourgeois economist of fetishism? If he simply wanted to intimate that the second stage of theoretical explanation constituted a necessary complement to the first, the modern theorist will heartily agree with him and point to the Walrasian theory of general equilibrium or the recently developed theory of monopolistic competition as two outstanding examples of this type of analysis. It must have been the guardian angel of Marx, the prophet, who made some of the modern theorists introduce expectations, anticipations and various other *ex ante* concepts, thus justifying *ex post* some of the most vitriolic pages of the first volume of *Capital*. But I prefer to let these modern theorists settle their own account with Marx.

Should, however, the Marxian theory of fetishism be understood as a forthright condemnation of the first stage of our theoretical analysis – the stage which deals with conscious reactions of individual entrepreneurs and householders – his objection must simply be turned down as fundamentally erroneous.

Unlike the modern theory of prices the present-day business cycle analysis is clearly indebted to Marxian economics. Without raising the question of priority it would hardly be an exaggeration to say that the three volumes of *Capital* helped more than any other single work to bring the whole problem into the forefront of economic discussion.

It is rather difficult to say how much Marx actually contributed to the solution of the problem. After years of intensive controversy, there is still no solution. I expect that this statement will not elicit any open contradiction, although I do not remember having read or heard a business cycle theorist admit that he was unable to solve this or that problem; the nearest he comes to such an admission is when he declares that the particular problem is insolvable, which implies that not only he but that also no one else will be able to solve it.

The two principal variants of the Marxian explanation of business cycles, or rather 'economic crises', are well known. One is the theory of under-investment based on the famous law of the falling rate of profits, the other is the theory of under-consumption. Both might contain some grain of truth. Which business cycle theory does not?

Scanning the pages of Marxian writings it is easy to find numerous hints and suggestions which can be interpreted as anticipating any and every of the modern theoretical constructions. Here is a curious example of this kind – an excerpt from a letter to Friedrich Engels, dated May 31, 1875:

> I communicated to Moor a story (*Geschichte*) with which I wrangled privately for a long time. He thinks, however, that the problem is insolvable or at least insolvable at the present time because it involves many factors which must be yet determined. The issue is the following one: You know the tables representing prices, discount rates, etc., in the form of zigzags fluctuating up and down. I have tried repeatedly to compute these 'ups and downs' [the English expression is used by Marx] – for the purpose of business cycle analysis – as irregular curves and thus to calculate the principal laws of economic crises mathematically. I still believe that the task can be accomplished on the basis of a critically sifted statistical material.

Thus it appears that towards the end of his life Marx actually anticipated the statistical, mathematical approach to the business cycle analysis. An approach which, incidentally, only recently was declared by an authoritative Soviet Russian textbook on mathematical statistics to be nothing else but an insidious invention of the Intelligence Division of the French General Staff.

The significance of Marxian economics for the modern business cycle theory lies, however, not in such indecisive direct attempts towards the final solution of the problem but rather in the preparatory work contained mainly in the second and partly in the third volume of *Capital*. I have in mind the famous Marxian schemes of capital reproduction.

Whatever the ultimate clue to the final theoretical solution might be, an intelligent discussion, not to say explanation, of economic fluctuations must be based on some kind of a theoretical model revealing the fundamental structural characteristic of the existing economic system. In this field the original contributions of post-Marxian economics are rather uncertain. On the one hand, we have the Walrasian scheme of $m$ householders and $n$ individuals, each one buying from and selling to the other. It is pretty certain that in terms of a schematic picture of such extreme generality it would be hardly possible to give an adequate realistic description of the process of economic fluctuations.

On the other hand, there is the well-known Böhm-Bawerkian model of a simple linear flow of commodities and services, originating in some distant point where only land and labour are being applied and emptying itself, after a greater or smaller number of intermediate stages, into the final reservoir of finished consumer goods. The picture certainly does not lack concreteness. Unfortunately its concreteness is utterly misplaced.

The actual structure of the present-day economic system is anything but linear. The mutual interrelation of industries is anything but that of simple vertical succession and – what is particularly important – that initial stage characterized by exclusive application of the 'original factors of production' is non-existent. If Böhm-Bawerk did actually set out in search of this hypothetical first stage, he would find himself now still on the road.

The controversial issue is not of mean importance. It affects even such relatively simple problems as, for example, the question of substitution of machinery for labour. If approached without preconceived notions, the matter is a rather simple one. Should, let us say, the price of 'horse labour' increase in relation to the costs connected with the operation of a tractor, the farmer would substitute tractors for horses. The demand for horses would decrease. If horses were able and willing to exist on smaller hay rations the postulated price discrepancy would disappear and they would find complete employment at a lower level of 'forage rates'. Otherwise serious unemployment appears to be inevitable. Put the word 'workers' instead of 'horses', 'wage rates' instead of 'forage rates', and 'entrepreneur' instead of 'farmer' and you have a fairly accurate statement of the problem and its solution.

Now comes the compensation theorist and objects. According to him, the price of tractors could not fall in relation to the price of horses in the first place. Referring to the vertical structure of the Böhm-Bawerkian scheme he substantiates his objection but points out that 'in the last instance' – in the famous first stage – all mechanical instruments are produced by labour and land alone and concludes that an increase in the price of labour would necessarily cause an equivalent rise in the tractor price.

If a faulty structural picture of our economic system can produce confusion even in the discussion of a relatively simple theoretical problem, it is bound to raise havoc with the incomparably more complicated analysis of cyclical business fluctuations.

Marx successfully combated the Böhm-Bawerkian point of view in attacking the contemporary *théorie des débouches* of Jean Baptiste Say. He also developed the fundamental scheme describing the interrelation between consumer and capital goods industries. Far from being the *ultima ratio* of this line of analysis, the Marxian scheme still constitutes one of the few propositions concerning which there seems to exist a tolerable agreement among the majority of business cycle theories. It is interesting to note in this connection that even Professor Hayek, as can be seen from his recent articles, is busy reconstructing his own triangular investment diagram. One does not need to be a prophet to predict that sooner or later he will present to us a circular arrangement of the orthodox Marxian type.

The controversy which thus seems to be drawing towards a happy ending has incidentally put both disputing parties into a rather paradoxical situation. The dean of the bourgeois economists insisted on theoretical reduction of all capital goods to pure labour; he was opposed by the formidable proponent of the labour theory of value in the role of a defender of the independent, primary function of fixed capital.

However important these technical contributions to the progress of economic theory, in the present-day appraisal of Marxian achievements they are overshadowed by his brilliant analysis of the long-run tendencies of the capitalistic system. The record is indeed impressive: increasing concentration of wealth, rapid elimination of small and medium-sized enterprise, progressive limitation of competition, incessant technological progress accompanied by the ever growing importance of fixed capital, and, last but not least, the undiminishing amplitude of recurrent business cycles – an unsurpassed series of prognostications fulfilled, against which modern economic theory with all its refinements has little to show indeed.

What significance has this list of successful anticipations for modern economic theory? Those who believe that Marx has said the last word on the subject invite us to quit. The attitude of other somewhat less optimistic – or should I say pessimistic – critics is well expressed by Professor Heimann: 'Marx's work remains by far the most comprehensive and impressive model of what we have to do.' The whole issue of the significance of Marxian economics for modern theory is thus transformed into a methodological question.

I enter this higher plane of discussion with feelings of considerable reluctance and serious apprehension. Not that Marx and his followers were sparse in their contributions to controversial methodological questions; on the contrary, it is rather the over-abundance of contradictory and, at the same time, not very specific advice that makes it so difficult to find our way through the maze of divergent interpretations and explanations. It was in the same spirit of despair that Marx himself, in one of his lighter moods, exclaimed, 'I am not a Marxist.'

Roughly all these methodological prescriptions can be divided into two groups. On the one side are the general considerations, which, although highly interesting from the point of view of philosophy and the sociology of knowledge, are entirely non-operational from the point of view of practical scientific work. It might be true, for example, that a bourgeois economist, by the very virtue of his social and economic position, is essentially unable to recognize the driving forces and to discern the fundamental relations which govern the rise and fall of capitalist society. But what can he do about it? Give up teaching and investigating and join the proletarian ranks? This might render him a more useful member of society, but will anybody seriously maintain that such a change could improve his economic theory?

Into the same group of essentially non-operational prescriptions I would also place all references to the efficiency of the dialectical method. It might be true that the concept of unity of opposites inspired Newton in his invention of infinitesimal calculus and helped Marx in his analysis of capital accumulation – at least it would be rather difficult to disprove such contentions – but it is very doubtful whether even a most careful reading of Engel's exposition of this principle could help Mr Keynes, for example, with his solution of the unemployment problem.

On the other hand, Marxian methodology seems to contain some more concrete principles and concepts which deserve serious and detailed consideration. It is this aspect of the problem which was so ably brought to light by Dr Lange in his brilliant article on 'Marxian Economics and Modern Economic Theory'.[1] Translating the Marxian slang into the vernacular of modern economics, he defines the issue at stake as the problem of data and variables in economic theory.

Admitting the superiority of the modern equilibrium theory, Dr Lange tries to explain the marked success of Marxian prognostications by the particular attention which the author of *Capital* gave to the treatment of his data. It is an interesting thesis and it deserves a closer, critical scrutiny.

Data comprise all those elements of a theory which are used in the explanation of the variables but are not explained themselves within the system of the same theory, i.e. they are simply considered as being 'given'.

Among these there are first of all those general propositions which indicate whether we are going to talk about cabbages or kings and thus describe the general 'universe of discourse', as the logician calls it. These data are predominately qualitative in character. The so-called institutional assumptions of economic theory belong to this first category.

Marx persistently derided contemporary classical economists for their failure to specify explicitly the institutional background of their theories. He was doubtless right and the same criticism

[1] *Review of Economic Studies*, June 1935. (See p. 68 in this volume.)

applies equally well to some of the modern theorists. Fortunately enough in the process of their actual work the bourgeois economists implicitly and maybe even unconsciously framed their theories in complete accordance with the fundamental, relevant facts of the institutional background of capitalist society. Thus the subjective methodological short-comings did not impair the objective validity of their theoretical deductions.

The second type of data comprise statements of basic inter-relations which constitute the immediate point of departure for derivation and formulation of specific propositions of our theoretical system. Technical production functions, shapes of the demand curves describing the consumers choice, schedules of liquidity preferences – all these are examples of this second type of data. They are predominately quantative in character.

It is this category of data which was meant by Clapham in his famous reference to the 'empty boxes of economic theory'. The boxes are not much fuller now than they were twenty years ago, but the Marxian theory hardly contains the stuff which could be used to fill the vacuum.

Dr Lange seems to be of a different opinion. He points out in this connection the concept of technological progress as the mainstay of the Marxian theory of economic evolution of the capitalist society. This progress is being made responsible for the formation of a permanent army of unemployed which in its turn is supposed to prevent the otherwise unavoidable absorption of all profit by an ever increasing national wage bill. Dr Lange's statement of the problem suffers, however, from serious ambiguity.

As indicated before, substitution of machinery for labour can easily take place without new inventions, simply through movement from one point of a given production function to another. Reduced interest rate due to ever-increasing supply of accumulated capital might easily lead to such a result. The technical datum – the technical horizon of the entrepreneur – will remain in this case as stable as for example the cost curve of a monopolist might remain stable while he is changing his position by sliding along his curve in response to some demand variations.

A quite different phenomenon takes place when an entrepreneur reduces his demand for labour not in response to changing interest or wage rates but because a previously unknown new

invention makes it profitable to use less labour and more machinery, even if interest as well as wage rates were to remain the
same as before. Here we are facing a genuine change in primary
technological data.

Both types of adjustment mark the evolution of capitalist
economics. Dr Lange does not seem to make a clear-cut distinction between the two, but the general drift of his argument
points towards the second rather than first type of labour displacement. Neither is the position of Marx himself particularly
clear. The great stress put upon the process of progressive
accumulation, which the author of *Capital* considers to be a
necessary condition of the very existence of the present economic system, indicates that it is rather the first type of substitution
which he has in mind.

Anyway, the fact that the Marxian theory lends itself on this
point to so many different interpretations, shows that in so far
as the careful specifications and analysis of basic data is concerned, it is rather the Marxist who can learn from modern
economists than vice versa.

Finally we come to the third and last aspect of this methodological conflict. Modern economic theory limits itself to a much
narrower set of problems than that which is included in the
scope of Marxian economics. Many items treated as data in the
first system are considered to be in the group of dependent
variables in the second. In so far as the general methodological
principle is concerned any effective extension of a theoretical
system beyond its old frontier represents a real scientific progress.

To avoid a misunderstanding it must be kept in mind that
such extension cannot possibly result in a complete liquidation
of independent data. It simply replaces one set of data by another. So, for example, if we were to include governmental
action as a dependent variable within the system of economic
theory, the amount of public expenditure of the height of import
tariffs had to be considered as a function of some other economic
variables in the same way as the output of a firm in competition
is considered to be a function of the prevailing market price. It
is perfectly obvious, however, that the first type of relationship
is much less definite in its character than the second. This, I
think, is the reason why the modern economist is reluctant to
discuss both types of interrelations on the same plane. And he

is right because neither part can profit from such artificial connection, which does not mean that the result of the two types of investigation could not and should not be fruitfully combined in attempts toward some kind of a wider synthesis. Occasional alliances and frequent co-operation are, however, something quite different than radical unification accompanied by complete obliteration of existing border lines.

Neither his analytical accomplishments nor the purported methodological superiority can explain the Marxian record of correct prognostications. His strength lies in realistic, empirical knowledge of the capitalist system.

Repeated experiments have shown that in their attempts to prognosticate individual behaviour, professional psychologists systematically fall behind experienced laymen with a knack for 'character reading'. Marx was the great character reader of the capitalist system. As many individuals of this type, Marx had also his rational theories, but these theories in general do not hold water. Their inherent weakness shows up as soon as other economists not endowed with the exceptionally realistic sense of the master try to proceed on the basis of his blueprints.

The significance of Marx for modern economic theory is that of an inexhaustible source of direct observation. Much of the present-day theorizing is purely derivative, second-hand theorizing. We often theorize not about business enterprises, wages, or business cycles but about other people's theories of profits, other people's theories of wages, and other people's theories of business cyles. If before attempting any explanation one wants to learn what profits and wages and capitalist enterprises actually are, he can obtain in the three volumes of *Capital* more realistic and relevant first-hand information than he could possibly hope to find in ten successive issues of the *United States Census*, a dozen textbooks on contemporary economic institutions, and even, may I dare to say, the collected essays of Thorstein Veblen.

## SELECTED BIBLIOGRAPHY

BLAUG, MARK. *Economic Theory in Retrospect*. London: Heinemann, 1962.

DOBB, MAURICE. 'A Note on Some Aspects of the Economic Theory of Marx', *Science and Society:* Vol. 3, 1937–8.

ROGIN, LEO. *The Meaning and Validity of Economic Theory*. 1954.

SCHUMPETER, J. A. *History of Economic Analysis*. 1954.

STRACHEY, JOHN. *The Nature of Capitalist Crisis*. London: Gollancz, 1935.

# 2. Marx and Keynes

# Marx and Keynes

*Joan Robinson*

THE RELATIONSHIP between Marxist and academic economists has changed in recent years. During the time of Marshall
an impassable gulf still divided them. The one party was engaged in exposing the evils of the capitalist system, the other in
painting it in an agreeable light. One regarded the system as a
passing historical phase, containing within itself the germs of its
own dissolution; the other regarded the system as a permanent,
almost a logical, necessity. This fundamental difference of outlook was supported by a difference of language, each party using
terms strongly coloured by its own point of view. Thus, the
academics described the interest obtained by owning capital as
the *reward of abstinence*, or *waiting*, and profit as the *reward of
enterprise*, while Marx treats interest and profit (and rent) as *unpaid labour*, or *surplus value* (the surplus of the value produced
by labour over the value paid to labour). This complete difference of attitude made inter-communication between the two
schools impossible.

Latter-day academics have, for the most part, undergone a
striking change. The circumstances of the times have forced
them to concentrate on two problems, monopoly and unemployment, which naturally raise doubts as to whether all is for the
best in the best of all possible economic systems, and they are
more inclined to analyse the defects of capitalism than to dwell
upon its merits. The attempt to represent merely owning capital
(waiting) as a productive activity has been abandoned, and the
view is gaining ground that it is misleading to treat capital itself
as a factor of production, on the same footing as labour. 'It is
preferable to regard labour . . . as the sole factor of production,

This paper appeared in Italian in *Critica Economica*, November
1948. The first two paragraphs are taken from an article which
appeared in the *Economic Journal*, June–September 1941. Reprinted
from Collected Economic Papers 1. Oxford: Blackwell, 1950.

operating in a given environment of technique, natural resources, capital equipment, and effective demand'.[1] What is more
important, capitalism is no longer regarded as an eternal necessity. Thus, Keynes writes: 'I see the *rentier* aspect of capitalism
as a transitional phase which will disappear when it has done its
work'.[2] And Professor Hicks: 'I do not think one could count
upon the long survival of anything like a capitalist system [in
the absence of a trend of innovations sufficiently strong to maintain investment] . . . one cannot repress the thought that perhaps
the whole Industrial Revolution of the last two hundred years
has been nothing else but a vast secular boom'.[3] These *dicta* are
much closer to Marx than anything that can be found in Marshall,
while Mr Kalecki's epigram: 'The tragedy of investment is that
it causes crisis because it is useful',[4] has a close affinity with
Marx: 'The real barrier of capitalist production is capital itself'.[5]

This change, however, had no direct relation to Marxism. It
was rather the result of an explosion of academic economics from
within.

The system of thought which dominated academic economic
teaching (and greatly influenced policy) even after the onset of
the great slump in 1930, allowed no place for unemployment as
more than a mere accident or friction. 'Natural economic forces'
tended to establish full employment. Crises were treated as a
special problem, and kept, as it were, in quarantine, so that
theory of crisis did not infect the main body of economic doctrine. Confronted with massive and persistent unemployment in
the first post-war period, the orthodox theory was baffled and
ran into a tangle of unconvincing sophistries. Out of this situation arose Keynes' General Theory, by which I do not mean
simply the book called *The General Theory of Employment,
Interest, and Money*, but the whole stream of ideas, or rather the
analytical system, to which that book made the main contribution, but which is still in process of developing and perfecting

[1] Keynes, *General Theory of Employment, Interest and Money*,
p. 213.
[2] Ibid., p. 376.
[3] *Value and Capital*, p. 302.
[4] *Essays in the Theory of Economic Fluctuations*, p. 149.
[5] *Capital*, Vol. III, Ch. 15, 2.

itself, finding new applications and modifying its methods to treat new problems.

Keynes' main achievement was in a sense negative (though it has many positive consequences both for theory and for policy). It was to show that there is no automatic self-righting mechanism tending to establish full employment in an unplanned private-enterprise economy.

The basis of the orthodox doctrine was Say's Law of Markets – the theory that supply creates its own demand – production and sale of one lot of commodities provides the purchasing power to buy other commodities. Thus general over-production cannot occur. This doctrine was accepted generally without much criticism. Marshall called it an axiom – that is, something self-evident.[1] But it was also elaborated and defended by a sophisticated argument.

The orthodox conception of a natural self-equilibrating mechanism in the *laisser-faire* system had two branches.

According to the first, the rate of money-wages provides the mechanism. If men are unemployed they will be prepared to accept lower wages. The fall in wages will increase demand for labour, and so unemployment will quickly disappear. If it does not disappear, that is due to the stupid obstinacy of trade unions in refusing to accept a cut in wages. Keynes showed that this theory was based on a very simple fallacy – the fallacy of composition. It is true for any one employer, or for any one industry – to a lesser extent for any one country in international trade – that a cut in wages, by lowering the price of the commodity produced, will increase its sales, and so lead to an increase of employment in making it. But if all wages are cut, all prices fall, all money incomes fall, and demand is reduced as much as costs. No one employer then has any motive to take on more men. In a crowd, anyone can get a better view of the procession if he stands on a chair. But if they all get up on chairs no one has a better view.

The second line of orthodox argument concerned the rate of interest. If the demand for consumer goods falls, this causes unemployment in making consumer goods. But, according to the orthodox argument, reduced demand for consumer goods means

[1] *Pure Theory of Domestic Values*, p. 36.

increased saving. An increase in saving means that there is more money to be lent to industry, so that the rate of interest falls. As a consequence, industry will want more capital (as it can now borrow on cheaper terms) and so there will be an increase of employment in making capital goods. This will exactly compensate the fall of employment in making consumer goods.

Here again Keynes pointed out a very simple error; this time the error of assuming what it is required to prove. If employment, and incomes, are unchanged, then a fall in consumption entails an increase in saving. But the first effect of a fall in consumption is to reduce incomes and cause losses, and with lower incomes there is less saving. If the rate of investment in new capital does not increase, incomes will fall to the point at which saving is no greater than before, and there is no tendency for the rate of interest to fall. (This led to discarding the theory that the rate of interest is determined by the supply and demand of saving, and putting in its place a totally different theory of the rate of interest based on demand for the stock of money.)

In so far as it is possible to summarize a complex system of thought in a few words, we may say that the essence of Keynes' theory is as follows: an unequal distribution of income sets up a chronic tendency for the demand for goods to fall short of the productive capacity of industry. Those who desire to consume have not the money to buy, and so do not constitute a profitable market. Those who have the money to buy do not wish to consume as much as they could, but to accumulate wealth, that is, to save. So long as there is a sufficient demand for new capital investment (in houses, industrial equipment, means of transport, growing stocks of goods, etc.), savings are utilized, and the system functions adequately. But saving in itself provides no guarantee that capital accumulation will take place; on the contrary, saving limits the demand for consumption goods, and so limits the demand for capital to produce them. Booms occur when there are profitable outlets for investment. Long periods of prosperity could occur in the nineteenth century when there were large opportunities for profitable investment in exploiting new inventions and developing new continents. Pseudo-prosperity occurs in wartime because war creates unlimited demand. But prosperity is not the normal state for a highly-developed capitalist system, and the very accumulation of capital, on the one hand by increasing wealth and promoting saving, and on the other by saturating the demand for new capital, makes prosperity harder to attain.

Thus crises appear, not as a superficial blemish in the system of private enterprise, but as symptoms of a deep-seated and progressive disease. Though Keynes' theory arose out of the problem of unemployment, it has many other applications. It has proved invaluable in the analysis of post-war inflation. It has revolutionized the theory of international trade. And it has implications, not yet fully worked out, which undermine the traditional academic theory of the long-run supply of capital and of the distribution of the product of industry between labour and capital.

Academic theory, by a path of its own, has thus arrived at a position which bears considerable resemblance to Marx's system. In both, unemployment plays an essential part. In both, capitalism is seen as carrying within itself the seeds of its own decay. On the negative side, as opposed to the orthodox equilibrium theory, the systems of Keynes and Marx stand together, and there is now, for the first time, enough common ground between Marxist and academic economists to make discussion possible. In spite of this there has still been very little serious study of Marx by English academic economists.

Apart from political prejudice, the neglect of Marx is largely due to the extreme obscurity of his method of exposition. There are two serious defects in the Marxian apparatus, which are quite superficial in themselves, and can easily be remedied, but which have led to endless misunderstandings.

In Marx's terminology $C$, constant capital, represents productive equipment (factories, machinery, etc.), and raw material and power; $V$, variable capital, represents the wages bill; and $S$, surplus, rent interest, and profits. Now, if we write (as Marx habitually does) $C + V + S$ to represent the flow of production, say per year, then $C$ is not the stock of capital invested, but the annual wear-and-tear and amortization of capital.

$$\frac{S}{C + V}$$

is the share of profits in turnover, and not the rate of profit on capital invested. The rate of profit which (for Marx as in orthodox systems) tends to equality in different lines of production, and the rate of profit which tends to fall as capital accumulates is not

$$\frac{S}{C + V}$$

but the rate of profit on capital invested.

Marx himself was well aware of this point, but his habitual use of the expression:

$$\frac{S}{C + V}$$

for the rate of profit on capital is excessively confusing. Moreover, lumping raw material and power along with equipment in the single concept of constant capital makes it impossible to distinguish between prime and overhead costs, since prime costs consist of $V$ and part of $C$ (raw materials and power), while another part of $C$ is overhead. Thus Marx's apparatus is useless for many of the problems in which academic economists have interested themselves, especially in connection with short-period supply price and the influence of monopoly on the share of wages in output.

The second main difficulty arises from Marx's method of reckoning in terms of *value* or labour time. With technical progress and capital accumulation, output per man-hour tends to rise, so that the *value* of commodities is constantly falling. Academic economists are much concerned with output, and with concepts such as the 'real national income', the 'level of real wages', and so forth. To measure these in terms of *value* is to measure with a piece of elastic. Thus academic economists, if they get as far as considering Marx at all, are apt to form the impression that his methods of thought are quite useless, and to dismiss the whole of his analysis as an inextricable mass of confusion, which it is not worth the trouble of understanding.

This impatience has been further encouraged by the perennial controversy over the labour theory of value. In my opinion, this has been much ado about nothing, and the pother that there has been over it has disguised both from the academics and from the Marxists the real nature of the question at issue. To the academic economist, the 'theory of value' means the theory of *relative*

prices – the prices of commodities in terms of each other. Now
Marx's theory of relative prices, as set out in Volume III of
*Capital*, is quite simple. The rate of profit on capital tends to
equality in all lines of production. Wages of labour also tend to
equality in all occupations (allowing for differences in skill). The
amount of capital per unit of labour employed is governed by
the state of technical development. The normal price (apart from
errors and perturbations of the market) for, say, a year's output
of any commodity, is equal to the wages of the labour employed
in producing it *plus* cost of raw materials, power, and wear and
tear of plant *plus* profit, at the ruling rate, upon the capital
invested. Prices would be proportional to *values* if capital per
unit of labour (the organic composition of capital) were the
same everywhere, but, in fact, for technical reasons, proportionately more capital is employed in some industries than in others,
and since the rate of profit on capital invested tends to equality,
profits, relatively to wages, tend to be high where the ratio of
capital to labour is high. Thus normal prices are equal to long-
run costs of production, and the ruling average rate of profit on
capital is the supply price of capital to any particular line of
production. Conditions of demand determine the amount of
each commodity produced.

There is nothing in this that contradicts orthodox theory. It
leaves out such refinements and complications as price rising or
falling with the scale of output (much emphasized by Marshall),
and it does not touch upon questions of oligopoly and imperfect
competition (which have been elaborated in recent years), but it
is the obvious first starting-point for any theory of relative
prices. The academic economist may consider it too simple and
primitive to be of much interest to him at this time of day, but
he has no reason to regard it as either mysterious or fundamentally erroneous. Equally, the Marxist has no reason to regard
the labour theory of value, *as a theory of relative prices*, either as
particularly important or as fundamentally opposed to orthodoxy.

What divides Marx's theory from others is not at all the
question of relative prices of commodities but the question of
the *total* supply of capital and the rate of profit on capital *as a
whole*. On this question there is a sharp difference between Marx
and the pre-Keynesian academics.

In the Austrian theory of value, the supply of capital is some-how given. For Marshall, capital accumulation represents a 'real cost' to capitalists – the 'sacrifice of waiting' – and accumulation goes on so long as profit exceeds this cost. In equilibrium, the rate of profit is just sufficient to cover the real cost of waiting. Thus there is a supply price for capital as a whole, and the amount of capital tends to be such that the rate of profit is equal to this supply price.

In Marx's system an urge to accumulate is inherent in the capitalist economy, the amount of capital, at any moment, is the result of the process of accumulation which has been going on in the past, the total of profits is the difference between total net receipts and the amount which it is necessary to give to the workers to ensure their reproduction, and the rate of profit is simply this total of profits averaged over the total of capital in existence. Thus the real differences between Marx and the ortho-dox schools concern the question of what governs the accumu-lation of capital and the distribution of the total product of industry between workers and capitalists. Compared to these problems, the determination of relative prices of commodities appears as a secondary question which has been too much flat-tered by all the attention that has been paid to it. It is precisely upon these large questions that the old orthodox system has been profoundly shaken. Thus, as between Marxists and Keynes-ians, the labour theory of value is a totally irrelevant issue.

What remains to divide them? Primarily, of course, a differ-ence in philosophical and political outlook, but here I wish to discuss the question as far as possible on the plane of ideas rather than of ideologies, and to confine the argument to problems of economic analysis, for I believe, with Professor Schumpeter,[1] that Marx was a great economist, in just the same sense as Ricardo, Marshall and Keynes were great economists, and that his merits simply as a theorist have been concealed by the prophetic robes in which he has been dressed up.

The central issue is the theory of crises. I have argued else-where[2] that the theory adumbrated in Volume II of *Capital* has close affinities with Keynes. But it is possible that I have over-

---

[1] Cf. Schumpeter, *Capitalism, Socialism and Democracy*, 1942
[2] *An Essay on Marxian Economics*, Chapter VI.

emphasized the resemblance. The last two volumes of *Capital*, which Marx did not complete, are excessively obscure and have been subjected to many interpretations. The waters are dark and it may be that whoever peers into them sees his own face.

Here I wish to concentrate on the differences rather than the resemblances between the two systems. In Keynes' system the clue to crises is found in variations of the *inducement to invest*, which depends primarily upon the prospect of future profit from new investment. As capital accumulates, the profitability of further investment declines. This accounts both for the sharp onset of a slump after a period of high investment, and for the secular tendency for unemployment to develop with growing wealth and productive capacity. Of this there are only scattered hints in Marx, and it is incompatible with his main argument. For in Marx's system the amount of investment is governed by the amount of surplus which the capitalists succeed in extracting from the system, that is to say, it is the rate of saving out of profits which governs the rate of investment. Competition and technical progress set up an urge to accumulation, for each capitalist fears to fall behind in the race if he does not continuously invest in new capital equipment embodying the latest developments. Thus the problem of effective demand does not arise, and though Marx explicitly repudiated Say's law as childish nonsense, yet he no more than Mill or Marshall admits the divorce between decisions to save and decisions to invest, which, in Keynes' system, appears as the root cause of crises and unemployment.

This does not mean, however, that Marx neglects the problem of unemployment. On the contrary, 'the reserve army of labour' is an essential feature of his system. In his view, the amount of employment offered by capitalists depends upon the amount of capital in existence, and there is unemployment because there is insufficient capital to employ all the potentially available labour. When accumulation catches up upon population growth (and the growth of the supply of 'free' labour as peasants and artisans are sucked into the labour market by the spread of the capitalist system), a temporary relative shortage of labour stimulates labour-saving inventions and so replenishes the reserve army once more. Now, unemployment of this type, in the world at large, is a phenomenon of the greatest importance. It exists in the backward, over-populated countries of the east, and, indeed, everywhere except amongst the most developed industrial nations. And something analogous has reappeared in war-shattered economies where unemployment results from the mere lack of equipment and material to work with. Unemployment of this kind is radically different from unemployment due to a deficiency of demand. It seems, then, that Marx and Keynes are discussing two different problems, and that each theory is required to supplement the other. Marx, however, regarded his system as all-inclusive, and he purported to derive from it an explanation of the crises which develop in advanced capitalist economies. It is here that, in the light of Keynes' argument, Marx's analysis appears inadequate and unconvincing.

There are two distinct strands of thought to be detected in *Capital*. According to the first, which is fully developed in Volume I, real wages (broadly speaking, with exceptions and reservations) tend to remain constant at subsistence level (though the subsistence level contains a 'moral and historical element' due to the customary standard of life). As productivity increases with capital accumulation and technical progress, the rate of exploitation (the ratio of profits to wages) therefore tends to rise. Capital at the same time tends to be concentrated in ever fewer hands as large units prevail in the competitive struggle over smaller units. Thus there is an ever-growing difference between the wealth of the few and the poverty of the many which in the end will lead to an explosion – the overthrow of capitalism and the 'expropriation of the expropriators'.

Now, the course of history since Marx's day has disproved this prediction. In the foremost capitalist countries the level of real wages has indubitably risen, and the gap in the standard of life of the workers and the capitalists has narrowed, most markedly in England and the Scandinavian countries, but to some extent in all capitalist nations. Marx did not foresee to what an extent capitalism would be able to buy off the workers with refrigerators and Ford cars.

Marxists often seek to explain away the rise in the standard of life of the industrial workers in the advanced countries by attributing it mainly to the exploitation of colonial peoples. The white workers are fatted 'palace slaves', and the capitalists can afford to pamper them so long as they extract profit from the exploitation of the coloured peoples. But this theory is unconvincing. If the profit obtainable abroad is high, there is no reason why any individual capitalist should be willing to accept a lower rate at home. Investment in colonial regions will be kept up and investment at home retarded, so that the bargaining position of home labour is weakened, not strengthened, by the existence of cheap labour abroad.

Colonial exploitation clearly does raise the level of real wages of home labour, but it does so by a different mechanism from that postulated by the theory of 'palace slaves'. The low wages of the colonial workers influence the standard of life of the home workers through low prices of raw materials and foodstuffs relatively to manufactures. (At the present moment, when the terms of trade are relatively favourable to primary producers, the industrial workers are feeling the difference.) This advantage is not confined to workers in the imperial nations. The innocent Swedes gain as much from favourable terms of trade for tropical raw materials as the British or the Dutch.

The importance of cheap colonial labour to the standard of life of the industrial workers has never, so far as I know, been systematically evaluated. But though it has been of obvious importance, particularly in England, it would be absurd to attribute to it a predominant share in the rise of the standard of life in the United States in the last fifty years, even if we extend the conception of colonies to include the Southern States, for raw materials 'imported' from regions of colonial exploitation play too small a part in the total of American consumption to account for more than a fraction of the spectacular rise in American wealth.

Thus it appears that Marx's prediction of 'increasing misery' of the workers has failed to be fulfilled. At this point Keynes once more supplements Marx, for he shows how increasing wealth brings its nemesis in a different way. Growing susceptibility to unemployment appears instead of growing poverty of the masses as the weakness at the heart of developing capitalism.

There is a second strand of thought in *Capital* which is quite different from the first, and which, indeed, is hard to reconcile with it. This is the Law of Falling Rate of Profit, elaborated in the third volume. In this argument (once more with exceptions and qualifications) it is the rate of exploitation, not the rate of real wages, which tends to remain constant. If the rate of exploitation is constant, real wages rise with productivity, the workers receiving a constant share in a growing total of real output. Now, according to Marx, there is a broad tendency for the organic composition of capital to rise as time goes by; that is to say, capital-using inventions are the predominant form of technical progress, so that capital per unit of labour employed is continuously rising. If capital per unit of labour is rising, but profit per unit of labour is constant (or rises more slowly) then the rate of profit on capital is falling. Thus capitalists undermine the basis of their own prosperity by their rage for accumulation. The connection between this theory and the theory of crises is made in the most tangled and confusing passages of Volume III, and has been the subject of many conflicting interpretations. Instead of plunging into that jungle, it is better to concentrate upon the first stage of the argument – the rising organic composition of capital.

Marx (or rather Engels for him) clearly admits that it is not the case that all technical progress increases capital per unit of labour. Historically, the key to development has been transport, and inventions which save time, save capital. It is therefore by no means obvious that organic composition has really been rapidly rising with the development of capitalism. Huge investments in machinery are obvious to the naked eye, but it is impossible to assess how far the saving in stocks and work in progress due to speeding up communications and speeding up processes has in the past offset growing investment in equipment. And it is impossible to tell what the predominant type of invention will be in the future. Certainly many great capital-saving inventions (such as wireless in place of cables) have been made in recent times. This is a question to be investigated. Meanwhile, it is at least possible to imagine, for the sake of argument, that from now on capital-saving inventions will balance capital-using inventions, so that organic composition ceases to rise (capital per unit of labour employed will tend to remain constant), while technical progress continues to raise productivity just as rapidly as before. A world in which organic composition is constant (or, for that matter, falling) is perfectly conceivable. To such a world, Marx's analysis would have no application, and the whole of that part of his theory of crises which depends upon the declining tendency of profits would fall to the ground. His case for a tendency to ever-deepening crises as a necessary and inevitable feature of capitalism therefore cannot be sustained. If there is a fundamental defect in capitalism it must have deeper roots than in a mere accident of technique.[1]

Keynes' theory does not depend upon any particular tendency in organic composition. Capital-saving inventions are likely to offer less outlet for investment than capital-using ones, and so tend to make a smaller contribution to maintaining effective demand. At the same time they may reduce the share of a given output going to capital (for in Keynes' system there is no reason why the rate of exploitation should be constant) and so tend to reduce the excessive propensity to save. But, either way, the question, in Keynes' system, is of secondary importance, and his theory is equally cogent whichever form technical progress in the future may happen to take.

Thus it appears that whichever branch of Marx's theory of crises we follow, it is necessary to call in Keynes' analysis to complete it, and neither part of Marx's argument can stand up by itself.

At the same time, Keynes' system of thought operates within a restricted field. He does not touch at all upon the major questions with which Marx was concerned, and he has undermined the orthodox theory of long-period equilibrium without putting anything very definite in its place. Thus Marx's theory, or at any rate some theory on the questions which Marx discussed, is as much required to supplement Keynes as Keynes' theory is to supplement Marx.

[1] In my *Essay on Marxian Economics* I have tried to show that even granted the assumption of rising organic composition, the theory still fails to be convincing.

## SELECTED BIBLIOGRAPHY

KLEIN, L. R. *The Keynesian Revolution*. New York: Macmillan, 1947.

MEEK, R. L. *Studies in the Labour Theory of Value*. London: Lawrence and Wishart, 1956.

ROBINSON, J. 'Open Letter from a Keynesian to a Marxian', *On Re-reading Marx*. Cambridge, 1953.

SHOVE, G. 'Mrs Robinson on Marxian Economics', *Economic Journal*. April 1944.

SWEEZY, P. M. 'John Maynard Keynes' in Lekachman (ed.) *Keynes' General Theory: Reports of Three Decades*. New York: Columbia University Press, 1963.

# Keynes and Marx on the Theory of Capital Accumulation, Money and Interest[1]

*Fan-Hung*

IN THE course of his criticism on the 'classical' economists, Mr J. M. Keynes has come, as it were, to occupy much common ground with Marx. It is the purpose of this paper to re-examine Marx's theory of capital accumulation and of the rate of interest contained in Volumes II and III of *Capital* in the light of what Mr Keynes has to say on these subjects.

## I. CAPITALIST PRODUCTION AND ACCUMULATION

By the term capitalist production Marx means the process by which property-owners advance their assets in the shape of money with the sole intention of getting back the money form of their assets advanced plus a surplus. Marx described the typical form of capitalist production in the following formula:

$$M \rightarrow C \left\{ \frac{m}{1} \ldots p \ldots C' \text{ or } \left\{ \frac{c}{\triangle c} \rightarrow M \left\{ \frac{M}{\triangle M} \right. \right. \right.$$

This means that capitalist production consists of three stages: (1) $M \rightarrow C$, the transformation of money–capital, $M$, into the elements of production, $C$, namely the means of production, $m$, and labour–power, l; (2) $p$, the activity of production, i.e. the creation of new utilities by the application of labour–power;

[1] I am very much indebted to Mr Maurice Dobb for his constant supervision and advice, and also to Dr Michael Kalecki for his encouragement and constructive criticisms. I have also had much help from Mr H. S. Furns and, also, from Mr Brian Tew for reading all and the latter part of this paper respectively. But none of them has any responsibility for errors which remain or for any of the opinions I have expressed. I must add that my research work was undertaken while a research fellow of the China Foundation for the Promotion of Education and Culture.

Reprinted from *The Review of Economic Studies*, October 1939.

(3) $C' \rightarrow M'$, the re-transformation of the newly created utilities into their money form, i.e. the sale of finished goods at a profitable price. Of these three stages the first and last, $M \rightarrow C$ and $C' \rightarrow M'$, belong to the sphere of circulation, while the second, $p$, belongs to the sphere of production.

Marx intended this formula to indicate the source from which the capitalists' additional income, $\triangle M$, arose. Many economists had suggested that $\triangle M$ was created in the sphere of circulation, $C' \rightarrow M'$, by buying cheap and selling dear. Marx rejected this view on the ground that if one man gets more by $\triangle M$ by selling, another man must get less by $\triangle M$ by purchase, so that, given the value of finished goods as determined in a competitive situation, $\triangle M$ cannot be created from $M$ merely by an act of exchange. Hence, it was evident that $\triangle M$, though realized in the sphere of circulation, was firstly created as $\triangle c$ in the sphere of production by the application of labour–power. In other words, for the system as a whole, $\triangle M$ is a function of the expenditure of current labour–power, l, at any given ratio of productivity to wages.

Concerning the cost-value relation, it is easy to see that in the process of production $C$ represents the aggregate capital value, $M$, which is composed of two portions: the one is money–capital which has been invested in the means of production, namely, the value of capital equipment, while the other is money–capital which has been invested in labour–power, namely, wages. Marx called the first portion constant capital, designated as $c$, and the latter portion variable capital, designated as $v$, on the grounds, as we have just stated, that $\triangle M$ varies as the expenditure of current labour–power, l, and, therefore, as 'wage–capital'. The value of $\triangle c$, namely, $\triangle M$, is called by Marx surplus value, designated as $s$, the only source of the revenue of the capitalist class. Thus the total value of finished goods $C'$, or $c + \triangle c$, namely $M'$, or $M + \triangle M$, or $c + v + s$, is called by Marx the total value of finished goods ready to be sold, designated as $V$. Since the aggregate of finished goods consists of two kinds, means of production and means of consumption, Marx constructs two equations:

Department I of Means of Production
$$c_1 + v_1 + s_1 = V_1 \qquad \qquad \ldots (1)$$

Department II of Means of Consumption

$$c_2+v_2+s_2 = V_2 \qquad \ldots (2)$$

For the sake of analysis, Marx made use of two models of capitalist production: (1) 'simple reproduction', and (2) 'enlarged reproduction'. In the former the relationship between the two departments is so arranged that at the beginning of every cycle of production the same scale of production is repeated. In the latter the relationship between them is so modified that at the beginning of every cycle of production the scale of production is expanded. 'Enlarged reproduction' is what Marx describes as capital accumulation.

According to Marx smoothly running 'simple reproduction' depends upon three conditions:

(*a*) The means of production produced by Department I must be as much as is demanded by the two departments for replacement, neither more nor less, namely:

$$c_1+c_2 = V_1 \qquad \ldots (3)$$

(*b*) The total value of consumption goods produced by Department II must exactly correspond to the total value of the consumption goods demanded by both departments, namely:

$$(v_1+v_2)+(s_1+s_2) = V_2 \qquad \ldots (4)$$

(*c*) From the above two necessary conditions, we derive a third, namely: if each department has purchased that part of its own products for its own use, they must be able to sell to each other the remainder of their products, i.e.

$$c_2 = v_1+s_1 \qquad \ldots (5)$$

or, more directly:

since $\quad V_1-c_1 = c_2 \qquad \ldots (3)$

and $\quad V_2-(v_2+s_2) = v_1+s_1 \qquad \ldots (4)$

but $\quad V_1-c_1 = v_1+s_1 \qquad \ldots (1)$

hence $\quad c_2 = v_1+s_1 \qquad \ldots (5)$

In the case of accumulation we have three different conditions.

(*a*) Since the capitalists increase their investment, they do not consume their income completely. Therefore,

$$V_2 < (v_1+s_1)+(v_2+s_2) \qquad \ldots (5)$$

(*b*) The total value of the products of Department I in the form of the means of production will be larger than the sum of the means of production required by the two departments for replacement use; namely,

$$V_1 > c_1 + c_2 \qquad \qquad \dots (7)$$

(*c*) From the above two equations we derive a third:

$$c_2 < v_1 + s_1 \qquad \qquad \dots (8)$$

In economic terms this means that the difference between the sum total of the means of production produced by Department I and that part of the means of production reserved for replacement use by the same department must be larger than that part of the means of production required by the second department for replacement use.

Marx is here assuming that when capitalists refrain from spending the whole of their income ($s$) on consumption goods, the difference is forthwith compensated by an equivalent increase in investment; so that the aggregate demand for and supply of commodities in terms of money will balance. Readers, however, are advised to refer to those numerical illustrations given by Marx in the last two chapters of Volume II of *Capital*.

It is easy to see that both of these simple models of reproduction imply two preliminary conditions. One is that all things required for the purpose of maintaining the smooth running of reproduction are being produced in certain definite proportions. For instance, in the case of simple reproduction, $v_1 + s_1 = c_2$ is one of the conditions which a central plan of social production must provide for keeping supply equal to demand. If this condition fails in such a way that $v_1 + s_1 > c_2$ as a result of lack of planning in the sphere of production, then a relative overproduction of means of production of Department I must happen and correspondingly a deficiency of effective demand for means of production of Department II. Or, if $v_1 + s_1 < c_2$, the converse will occur. Similarly in the case of enlarged reproduction, production must be so regulated as to make $c_2 + \triangle c_2 = V_1 - (c_1 + \triangle c_1)$. If this condition is not fulfilled a gap between aggregate supply and demand will be inevitable. The second preliminary condition implies that the things that have been produced in these requisite proportions must be able to be exchanged at their values. This implies a co-ordination of the sphere of circulation as well as of production. Or, to put it differently, no portion of money realized by selling must fail to be spent in re-purchase. Suppose that in the case of enlarged production the necessary condition $c_2 < v_1 + s_1$ by $\Delta s_1$ has been fulfilled. If, nevertheless, Department II fails to buy $\Delta s_1$ from Department I, after Department I has bought means of consumption from the second department, it will follow that this act of accumulation of money in the second department must lead to a relative over-production of means of production $\Delta s$ in the first department, no matter how correctly the relationship between the two departments in the sphere of production has been maintained. Under a system of capitalist production, as Marx remarks, 'because nothing is undertaken according to social plans, but everything depends on the infinitely different conditions, means, etc., with which the individual capitalist operates'[1] great disturbances will inevitably occur either as a result of relative over-production or as a result of money-hoarding or increase of saving.

It is interesting to note that Mr Keynes' principle of effective demand has many points in common with the second aspect of Marx's analysis. Mr Keynes emphasizes that the realization of the entrepreneur's profit depends on the existence of an adequate effective demand. Leaving aside the question of cost due to the deterioration of capital equipment, the aggregate supply price, according to Mr Keynes, consists of two quantities: one is factor cost, $F$, while the other is the entrepreneur's profit, $P$. On the other hand, effective demand, $D$, also consists of two quantities, namely the amount which the community is expected to spend on consumption, $C$, and the amount which the community is expected to devote to new investment, $I$. Symbolically, this means that if $Z = F + P$ and $D = I + C$, then the condition $Z = D$ depends upon $F + P = I + C$. Given $I$: if $C < (F + P) - I$ then $D < Z$. This means that capitalists will lose money owing to a deficiency of demand for consumption goods. Or, given $C$: if $I < (F + P) - C$, then $D < Z$, namely, the capitalists will fail to realize their profit owing to a deficiency of effective demand for investment goods.

[1] *Capital*, Vol. II, Ch. VIII, p. 196.

To return to Marx's analysis of enlarged production: if we abstract the value of replaced capital, i.e., the deterioration of capital equipment, by deducting $c$ from both sides of the equation $c+v+s = V$, then $v+s = V-c$. This equation, then, virtually becomes Mr Keynes' equation $F+P = Z$. As to the other equation, $D = C+I$, Mr Keynes and Marx agree to the extent that both of them assume that the realization of the profit-expectations of capitalists depends upon the condition that (assuming labourers spend all their incomes on consumption goods) the capitalists must *either* consume all their surplus value *or* consume one part of it and directly invest the remainder of it, so that no gap between supply and demand is created by the act of saving. Therefore, the proposition that saving will check effective demand unless there is corresponding investment, as elaborated by Mr Keynes, is also implied in the theory of Marx.

There is still another aspect of hoarding which reveals common ground on which Mr Keynes and Marx stand. This concerns the deficiency of effective demand that is caused by a decrease of current expenditure on replacement and renewal. Thus, Mr Keynes says:

> 'All capital investment is destined to result, sooner or later, in capital disinvestment [by which Mr Keynes means the sale of an old investment]. Thus, the problem of providing that the new capital investment shall always outrun capital disinvestment sufficiently to fill the gap between net income and consumption presents a problem which is increasingly difficult as capital increases. New capital investment can only take place in excess of capital disinvestment if future expenditure on consumption is expected to increase.'[1]

According to Marx's analysis, in the case of enlarged reproduction, if gross investment made by the two departments is not larger than $c_1+c_2$, other things being equal, there would be no net accumulation of capital at all. If it is smaller than $c_1+c_2$, other things being equal, there would be even a net decrease of accumulation. Once again, Marx and Mr Keynes are in agreement. Actually the main equations of Mr Keynes' 'General

[1] *General Theory of Employment, Money and Interest*, Ch. 8, p. 105.

Theory of Employment' can be deduced from Marx's two main equations of enlarged production. Where Marx speaks of constant capital imparting its value to the product, he is using a conception parallel to Mr Keynes' deterioration of capital equipment, namely, user cost plus supplementary cost, and, if Mr Keynes' conception of investment is taken to mean net investment, namely, 'the net additions to all kinds of capital equipment', it becomes obvious that Mr Keynes' aggregate supply price gross of user cost and supplementary cost and Marx's total value of product are the same thing. It may also be of interest to note other similarities in the use that the two theories make of the following concepts:

(1) Mr Keynes' Aggregate Supply Price and Marx's Total Value of Product. According to Mr Keynes, aggregate supply price (gross of user cost and supplementary cost) is factor cost plus normal profit plus user cost plus supplementary cost, designated as $A = F+P+U+W$. According to Marx, the total value of the product is constant capital plus variable capital plus surplus value designated as $V = c+v+s$. Since $F+P = v+s = w+r+i+p$ (where $w$, $r$, $i$, and $p$ represent wages, rent, interest, and profit) and $c = u+w$, it follows that Mr Keynes' $A =$ Marx's $V$.

(2) Income and Revenue. According to Mr Keynes, income is aggregate supply price (gross of user cost and supplementary cost) minus user cost minus supplementary cost, designated as $Y = A-U-W$. According to Marx, revenue is the total value of the product minus constant capital, namely, $R = V-c$. Since $A-U-W = F+P = V-c = v+s$, it follows that Mr Keynes' 'income' is Marx's 'revenue', i.e. $Y = R$.

(3) Investment and the Purchase of the Means of Production. Mr Keynes has described investment as total sales between entrepreneurs, i.e. $I = U+W+\Delta I = A_1$. Marx describes the purchase of means of production as consisting of old constant capital plus current additional constant capital and designates this as $c + \Delta c$. The identity of the two is clear. Mr Keynes' net investment is total sales between entrepreneurs minus user cost minus supplementary cost, i.e. $\Delta I = A_1 - U - W$; while Marx's additional purchase of means of production is the difference between total purchase of the means of production and that part of the purchase of the means of production which is used for

replacement, i.e. $\triangle c = (c + \triangle c) - c$; so that $\triangle I$ and $\triangle c$ are identical.

(4) Consumption. Mr Keynes equates consumption to aggregate supply price minus investment, i.e. $C = A - A_1$. Marx equates it to total value of product minus constant capital, old and new, i.e. $C = V - (c + \triangle c)$. As $A - A_1 = V - (c + \triangle c)$ it follows that Mr Keynes' 'consumption' is the same as Marx's.

(5) Income and Revenue Reconsidered. Mr Keynes' 'income' equals consumption plus net investment, i.e. $Y = A - A_1 + \triangle I$. Marx's 'revenue' is equal to consumption plus net purchase of the means of production, i.e. $R = [(v + \triangle v) + (s + \triangle s)] + \triangle c$. Hence, Mr Keynes' income $A - A_1 + \triangle I$ equals Marx's revenue $(v + \triangle v) + (s + \triangle s) + \triangle c$.

(6) Net Saving and Net Investment. Mr Keynes' net saving is income minus consumption and is also net investment, i.e. $S = Y - C = (A - A_1 + \triangle I) - (A - A_1) = \triangle I$. It is obvious that Mr Keynes' '$S$' is Marx's '$\triangle c$', the additional purchase of means of production representing the difference between income and consumption.

From the above discussions it will be seen that the deficiency of effective demand, which arises from absence of planning in the sphere of circulation can be explained with equal clarity by means of either Mr Keynes' analysis or Marx's. Mr Keynes, however, does not deal with the deficiency of effective demand that arises from the absence of planning in the sphere of production which occupies so prominent a place with Marx. Furthermore, Mr Keynes' contention that Marx's theory of Capital is based on an acceptance instead of on a refutation of the classical hypothesis[1] and also Mrs Joan Robinson's assertion that Marx's theory is based on Say's Law[2] that supply creates its own demand, are both of them invalid, since Marx's theory of accumulation, far from following Say's Law, rests on the proposition that supply will correctly correspond to demand *only if* both production and circulation are controlled according to some social plan in which all the necessary conditions that he enunciates are embodied. In Marx's view, however, within a capitalist

---

[1] *General Theory of Employment, Money and Interest*, Ch. 23, p. 355.

[2] *Essays on the General Theory of Employment*, pp. 246–55.

society, no such social planning of production and circulation is possible; and he accordingly emphasizes that total demand under capitalism is always tending to be smaller than supply. He conceived it to be contrary to their very nature, that the capitalists should consume the whole of their income: their compelling motive was increase of wealth and not enjoyment. Hence the capitalist class was continually under an obligation, not only to 'form a reserve fund as protection against fluctuations of value and as a fund enabling them to wait for favourable conditions of the market for sale and purchase, but also accumulate capital', in order to extend production and extend its acquisition of surplus-value in the future.[1] It is quite clear that Marx fully realized that within capitalist production supply never can create its own demand as Say's Law states.

But here we come upon another contradiction that Marx was concerned to emphasize, and it is important to realize that Marx's theory did not hold that the contradictions of capitalist production were confined to maladjustments between various departments of production either in the sphere of production or in the sphere of circulation as some writers have supposed. Marx further emphasized that as capital accumulation proceeded, this produced a tendency for the rate of profit to fall. For the demonstration of this tendency Marx relied on his main equation, $c+v+s = V$. Let us first abstract rent from $s$ by assuming that production is carried on upon marginal land. $s$ will then represent profit, including interest, while $s/(c+v)$ will represent the rate of profit. Given $s$ as being uniquely determined by $v$, if the productivity of labour measured in terms of wage-units is constant, it will follow that when, as a result of capital accumulation, $c$ increases faster than $v$, the *rate* of profit must fall. Mr Keynes' theory also refers to this tendency to a falling rate of profit in the form of the tendency for the schedule of the marginal efficiency of capital to fall as the stock of capital grows. In Mr Keynes' view this declining tendency of marginal efficiency of capital develops, partly because the prospective yields fall as the supply of the same type of capital increases, and partly because, as a

[1] Marx pointed out that 'so long as the formation of a hoard continues, it does not increase the demand of the capitalist'; while if the worker saves a part of his wages, he converts this part into a hoard and does not perform the function of a purchaser.

rule, pressure on the facilities for producing capital goods will cause their supply price to increase. The validity of Mr Keynes' argument, therefore, depends on two conditions: (1) that the types of capital equipment are fixed in number; and (2) the shape of the supply curve of each type of capital good is increasing.

Yet we must note that Marx's analysis of capitalist accumulation has its own limitations. Concentrating his energy on the analysis of a closed economy in which only two classes have been assumed, Marx has reached the conclusion that in a capitalist society the process of capital accumulation cannot be enlarged beyond the limit set by the total expenditure of both the capitalist class and working class on means of production and means of consumption. Marx only touches incidentally on the possibility of the capitalists raising their average rate of profit by investment in foreign countries and particularly in colonial areas where the productive forces are less developed. It is at this point that Lenin developed Marx's analysis of foreign investment, by showing that a capitalist society surrounded by non-capitalist and undeveloped capitalist countries can expand its profits (and hence, subsequently its accumulation) beyond the limit set by the aggregate demand of the society itself by means of exporting capital. Highly developed capitalist societies, which suffer from a sharp limitation of the home market in the shape of saving or hoarding or of relative over-production of means of production and/or suffer a marked decline in the general rate of profit, are compelled to treat the export of capital as a question of life and death so far as the continuance of capitalism is concerned.[1] Mr Keynes has come to occupy much the same position as Lenin on this question. He maintains that the 'balance of foreign countries' expenditure' may be regarded as an addition to net investment from the point of view of capitalist society. Like Lenin, he holds that the export of capital may be correctly interpreted as the 'balance of foreign countries' expenditure'; meaning by this an export of goods in terms of money without any corresponding import. The future of economics, therefore, depends mainly upon the extent to which our knowledge of the export of capital and its significance as elaborated by Marx,

[1] V. I. Lenin, *Imperialism*, Ch. 6, pp. 69–75.

Lenin, and also by Mr Keynes, can be extended, in the direction of enabling us (I hope) to understand the influence exerted on the feelings, thoughts and actions of different classes of both the capital-exporting and capital-importing countries by the manner in which capital is exported and also by the forms that this capital-export assumes.

## 2. MONEY AND THE RATE OF INTEREST

So far we have analysed only the pure relation between effective demand and the smooth running of the system of capitalist accumulation. Marx, however, extended the sphere of his research to include a study of money, the rate of interest and financial crises; and one can say that Marx was the first to indicate the antagonistic relation between industrial profit and the rate of interest, which Mr Keynes has re-examined in his *General Theory*. It is of interest in this connection to note how much Mr Keynes' criticism of the Bank Act of 1925 has in common with Marx's criticism of the Act of 1844. Mr Keynes attacked the 1925 Act which provided that '£120 millions must be held in gold against the active Note Circulation of the Bank Notes and Currency Notes amounting to £387 millions' on the grounds that 'the £120 millions must be held (in gold) to satisfy the law is absolutely useless for any other purpose; indeed, it intensified depression through the curtailment of credit in conforming with all the rules of the Gold Standard'. Similarly, Marx criticized the 1844 Act which divided the Bank of England into an issue department and a banking department, and provided for a stringent control of the note issue in relation to the gold reserve.[1]

According to Marx (as interpreted by Engels), 'the separation of the Bank into two departments robbed the management of the possibility of disposing freely of its entire available means in critical moments, so that cases might occur in which the banking department might be confronted with bankruptcy, while the issue department still possessed several millions in gold and its entire £14 millions of securities untouched. And this could take place so much more easily, as there is one period

[1] *Capital*, Vol. III, Ch. XXXIV, pp. 651-2, English Translation. Also Ch. XXXIII, pp. 606-7.

in almost every crisis, when heavy exports of gold flow to foreign countries, which must be covered in the main by the metal reserve of the Bank. But for every five pounds in gold, which then go to foreign countries, the circulation of the home country is deprived of one five pound note, so that the quantity of the currency is reduced precisely at the time when the largest quantity of it is most needed. The Bank Act of 1844 thus directly challenges the commercial world to think betimes of laying up a reserve fund of bank-notes on the eve of crisis; by this artificial intensification of the demand for money accommodation, that is for the means of payment and its simultaneous restriction of the supply, which takes place at the decisive moment, this Bank Act drives the rate of interest to a hitherto unknown height; hence, instead of doing away with crises, the Act rather intensifies it to a point where either the entire commercial world must go to pieces, or the Bank Act.' For this reason, Marx dismissed the Bank Act of 1844 as the 'crazy' policy of Lord Overstone in much the same way as Mr Keynes stigmatized the Bank Law of 1925 as the 'sound' policy of Mr Churchill.

Let us consider the theoretical foundations of Marx's criticisms. The first problem which arises here is this: Is the rate of interest a reward for saving or abstinence as such? The answer of Marx is in the negative. He rejects for two reasons the validity of Nassau W. Senior's abstinence theory of capital. One of them is exactly the same as that of Mr Keynes when he makes an examination of the same abstinence theory of Marshall and his contemporaries, while the other, though not contained in Mr Keynes' system, yet supplements rather than contradicts it. In Marx's view, the pure act of saving or abstinence, either in the shape of hoarding money or in the shape of hoarding commodities will not create interest at all, because the 'exclusion of money from circulation' in consequence of hoarding money in cash 'would also exclude absolutely its self-expansion as capital, while accumulation of a hoard in the shape of commodities will be sheer tomfoolery'.[1] Therefore, he adds, in the section dealing with interest, 'so long as a money capitalist is keeping money capital in his own hands it collects no interest, it does not act in

[1] *Capital*, Vol. I, Part II, Ch. vii, p. 599, English translation, edited by Dona Torr.

the capacity of capital; and so long as it gathers interest and serves as capital, it is not in his hand.'[1] This form of statement is comparable to what Mr Keynes has said about the same point: 'It should be obvious that the rate of interest cannot be a return to saving or waiting as such. For if a man hoards his savings in cash, he earns no interest, though he saves as much as before.'[2] The second reason of Marx is that the abstinence theory is illogical in the sense that 'it has never occurred to the vulgar economist to make the single reflection that every human action may be viewed as abstinence from its opposite. Eating is abstinence from fasting, walking is abstinence from standing still, working, abstinence from idling, idling, abstinence from working, etc. These gentlemen would do well to ponder, once in a way, over Spinoza's *Determinatio est Negatio*.'

Hence, a second question arises. If Marx's statement is true that the rate of interest is not a return for saving as such, then, from Marx's point of view, for what kind of thing is the rate of interest a reward? According to Marx, as soon as the social functions of money are understood this question is solved. Admitting that money is a standard of value, Marx points out that it has three other social functions: (1) as a means of purchase; (2) as a means of payment; and (3) as a means of hoarding. If in the sphere of circulation $C \to M \to C$ (selling followed by purchase), commodity and money must confront each other at the same time. Money then circulates as a means of purchase. But if at the two poles of exchange there is a commodity on the one hand, but on the other hand not money but credit or a bill of exchange, money then functions, not as a means of purchasing, but as a means of payment. In this case money will not appear of itself in the sphere of circulation until such time as the term of contract expires. Thus in the whole market when the transfer of commodity-capitals between capitalists is promoted by bills of exchange, money, then, plays its well-known role as a means of payment. To the above two functions it is necessary to add a third, i.e. money as a means of hoarding or as a store of value. If in the course of circulation $C \to M \to C$ (selling to buy again),

[1] *Capital*, Vol. III, Ch. XXIII, p. 435, English translation.
[2] *The General Theory of Employment, Interest and Money*, Ch. 13, p. 167.

the first phase (selling, $C{\rightarrow}M$) is not followed immediately by the second phase (purchase, $M{\rightarrow}C$), but only after an interval of time, then money becomes a means of hoarding. We must, however, note that there are two different kinds of hoarding corresponding to two different historical periods. In ancient society, hoarding occurs generally in the form of a store of wealth for its own sake, the impulse to hoard being greed, or the satisfaction of social aspirations. Those who held wealth in its money form did so neither for enjoyment nor for making profit. With the development of capitalist production, however, this sort of hoarding declined as a source of enrichment and there grew up a new species of hoarding directly required by the productive process as a reserve fund of means of payment. The fact that at times of disturbance the whole commercial world clamours for hard cash essentially expresses the fact that money is being required as a means of payment. On the other hand, at times of expansion money is chiefly required as a reserve fund of means of purchase, for the expenditure of incomes. In view of the fact that the industrial capitalists require to borrow money from money capitalists to employ it either as a means of payment or as a means of purchase in the course of real production, Marx defines the rate of interest mainly as a proportional sum which the industrial capitalists have to pay to the money capitalists for the use of a certain amount of money capital over a given interval of time.[1]

With regard to the determination of the rate of interest, Marx was perfectly clear that it was a *money* rate, and treated it as something distinct from the rate of profit on real capital, already invested in the productive process, and as being determined by the supply and demand for money–capital in contrast to other forms of capital. But one might ask furthermore: How did he regard the demand and supply of money–capital as being determined? 'It is doubtless true,' he says, 'that a tacit connection exists between the supply of commodity–capital and the supply of money–capital, and also that the demand of the industrial capitalist for money–capital is determined by the actual conditions of real production.'[2] It is evident that the total sum of

[1] *Capital*, Vol. III, Ch. 23, p. 435.
[2] *Capital*, Vol. III, Ch. 23, p. 495.

money required by capitalist society in the course of capitalist production consists of two portions: one is required as a means of purchase for the expenditure of revenue between consumers and retail dealers, while the other is required for the transfer of capital between capitalists. Thus the total sum of money in circulation at a given time, given the rapidity of the circulation of money, will depend on the sum of these two portions, subject to the condition that commercial credit, or bills of exchange, can be substituted for money as a means of payment.

We may now turn our attention to the question of the way in which the demand of industrial capitalists for money varies with the conditions of prosperity and crisis.

'In times of prosperity, great expansion, acceleration and intensity of process of reproduction,' says Marx, 'the labourers are fully employed. Generally there is also a rise of wages which makes up in a slight measure for their fall below the average level in the other periods of the commercial cycle. At the same time the revenue of the capitalists grows considerably. Consumption increases universally. The prices of commodities also rise regularly, at least in various essential lines of business. Consequently the quantity of the circulating money grows, at least within certain limits, since the increasing velocity draws certain barriers around the quantity of the currency. Since that portion of the social revenue, which consists of wages, is originally advanced by the industrial capitalist in the form of variable capital, and always in the form of money, he requires more money in times of prosperity for his circulation.

'The final result is that the mass of currency required for the expenditure of revenue increases decidedly in periods of prosperity. As for the currency, which is necessary for the transfer of capital for the exclusive use of the capitalists, a period of brisk business is at the same time a period of most elastic and easy credit.'[1] On the one hand, an enlarged proportion of payments is handled by commercial credits in the form of bills of exchange which circulate among the industrial capitalists, as a means of payment, by successive endorsement without the intervention of any money at all; on the other hand, owing to the great fluidity of this process, the same quantities of money

[1] *Capital*, Vol. III, Ch. 28, p. 528.

have a greater velocity. Thus the mass of currency required for the transfer of capital decreases relatively, although its absolute quantity may increase.

In a period of crisis, however, the position is reversed. Both reinvestment and new investment contract, prices fall, likewise the wages of labour; the number of employed labourers is reduced, the mass of transactions decreases. On the other hand, in consequence of the sudden paralysis of the capitalistic process of production, confidence is shaken, commercial credit becomes scarce and contracted, and the demand for the conversion of bills of exchange into cash will necessarily increase in a similar degree. In other words, the need for money as a means of payment will increase as commercial credit decreases. At the same time, since the demand for money to meet obligations to pay cash for maturing bills increases much more than can be counter-balanced by the contraction of liquid resources required for the expenditure of incomes, the volume of money required for business transactions increases as a whole. Therefore, Marx remarks 'that a low rate of interest generally corresponds to periods of prosperity, or of extra profit, a rise of interest to the transition between prosperity and its reverse, and a maximum of interest up to a point of extreme usury to the period of crisis'. It is in times of stringency (and only then), as he emphasizes, that 'the absolute quantity of circulation has a determining influence on the rate of interest'.[1]

It is now proper to consider Marx's analysis of the supply of money capital. According to him the supply of money capital depends roughly on three facts: (1) the growth and development of the banking system; (2) imports of gold; and (3) banking legislation and its enforcement.

(1) In countries with a developed banking system a growing proportion of the total money in circulation, which would otherwise slumber as a reserve fund, is absorbed in the hands of bankers, whereby either a greater economy in the use of money or a relaxation in the flow of bank credit is realized. Thus, the more concentrated is the banking system the smaller are the reserve funds which every producer and merchant must keep as a hoard for gradual consumption or for gradual investment or

[1] *Capital*, Vol. III, Ch. 33, p. 622.

for the purpose of counterbalancing disturbances in the circulation of productive capital, etc. The banks are thus enabled by concentrating all kinds of reserve funds of the commercial world into something like a common treasury, to lend money at a lower rate of interest than would otherwise prevail.

(2) In the second place, the supply of money, as Marx says, depends on 'the extraordinary imports of gold such as those of 1852 and 1853 resulting from the output of the new Australian and Californian mines. This gold was deposited in the Bank of England. The depositors took notes instead, which they did not redeposit in banks. By this means the circulating medium was usually increased. The Bank strove then to utilize these deposits by lowering its discount to 1 per cent.'[1]

(3) Finally, the supply of money depends on banking legislation and its enforcement. Before the Act of 1844, as Marx remarks, no limit was set to the issue of Bank of England notes. If the exchange rates were in favour of England, and unrest, or even panic, reigned in the country, the condition of stringency could be relieved by the issue of notes. But with the Act of 1844, which set a rigid limit to the issue of bank-notes, the supply of money became scarce in times of emergency. Thus, during the period of crop failure in 1847, when England had to pay millions of gold to foreign countries for imported corn and potatoes, 'there was no rate of interest which the Bank could ask from creditable firms, which they would not have paid willingly in order to continue their payment'.[2] Eventually, the Government had to face the fact that the Bank itself was in danger and, yielding to the universal demand, suspended the Bank Act on October 25, 1857, thereby breaking the legal pattern on the Banks policy. The Bank was now enabled to put its supply of bank-notes into circulation without any interference, and the Bank Rate fell once more to the normal level. Following this close examination of the Bank Act of 1844, Marx remarks: 'All history of modern industry shows that metal would indeed be required only for the balancing of international commerce, whenever its equilibrium is disturbed momentarily, if only national production were properly organized. That the inland

[1] *Capital*, Vol. III, Ch. XXXI, pp. 589–90.
[2] *Capital*, Vol. III, Ch. XXIV, pp. 656–7.

market does not need any metal even now is shown by the suspension of cash payments of the so-called national banks, that resort to this expedient whenever extreme cases require it as the sole relief.'[1] It is obvious that time has proved the correctness of Marx's prediction.

Three final questions remain: (*a*) What is the position of Marx in respect to modern controversies on the rate of interest? (*b*) What can modern economists learn from Marx's theory of interest? (*c*) Is it likely that the smooth running of capitalist production can be attained by reducing the rate of interest to zero?

(*a*) My answer to the first question is that, in his analysis of the rate of interest in times of crisis, Marx has much in common with Mr Keynes, to the extent that he regards the rate of interest as being primarily determined by the supply and demand of money. In his analysis of the rate of interest over the whole period of a trade cycle, Marx's work is more akin to that of Professor Robertson, in the sense that he considers the rate of interest as being determined by the supply and demand of loanable money. On the whole, however, Marx's theory can be correctly interpreted as a typical bank-loan theory, since he says, in a certain place, that 'the variations of the rate of interest depend upon the supply of loan-capital, that is of the capital loaned in the form of money, hard cash, and notes ... However, the mass of this loanable capital is different from and independent of the mass of circulating money. If twenty pounds sterling were loaned five times per day, a money capital of 100 pounds sterling would be loaned.'[2] Although Marx argues that in times of stringency the rate of interest is primarily determined by the absolute quantity of money in circulation, this must not be taken out of the whole context of his work. Marx seems to assume that during a financial panic, loanable capital decreases in proportion to the increase of hoards, because everyone takes good care not to convert money into loanable capital.

---

[1] *Capital*, Vol. III, pp. 607–8.

[2] *Capital*, Vol. III, Ch. 31, pp. 586–7. (Marx excepts from this statement changes in the rate of interest 'occurring in long periods'. These he thinks are to be explained in terms of changes in the rate of profit or in general credit facilities.)

Whether Marx's theory of interest belongs to the loanable-funds approach or the cash-balances approach is a question that is probably more important in form than in substance. 'For over any short period,' as Professor J. R. Hicks has said, 'the difference between the value of things an individual acquires (including money) and the value of things he gives up (including money) must, apart from gifts, equal the change in his net debt – his borrowing and lending. The same will apply to a firm. If then, the demand for every commodity and factor equals the supply, and if the demand for money equals the supply of money, it follows by mere arithmetic that the demand for loans must equal the supply of loans. Similarly, if the equations of supply and demand hold for commodities, factors and loans it will follow automatically that the demand for money equals the supply of money.'[1] This clearly shows that in equilibrium the rate of interest is determined simultaneously both by the supply and demand of cash and the supply and demand of loanable funds.

However, we must emphasize that the superiority of Marx's theory of interest compared with that of the neo-classical economists is that from the outset he regards the rate of interest as a money rate. The determination of the rate of interest is, therefore, specifically a monetary problem. Marx probably is the first who has been able to distinguish money capital from commodity–capital, and even from short-term bills and other securities. Thus the antagonistic relation between industrial profit and the money rate of interest on the one hand, and also the institutional conflict of interests between industrial capitalists and money capitalists on the other, are greatly clarified.

(b) The most valuable contribution of Marx's theory of the rate of interest is the way in which it has clarified the relation between 'debts' and money. In Marx's view 'debts' are themselves only money in so far as they absolutely take the place of actual money to the amount of its normal value as a means of purchase or as a means of payment. He also informs us that 'debts' can take the place of actual money both for the transfer of capital between capitalists and for the settlement of mutual

[1] J. R. Hicks: 'Mr Keynes' General Theory of Employment', *Economic Journal*, June 1936.

claims of indebtedness only at times of prosperity, when the state of confidence is very strong, the sale of commodities at profitable prices being assured. The extent to which 'debts' act as money will finally be determined by the smooth inter-relationship of production and circulation. Hence it follows that if the relationship between the various lines of production were so correctly balanced that no interruptions of the kind that we have spoken of above could occur in an exchange-society, money required for business transactions might be entirely replaced by the employment of 'debts' either as a means of purchase or as a means of payment. Therefore 'debts' like bank-notes, would not be able to earn any interest for their keepers and the rate of interest would be zero. This clearly shows that the realization of a zero rate of interest will uniquely be deter-mined by the zero rate of deviations between aggregate supply and demand price in the long run, which, however, can only be the result, as we have shown, of a central co-ordination of production and circulation. Under the conditions of capitalist production where no central planning of the economy is possible, and periodic ruptures of confidence are inevitable, cash is nor-mally preferred to 'debts', and, therefore, the antagonistic relation between the rate of interest and industrial profit is and remains a question unsolved and insoluble despite any monetary manipulation that may be desired and even occasionally brought into force.

(c) In view of the fact that the result of any money panic is certainly more in favour of the money capitalists than in favour of industrial capitalists, those who are friends of the industrial capitalists naturally hope to see the rate of interest reduced, particularly at the height of a crisis, to an insignificant amount approaching to zero, in order to ensure the convertibility of maturing bills and hence the saleability of commodities at profitable prices. It is impossible to imagine money capitalists accepting a zero rate of interest in direct contradiction to their own interests. Even if they were to do so, periodical crises would still happen, owing to the fact that the causes of capitalist crises are numerous: firstly, the keen competition between industrial capitalists and their financial superiors; secondly, maladjustments between the various departments of production; thirdly, the disproportion of consumption of capitalists and the accumulation of their capitals; and, finally, the poverty and the restricted consumption of the masses in consequence of the relative and progressive growth of capital equipment compared to wages, combined with that grand tragedy of capitalist production, the falling rate of profit.

## SELECTED BIBLIOGRAPHY

GILLMAN, J. M. 'An Evaluation of John Maynard Keynes', *Science and Society:* Vol. XIX, p. 107.

MATTICK, P. 'Marx and Keynes', *Cahiers de L'Institut de Science Economique Appliquée, Etudes de Marxologie:* 5. M. Rubel, dir. January 1962.

# Theories of Effective Demand and Employment[1]

*Lawrence R. Klein*

THERE is much talk about such matters as the downard rigidity of wage rates, the relationship of wages to employment and output, the influence of liquid assets on the level of economic activity, and the stage of maturity of the American economy. The various theories of employment must be examined in the light of these concepts in order to get some clear answers to important economic problems. The Keynesian theories are often accused of being based on assumptions of rigid wage rates or interest-elastic liquidity preferences, but there may be much less truth in these assertions than is commonly thought to be the case. The purpose of this paper will be to study three theories of employment – (1) the classical, (2) the Keynesian, and (3) the Marxian – in order to attempt to clear up some confusions that still exist. One of the main objectives will be to try to show the distinctions between necessary and sufficient assumptions that underlie each theory.

## I. THE CLASSICAL THEORY

Since the publication of the *General Theory*, there have been numerous discussions in the professional literature comparing Keynes and the Classics. As a result of these discussions, we now have a good idea as to the form of the classical model. The simplest version is as follows: (1) The supply of and demand for labour determine the real wage rate and the level of employment. (2) The technological input–output relationship determines the level of real output since the input of labour services has been

---

[1] Some of the ideas on Keynesian economics contained in this article are more fully discussed in the author's book, *The Keynesian Revolution* (New York: Macmillan Co.).

Reprinted from *The Journal of Political Economy*, April 1947.

determined by step 1. It is, of course, assumed that the stock of fixed capital is given. (3) The equation of savings and investment determines the rate of interest. (4) Given output from step 2, the constant velocity of circulation and the given supply of cash determine the absolute price level (quantity theory).

The mathematical version of this system is:

$$M = kpY \text{ (quantity equation)} \qquad \ldots (1.1)$$

$$S(i) = I(i) \text{ (savings-investment equation)} \ldots (1.2)$$

$$Y = Y(N) \text{ (production function)} \qquad \ldots (1.3)$$

$$\frac{dY}{dN} = \frac{w}{p} \text{ (demand for labour)} \qquad \ldots (1.4)$$

$$N = f\left(\frac{w}{p}\right) \text{ (supply of labour)} \qquad \ldots (1.5)$$

where $M$ = cash balances, $p$ = price, $Y$ = output, $i$ = interest rate, $N$ = employment, $w$ = wage rate. Given the amount of money, there are five equations to determine $p$, $Y$, $i$, $N$, and $w$.

The classical economists not only counted relations and variables; they also assumed that the forms of their relations were such that a unique solution was possible. This solution will always be one of full employment because all who want to work at the going real wage rate can find a job; equation (1.5) tells us that. This equation shows how much employment will be offered at any real wage rate. If all the equations of the system are consistent, as was classically assumed, equation (1.5) must hold, i.e. all who offer their services at prevailing real wages can find employment. In this model, since all equations hold simultaneously, the solution must be on the supply curve of labour, which is what is meant by full employment.

It is easy to make a slight generalization of this model and still get the same results. Those defending the classical doctrine against Keynes' 1936 attack were quick to point out that the classical economists did not neglect the fact that the demand for money depends on the rate of interest or that savings and investment depend on income. The same results, so far as the level of employment is concerned, follow even if the quantity equation and the savings-investment equation are modified. Steps 1 and 2 of the process of solving the classical model remain as before. Steps 3 and 4 become: (3') Given the level of output from step 2, the equation of savings and investment determines the rate of interest. (4') Given the level of output from step 2 and the level of the interest rate from step 3', the given supply of cash determines the absolute price level.

Equations (1.1) and (1.2) are replaced by:

$$\frac{M}{p} = L\,(i,\,Y), \qquad\qquad \ldots (1.1')$$

$$S\,(i,\,Y) = I\,(i,\,Y). \qquad\qquad \ldots (1.2')$$

The other equations remain as before.

As presented here, the classical system is static and should be looked upon as the equilibrium solution of a more general dynamical system. It is evident that the equilibrium will always be one of full employment. In the general case – when the system is not at its equilibrium position – there may be unemployment, but this unemployment will be only temporary if the dynamic movements are damped, as the classical economists implicitly assumed. When unemployment does occur in the state of disequilibrium, there is always an appropriate remedial policy available – namely, an increase in the amount of money or (its equivalent) a cut in prices or in wages. Every variable in the classical system can be expressed in terms of the autonomous supply of money as a parameter, and it is easy to calculate the effect upon the system of varying the quantity of money. The assumptions of the structure of the classical system are such that variations in the quantity of money tend to raise the level of output and employment when there is a deviation from the full-employment equilibrium.

## 2. THE KEYNESIAN THEORY

The Keynesian theory is quite different from the classical theory. The basic hypothesis of the Keynesian theory is that people make two kinds of decisions in our present type of economy. They decide, on the basis of their income, whether to spend or save; and they decide, on the basis of the rate of interest, the form in which they want to hold their accumulated savings – cash or securities. In the classical theory income is the strategic variable in the money equation (1.1), and interest is the strategic variable in the savings-investment equation (1.2). Exactly the reverse is true in the Keynesian system. Keynes's great contribution was to replace the classical savings-investment theory of interest with a savings-investment theory of the determination of income.

The simplest Keynesian theory is the following: Savings as a function of the level of income equals autonomous investment. This is one equation in one variable, namely, the level of income. Investment is considered to be autonomous because it depends upon such factors as the expectations of future market demand, innovations, fiscal policy, etc. It is obvious, however, that the validity of the Keynesian theory does not depend on the fact that investment is autonomous, for, if investment is also a function of income, the Keynesian theory of the savings-investment determination of the level of income still holds.

One pillar of support for the simplest Keynesian model is that it is not contradicted by the data. If the hypothesis is that savings as a function of income equals autonomous investment, there should be a close correlation between income and investment. The published data (United States) on disposable income (constant dollars, per capita) are very highly correlated with investment – defined as the difference between disposable income and consumer expenditures (constant dollars, per capita) – and lagged disposable income during the inter-war period. There is nothing artificial in this high correlation, and statisticians have never found a similar confirmation of the alternative classical theories from the available data.

The Keynesian revision of the savings-investment theory is of profound importance. Since the Keynesian theory does not involve the introduction of any new variables and since it merely involves a change of form of some of the classical equations, it would seem natural that the system (1.1)–(1.5) could be re-written with the suggested revisions, so that we would again have a model of full-employment equilibrium. However, this supposition is not correct. The revised model would be:

$$\frac{M}{p} = L\,(i) \text{ (liquidity-preference equation)} \quad \ldots (2.1)$$

$$S(Y) = I(Y) \text{ (savings-investment equation)} \quad \ldots (2.2)$$

$$Y = Y(N) \text{ (production function)} \quad \ldots (2.3)$$

$$\frac{dY}{dN} = \frac{w}{p} \text{ (demand for labour)} \quad \ldots (2.4)$$

$$N = f\left(\frac{w}{p}\right) \text{ (supply of labour)} \quad \ldots (2.5)$$

There is a basic contradiction and indeterminacy in this system. The supply of and demand for labour, plus the production function, determine the level of output. But the savings-investment equation also determines the level of output, and there is no obvious mechanism to insure that these two levels of output will be the same. Furthermore, the liquidity-preference equation cannot determine both the price level and the rate of interest.

There are various ways out of the difficulties that arise in the system $(2.1)$–$(2.5)$. The liquidity-preference and savings-investment equations can be generalized; the supply-of-labour equation can be changed; or possibly other changes may be suggested. It should be pointed out, however, that there is little that can be done to either the production function or the demand for labour. The production function cannot be changed, because it is a technological phenomenon. The laws of nature cannot be tampered with, while the hypotheses of economic behaviour can. Many empirical studies have show that the aggregate production function can be closely approximated by a linear-logarithmic relation. From the theories of profit maximization it follows that a linear-logarithmic production function implies a demand equation for labour such that the wage bill is proportional to the aggregate value of output. This constancy of labour's share of the national product is precisely what the data show. In dynamic econometric models this relation can be improved by saying that the wage bill is a linear function of the value of current output, lagged output, and a time trend. A demand equation for labour, of this generalized dynamic type, can be easily derived from empirical production functions. In various econometric models that the author has constructed, there is no relation that is more stable than the demand for labour; hence it seems unwise to attempt to clear up the theoretical difficulties of the above model by altering (2.3) or (2.4). We must concentrate our attention on (2.1), (2.2), and (2.5). This is precisely the Keynesian approach.

If the generalized forms of the money equation and the savings-investment equation presented in the previous section – (1.1') and (1.2') – were substituted for (2.1) and (2.2), the Keynesian theory would appear to be coincident with the classical theory. But such a conclusion would be hasty. Suppose that (2.1) and (2.2) are replaced by (1.1') and (1.2'). If there was formerly a contradiction between the level of output determined from one part of the model, (2.3)–(2.5), and from another part of the model, (2.2), a classical economist would argue that the contradiction is now avoided because the interest rate would adjust itself so that investment would offset savings out of the same income that is determined by (2.3)–(2.5). But, according to the Keynesian theory, an interest-rate adjustment is not generally possible. There is no assurance that the equation:

$$S\,(i,\,Y_0) = I\,(i,\,Y_0) \qquad \qquad \ldots (2.6)$$

has a solution in $i > 0$ when $Y_0$ is the full-employment level of income determined from (2.3)–(2.5). In fact, if savings and investment are both interest-inelastic, the chances are very great that there will be no solution to this equation. Interest-inelasticity of these schedules is one of the fundamental assumptions of modern Keynesian theory. The extreme case occurs when $i$ is omitted as a variable from the savings and investment schedules. Econometric and questionnaire investigations have always shown the influence of the interest rate on savings and investment to be small or absent; it remains for the opponents of Keynes to show that there is high interest-elasticity in these schedules.

One of the main reasons why savings are interest-inelastic is that some savings respond positively to variations in the interest rate (savings for wealth accumulation), while other savings respond negatively to variations in the interest rate (savings for annuities). On balance, the total effect is in doubt in regard to sign. In the modern society, savings are regulated largely by habits and considerations of economic security and have little to do with the rate of interest.

On the side of investment, it is well known that businessmen make capital outlays on the basis of a very short horizon (one to five years) and that the shorter the horizon the smaller is the effect of interest rates.[1] Furthermore, the increased use of internal financing – coupled with a failure to charge imputed interest – have intensified the neglect of the interest rate in the formation of investment decisions. These are two of the main reasons why the investment schedule is interest-inelastic.

There is a method of assuring a full-employment solution to the system, although it is highly artificial and unobserved in the real world. Professor Knight has suggested that the investment schedule be made infinitely interest-elastic. If this were assumed, there would always be full-employment equilibrium. Knight has written, 'The heart of a correct theory of interest is the fact, corresponding more or less to infinite "elasticity of demand for capital", that the investment market is capable of absorbing savings at the maximum rate at which they are forthcoming,...'[2] If the investment schedule possessed infinite interest-elasticity, equation (2.6) would always have a solution and the contradiction would be solved. However, Knight's assumption – which comes to exactly the same thing as Say's Law – is untenable in the light of statistical data or any other knowledge that we have of the facts in the savings-investment market.

Supporters of Knight's views on capital theory may point out that the foregoing quotation applies only to a long-run situation. In this event, the term 'elasticity of demand for capital' must take on a new connotation. Elasticities are ordinarily computed as logarithmic partial derivatives, which means that other variables are held constant. In the long run these other variables are not constant. If Knight is referring only to long-run processes in the quotation, his remarks are not related to the problem that we are discussing.

[1] See G. L. S. Shackle, 'Interest Rates and the Pace of Investment', *Economic Journal*, LVI (1946), pp. 1–17.

[2] Frank H. Knight, 'Capital, Time, and Interest Rate', *Economica*, N.S., I (1934), p. 285.

Professor Pigou[1] was one of the first classically minded economists to point out clearly that the amended system may be overdetermined with the added condition $i > 0$. Pigou acknowledged that savings and investment may be sufficiently interest-inelastic that the interest rate cannot be relied upon to bring them into balance at full employment. He suggested a further alteration in the savings-investment equation in order to salvage the classical doctrine of full-employment equilibrium. His suggestion would mean replacing the savings-investment equation by:

$$ S\left(i, Y, \frac{M}{p}\right) = I(i, Y) \qquad \dots (2.2') $$

with the assumption that savings vary inversely with the real stock of cash.[2] The solution to an unemployment disequilibrium is now obvious. If wages are cut with $M$ held constant by the banking system, $M/p$ can be pushed to sufficiently high levels so that savings and investment are in balance at full employment. Since prices (equally well, wages) enter as a denominator in real cash balances, there is no limit to the size of $M/p$ as a result of wage cuts and hence no limit to the extent to which savings can be lowered.[3] Thus, by always restoring the system towards its full-employment equilibrium, competitive wage cuts during periods of unemployment solve the problem for Pigou.

Equation $(2.2')$ rests on an unconfirmed hypothesis, namely, that savings vary inversely with the real stock of cash balances. Just as the classical assumptions about the influence of interest rates on savings and investment have never been discovered to hold empirically, so has it never been discovered that consumption

---

[1] A. C. Pigou, 'The Classical Stationary State', *Economic Journal*, LIII (1934), pp. 343–51.

[2] Other economists, notably Professor Haberler, have made the same suggestion, although none has been so explicit as Pigou.

[3] The 'real' models of this paper have been constructed in terms of the price level, $p$, as a deflator, but we could just as easily have constructed the system in wage units with $w$ as the deflator. If the system is written in wage units, the appropriate variable for $(2.2')$ is $M/w$. This form makes it possible to see more directly how wage cuts are used as a lever to raise the level of real balances.

or savings patterns are significantly influenced by the stock of cash balances. The data of the inter-war period show that cash balances, at best, had a very mild influence on consumption. If we adopt the following simple model for purposes of statistical investigation,[1]

$$S = a_0 + a_1 Y + a_2 Y_{-1} + a_3 \left(\frac{M}{p}\right)_{-1} = I = \text{autonomous} \ldots (2.7)$$

or

$$Y = \frac{-a_0}{a_1} - \frac{a_2}{a_1} Y_{-1} - \frac{a_3}{a_1} \left(\frac{M}{p}\right)_{-1} + \frac{1}{a_1} I,$$

the least-squares estimates of the parameters are:

$$Y = 186.53 + .30 Y_{-1} + .13 \left(\frac{M}{p}\right)_{-1} + 2.36 I . (.34)$$
$$\qquad\quad (.13) \qquad (.10)$$

The standard error of the estimate of $1/a_1$ is relatively small, $0.34$. On the other hand, the standard error of the estimate of $a_3/a_1$ is relatively large. The coefficient of $M/p$ could easily be close to zero, but since $1/a_1$ is definitely not zero, it follows that $a_3$ could be zero. Pigou's hypothesis is not confirmed. Even if the true value of $a_3$ is not zero, it may not be very large. The main point, however, is that the size (and sign) of $a_3$ is very uncertain. There is no 'proof' of Pigou's hypothesis.

The size of the coefficient relating savings to cash balances is very important for Pigou's theory. Recall that the systems of this paper are regarded as equilibrium solutions of more complex dynamical systems. The classical theory implicitly assumes that the system returns rapidly to its equilibrium when it is displaced to a position of disequilibrium. This implies that the dynamical system is damped. But do wage and price cuts always lead to damped processes in time? In order to insure that the classical assumption of dampening is correct, it will be necessary

---

[1] All variables are per capita in 1935–39 dollars. The time period is 1922–41. The figures in parentheses below the estimated parameters are standard errors of the estimates. $Y=$ disposable income, $S =$ personal savings, $I =$ net investment, $M =$ total cash balances (current dollars).

to assume that a small cut in wages, for example, will tend to restore the system immediately to its position of equilibrium. Thus it is required that the multiplier effect of wage cuts (or increases in the real stock of cash) be very large. The statistical calculations of (2.7) do not show this. There exists the possibility, but not the necessity, that the increase may be practically zero. Instability may develop in a model like this. There is an initial position of unemployment. Wages fall, but employment and income increase little or not at all. Wages fall still further, but unemployment is still not eradicated. This is a perfect setting for expectations of further wage cuts, the very conditions that make the system unstable and make it likely that wage cuts will push the system away from rather than towards its full-employment equilibrium.

If there are expectations of falling wages, entrepreneurs will postpone production until a time when labour costs will be lower yet. Wage-earners will feel very insecure and spend as little as possible. Hyperdeflation will never cure unemployment. The only way that unstable situations of hyperdeflation can be stopped is by direct, autonomous action on the part of the state or some other authoritative agency, as was the case in the period 1929–33 in the United States. Admittedly, the process of hyperdeflation is the worst set of circumstances that can arise in Pigou's system, yet – on the basis of the available data – an assumption of such unfavourable conditions is legitimate even though other assumptions can safely be made also. The problem, as yet, remains unsettled.

In the most general model – in which the savings-investment equation is (2.2') and the liquidity-preference equation is (1.1') – the expression for the rate of change of real income with respect to real cash balances is more complicated. Without going into the mathematics of this expression, it is possible to present certain results on an intuitive basis. If savings are insensitive to variations in $i$ and $M/p$ and if investment is insensitive to variations of $i$, then it will follow that real income will not be greatly stimulated by increases in real cash balances. These are the properties of the savings-investment equation that have already been discussed in the preceding pages. The conclusion about small variations in real income associated with variations in real balances is *reinforced* if we appeal to the Keynesian assumptions about the shape of the liquidity-preference equation. Keynes put forth the hypothesis that the demand for cash is infinitely elastic with respect to the interest rate in the neighbourhood of low interest rates. Some economists have singled out this hypothesis of Keynes as his strategic assumption which is necessary for the validity of his theories. The truth of the matter is that high interest-elasticity of liquidity preferences is sufficient in many cases but never necessary. The validity of the theory of employment does not depend on the validity of the assumption about the form of liquidity preferences. It is obvious that the simplest version of the Keynesian theory (savings as a function of income equals autonomous investment) has nothing to do with the theory of interest.

It is instructive to examine the empirical relationship between the interest rate and cash balances to see whether or not the Keynesian hypothesis is correct. If we identify active cash balances as circulating currency plus demand deposits, and idle cash balances as savings deposits, we find for the inter-war period very strong linear correlations (a) between active balances, net national product and trend, and (b) between idle balances, corporate-bond yield, lagged corporate-bond yield, lagged idle balances, and trend. The data also show that the corporate-bond yield is not a statistically significant variable in a and that net national product is not a statistically significant variable in b. These latter findings imply that the empirical split between active and idle balances is not bad.

The fact that idle balances are linearly related to the interest rate in the inter-war period implies that the Keynesian hypothesis of infinite elasticity cannot be correct. But the post-war data show something different. The current data are consistent with Keynes's hypothesis. While the inter-war demand relation for active balances is close to the post-war facts, the inter-war demand relation for idle balances gives a computed level of idle balances, for observed interest rates, much lower than the actual level. There are several explanations for the breakdown of this empirical function in the post-war years. One explanation is that the whole relation has shifted. Another explanation is that some variable, which was relatively unimportant in the past, is now important and accounts for the discrepancy. A third explanation, which is very appealing, is that the Keynesian hypothesis is correct. If the liquidity-preference function were approximately linear for interest rates above 3 per cent and asymptotic to the line, interest rate = 2·5 per cent, it would fit the inter war data, the post-war data, and the Keynesian hypothesis. There are a variety of simple mathematical functions which have the required properties.

The intuitive significance of the various assumptions about interest-elasticities can be summed up briefly. Assuming that the mechanism to maintain full-employment equilibrium is a fluctuating stock of real balances, it follows that these fluctuations will have little influence on the interest rate if the liquidity preferences are highly elastic, and it follows further that they will have little influence on savings and investment if these schedules are interest-inelastic. It may seem that much weight is attached to the interest rate, but the opposite is the case. The complex of elasticities assumed in the Keynesian theory makes the interest rate extremely unimportant. The same results can be obtained by altogether dropping interest as an independent variable from the system.

The other available alternative by which the contradictions of the system may be reconciled is the modification of the supply curve of labour. This is the alternative that Keynes chose for himself. Before discussing this alternative, however, several points should be made clear. We have been able to demonstrate a basic contradiction in the working of the capitalist system when the traditional supply curve of labour is used. The recognition of this contradiction represents a great step forward in economic theory, and this contribution has nothing to do with any special assumptions about wages. The truly important ideas of Keynes, contrary to much of popular belief, are independent of any special assumptions about the labour market. Keynesian theories of the savings-investment process superimposed on the classical theory of the labour market show that full employment is not automatic under capitalism.

Keynes recognized that full employment was not the equilibrium position for the real world, and he set about to develop a theory of an unemployment equilibrium by changing the classical supply curve of labour and by adopting a new definition of unemployment. It is this part of his theory that many of the modern Keynesians would like to give up while still retaining the savings-investment theory of income determination. The strict Keynesian approach amounts to replacing (2.5) by

$$N = F(w) \qquad \qquad \ldots (2.8)$$

and adopting the well-known definition of involuntary unemployment found in the early pages of the *General Theory*. It is assumed that the new supply curve of labour has infinite wage-elasticity up to the full-employment point. This system is rigged to get an unemployment equilibrium as much as the classical system is rigged to get a full-employment equilibrium. Neither approach is entirely acceptable.

There are at least two criticisms of the Keynesian solution. In the first place, Keynes' definition of unemployment has the unsavoury implication that the cause of unemployment is a money-illusion on the part of workers; if workers would only bargain in terms of real wages instead of in terms of money wages, there would be no problem of unemployment, other than the frictional variety. Surely, a small thing like a money-illusion cannot be responsible for the existence of unemployment. Second, the supply curve of labour given by (2.8) has never been tested against the facts and may not hold if it is tested. The behaviour patterns of recent years (since the Little Steel Formula) give the impression that workers do not bargain exclusively in terms of money wages. They are very conscious of the relation between wages and the cost of living, and it does not seem correct to assume that they are fooled by any money-illusion. Many of the parts of the Keynesian system have withstood the test of being consistent with observed data, but all that we can say about equation (2.8) is that we do not know about its validity. It must be re-emphasized, however, that the important parts of the Keynesian theory are independent of Keynes' own theories of wages and the labour market.

Joan Robinson has made a very important remark that holds the key to an answer to the problem. She said: 'Again, the orthodox conception of wages tending to equal the *marginal disutility* of labour, which has its origin in the picture of a peasant farmer leaning on his hoe in the evening and deciding whether the extra product of another hour's work will repay the extra backache, is projected into the modern labour market, where the individual worker has no opportunity to decide anything except whether it is better to work or to starve.'[1] The essence of capitalism is that there exists a definite legal respect for private ownership of the means of production. The owners of the means of production, the capitalists, make all the final decisions with regard to the use of the means of production. The workers have nothing to say about the amount of employment that will be forthcoming at any point of time. Either the entire concept of the supply curve of labour must be dropped, or the supply curve of labour must become a curve of *virtual* points on which observations do not occur. The first alternative means that the demand for labour is given by profit maximization (marginal productivity theory); the supply of labour is an exogenous variable represented by the labour force and determined by demographic factors; the wage rate is determined by a market adjustment between demand and supply (collective bargaining). The mathematical model would be:

$$\frac{dY}{dN} = \frac{w}{p} \quad \text{(demand for labour)} \qquad \ldots (2.4)$$

$$\overline{N} = \text{labour supply} \qquad \ldots (2.9)$$

$$\frac{d\left(\frac{w}{p}\right)}{dt} = g(\overline{N}-N) \qquad \ldots (2.10)$$

Equation (2.10) could be replaced by:

$$\frac{dw}{dt} = h(\overline{N}-N) \qquad \ldots (2.10')$$

if all the other equations of the system are used also. The same arguments about expectations and damping apply to the path by which this system approaches or diverges from equilibrium. If the system is damped and $g(0) = 0$ or $h(0) = 0$, we have a model of full-employment equilibrium.

It was pointed out above that equation (2.4) is based on sound empirical verification. Similarly, market adjustment equations like (2.10') are also consistent with the data. First

[1] Joan Robinson, *An Essay on Marxian Economics* (London: Macmillan & Co., 1942), pp. 2–3.

differences in the general wage rate (USA, inter-war period) are highly correlated (inversely) with unemployment and the lagged wage rate. The parameters of this empirical equation suggest that small wage cuts are not associated with large increases in employment and that $h(0) \neq 0$, from which we conclude that the system does not have a stable equilibrium of full employment.

If the concept of a supply curve of labour is to be retained, it must be interpreted in a new way. We can say that the supply curve of labour shows how much the people would *like* to work at any given real wage. It does not mean, as in the classical system, that people's desires become effective. In this situation the supply curve of labour exists as a set of virtual points which are never observed. However, it is known that the demand curve for labour represents a set of observed points. This means that we shall have an observed point on the demand curve and off the supply curve. If this point is such that supply exceeds demand (at the same wage) there is unemployment, and if this point is such that demand exceeds supply (at the same wage) there is over-employment. This concept of unemployment is not easily measurable, however, since it involves virtual, unobserved points. In order to measure unemployment in this model, we would have to sample the population, questioning them on the amount of employment that they would like to supply at prevailing wage rates.

Thus far we have attempted to point out the main differences between Keynesian and classical economics. But there is also an important aspect of similarity, namely, methodology. For both types of systems, macro-economic models have been studied in this paper. The macro-economic models are similar except for emphasis. A single model with one set of parameters yields the classical theory and with another set of parameters yields the Keynesian theory. However, the macro-economic models are not the basic elements of either system. It is necessary to analyse the considerations that lie behind the macrosystem, i.e. the microsystem. It will be found here, too, that the methodologies of classical and Keynesian economics do not differ. There are two steps in the formation of the macro-economic systems. First, it is necessary to formulate the behaviour pattern of individuals. Both theories are based on household utility-maximization to get the demand for consumer goods and household cash-holdings, and on business-firm profit- (or utility-) maximization to get the demand for producer goods, labour, and business cash-holdings. The second step is to show how to pass from a theory involving individual firms, households, factors, and commodities to a theory involving communities of individuals, composite factors, and composite commodities. This step involves the index-number problem. The discussion of both these subjects is important but lengthy. The reader is referred to other works for more extensive analysis.[1] The point to be emphasized at this stage is that the methodology is the same for classical and Keynesian economics at all steps in the process of deriving the macro-systems.

### 3. THE MARXIAN THEORY[2]

There are two important subsections of the modern theories of employment which need to be clarified. One subsection is the stagnation thesis, and the other is the relation between wages, profits, and employment. The modern version of the stagnation thesis is an outgrowth of the Keynesian developments in American economic thinking. The opposite theory of the stationary state is a natural outgrowth of the classical system. But neither model, as usually stated, gives an adequate analysis of the theory of economic development. It is possible to modify these theories with the introduction of trend variables, the stock of capital, etc.,

[1] On the problem of the theories underlying the Keynesian and classical macro-economic systems see Klein, *op. cit.* On the problem of aggregation see Francis W. Dresch, 'Index Numbers and the General Economic Equilibrium', *Bulletin of the American Mathematical Society*, XL (February 1938), pp. 134–41; Lawrence R. Klein, 'Macro-economics and the Theory of Rational Behaviour', *Econometrica*, XIV (April 1946), pp. 93–108; and 'Remarks on the Theory of Aggregation', *Econometrica*, XIV (October 1946), pp. 303–12; Kenneth May, 'The Aggregation Problem for a One-Industry Model', *Econometrica*, XIV (October 1946), pp. 285–98; Shou Shan Pu, 'A Note on Macro-economics', *Econometrica*, XIV (October 1946), pp. 299–302.

[2] The author is indebted to Professor Kenneth May for helpful criticisms in this section.

in order to get some information about the economic laws of motion of society; but it seems preferable to go to a theory which deals directly with this subject. From an historical point of view it is also fitting to use the theory which first tackled the problems related to the stagnation thesis. The Marxian theory of the falling rate of profit is one of the first, and probably one of the best, tools for analysing the stagnation theory. Since Marxian theory comes to conclusions similar to those of the modern stagnationists, but for different reasons, it will also be instructive to study it in some detail.

The other problem of the relation between wages, profits, and employment is of great current interest but also cannot be properly analysed within the customary frameworks of Keynesian and classical economics. These theories can also be modified by distinguishing in the consumption function between wage income and profit income. But the Marxian theory is based fundamentally on the interrelationships between wages and profits. The Marxian theories of reproduction are well suited for the study of this problem.

Here it will be necessary to digress for a few pages in order to show explicitly the structure of the Marxian model. This model will then be compared with the Keynesian model and used for the analysis of the stagnation theory and the relationship between wages, profits, and employment.

The methodology of the Marxian approach is quite different from that of Keynes and the Classics: Instead of studying the behaviour of individuals, Marx studied the behaviour of classes directly. His theory is probably the origin of macro-economics. But the Marxian system of macro-economics differs essentially from the Keynesian and classical systems. The macro-units in the latter systems are producers and consumers, and this overlapping fails to bring out some essentials. The macro-units of the Marxian system are not only producers and consumers but also workers and capitalists. The latter two groups are, practically speaking, exclusive, and their basic conflict of interests can more easily be singled out as one of the moving forces in the system.

The economic writings of Marx were not presented in the form of systems of simultaneous equations. The equation-system approach to economics came at a later date. There are various equations throughout Marx's writings, but these equations are mainly definitions. They state, for example, that total output can be broken up into three components: constant capital, variable capital, and surplus value. Various manipulations are carried out with these components, but complete systems of equations are not formulated. However, imbedded in Marx's literary discussion and numerical examples, there are several hypotheses and assumptions that can be used to build a system of equations. The validity of the equation system depends upon the validity of the hypotheses made. It is the function of the empirical studies to test the validity of these equations.

The supply-and-demand equations of orthodox economics also are based upon some assumptions the validity of which cannot be assumed *a priori*. The systems of supply-and-demand equations are usually based on the assumptions that households maximize their individual utility functions subject to certain constraints. The assumptions produce the maximization equations which are essentially the supply-and-demand equations. In the same way, we shall have to introduce Marxian assumptions in order to construct an equation system out of *Capital*.

A concrete example will demonstrate clearly the relation between definitional equations and behaviour equations (or refutable hypotheses). Suppose we write, as did Marx:

$$c + v + s = \text{total value} \qquad \ldots (3.1)$$

$$\frac{s}{v} = \text{rate of surplus value} \qquad \ldots (3.2)$$

$$\frac{c}{c+v} = \text{organic composition of capital} \qquad \ldots (3.3)$$

$$\frac{s}{c+v} = \text{rate of profit} \qquad \ldots (3.4)$$

where $c$ = constant capital, $v$ = variable capital, $s$ = surplus value.[1] Equations (3.1)–(3.4) are definitions. They define four different terms and hold, regardless of any economic behaviour patterns. We cannot test the validity of any of these equations

---

[1] For the individual firm, $c$ consists of depreciation and raw materials; $v$ consists of wage payments; and $s$ consists of profit, interest, and rent.

because they must hold by definition. They are not refutable hypotheses.

According to the simplest rules of algebra the following equation:

$$\frac{s}{c+v} = \frac{s}{v}\left(1 - \frac{c}{c+v}\right) \qquad \ldots (3.5)$$

must hold[1] because

$$\frac{s}{v}\left(1 - \frac{c}{c+v}\right) = \frac{s}{v}\left(\frac{c+v-c}{c+v}\right) = \frac{s}{c+v}$$

Equation (3.5) is not a refutable hypothesis either. It, too, must hold, regardless of the actual values of the variables $c$, $v$, $s$. Equation (3.5) merely states the truism that:

$$\frac{s}{c+v} = \frac{s}{c+v}$$

In so far as Marxian economics is based on equations (3.1)–(3.5) no real progress can be made. None of these equations tells us anything about fundamental economic behaviour. The extensive use by Marx and the Marxists of equations similar to (3.1)–(3.5) has undoubtedly led Oscar Lange to remark: 'This whole [Marxist] literature tries to solve the fundamental problems of economic equilibrium and disequilibrium without even attempting to make use of the mathematical concept of functional relationship.'[2]

But Marx was probably not so guilty as Lange's remark implies. In Volume III of *Capital*, when discussing the theory of the falling rate of profit, Marx[3] made specific assumptions in his numerical examples. He assumed that $s/v$ in equation (3.5) is constant. Thus he was able to say that the rate of profit, $s/(c+v)$,

---

[1] For the use of such equations in Marxian economics see Paul M. Sweezy, *The Theory of Capitalist Development* (New York: Oxford University Press, 1942), p. 68.

[2] Oscar Lange, 'Marxian Economics and Modern Economic Theory', *Review of Economic Studies*, II (June 1935), p. 196. (See p. 79 above.)

[3] Karl Marx, *Capital*, III (Chicago: Charles H. Kerr & Co., 1909), p. 247.

varies inversely with the organic composition of capital, $c/(c+v)$. Here is a refutable hypothesis, namely, $s/v =$ constant. This is an economic hypothesis that can be tested. We can examine data on wages, profits, interest, and rent to see whether or not $s$ and $v$ have a constant ratio. By making this assumption, Marx was able to develop the theory of the falling rate of profit which states that the rate of profit falls as the organic composition of capital rises. From equations (3.1)–(3.5) we can say nothing about the behaviour of the economic system, but from equations (3.1)–(3.5) and the assumption $s/v =$ constant we can say very much. However, the system is not yet complete even at this stage.

It is worth pointing out that this confusion is not peculiar to Marxian economics. It has arisen in non-Marxian economics in connection with the quantity theory of money. Let us define $M =$ total stock of money; $V =$ average number of times a monetary unit is spent in a given period on newly produced goods and services; $p =$ average price of newly produced goods and services; $X =$ aggregate output of newly produced goods and services.[1] It follows by definition that

$$MV = pX \qquad \ldots (3.6)$$

Equation (3.6) tells us nothing about economic behaviour. In its present form it is of the same nature as equation (3.5). There is no refutable hypothesis contained in either (3.5) or (3.6).

The classical economists did the same thing about (3.6) that Marx did about (3.5). They assumed that certain variables in (3.6) were known numbers. Specifically, they assumed $V =$ constant and $X =$ full-employment output. For them, $V$ was determined by institutional and psychological phenomena such as the frequency of wage payments, attitudes towards holding cash, etc. With $V$ and $X$ known, the classical economists could say that the price level varies directly with the amount of money. The validity of this theory depends upon the validity of the assumptions about $V$ and $X$.

These examples illustrate our method. We shall search through Marx's literary explanations and numerical examples

---

[1] The aggregates $p$ and $X$ are constructed so that their product, $pX$, is exactly equal to the total value of newly produced output.

for the strategic hypotheses that will produce a determinate system of equations.

First we must define the variables carefully. We shall retain Marx's notation of $c$, $v$, $s$. When referring to the individual firm, $c$ consists of depreciation and purchases of raw materials, $v$ consists of wage payments, and $s$ consists of profit plus interest plus rent. The aggregate value of output for the individual firm is $c+v+s$. When referring to the economy as a whole, we must redefine constant capital in order to avoid double counting. For the entire system, constant capital, denoted by $C$, is defined as the value of depreciation charges. Constant capital does not include raw materials for the system as a whole because such an inclusion would lead to excessive double counting in determining the value of output. Variable capital for the entire system will be denoted by $V$ and will include all wage payments. Surplus value for the entire system will be denoted by $S$ and will include total profits, interest, and rents. In modern terminology, we have:

$$C+V+S = \text{gross national income}$$

$$V+S = \text{net national income}$$

National income can be considered from two sides – production and factor payments. National income as the sum $V+S$ represents total factor payments.[1] From the side of production, national income can be considered as equal to the total production of two types of goods and services – consumption and investment (consumer goods and producer goods). Consumer goods are those that flow to households and producer goods those that flow to business firms. We shall denote consumption by $R$ and net investment by $I$. Net national income will be denoted, as usual, by $Y$. We have, thus far, the two following definitional equations:

$$V+S = Y \qquad \qquad \ldots (3.7)$$

$$R+I = Y \qquad \qquad \ldots (3.8)$$

[1] It is only in orthodox economics that $S$ represents a factor payment. In Marxian terminology, $S$ represents exploitation. The term 'factor payment' is used in the text only because it is customarily used today in discussions of national income statistics.

The variables $V, S, Y, R, I$, are all measured in real terms, for example, constant dollars.

It is now necessary to develop behaviour equations to show how these variables are determined. First consider $R$, consumption. Marx divided consumers into two strategic groups – workers and capitalists. He *assumed* that workers spend all their incomes on consumer goods and services. In fact, he wrote: '... the variable capital advanced in the payment of the labour–power of the labourers is mostly spent by them for articles of consumption; ...'[1] This assumption is also carried through in a purer form in his numerical examples of reproduction schemes in Part III, Volume II of *Capital*. In the numerical examples he always put workers' consumption exactly equal to wages (not approximately equal). In the quotation he said that wages are 'mostly spent' (but not entirely spent) on consumer goods and services. As a matter of fact, empirical data suggest that Marx's quoted assumption is the correct one. The marginal propensity to consume out of wages is not unity, although it is very close to unity.

It is less obvious how to determine the behaviour pattern for capitalist consumption in the Marxian system. The main clue comes from a study of numerical examples that Marx used to analyse capitalist reproduction schemes. The theory of simple reproduction is not much of a clue, for in that scheme a steady state is assumed in which variable capital (wages) and surplus value are always exactly spent on consumer goods and capital is replaced without any net investment taking place. The schemes of accumulation and reproduction on an enlarged scale, found at the end of Volume II of *Capital*, provide the basis for a theory of capitalist consumption.

In his examples on accumulation, Marx divided the economic system into two departments – the department (I) producing producer goods and the department (II) producing consumer goods. In the first department, workers were assumed to spend all their wage income on consumer goods produced by the second department, while capitalists were assumed to spend only a part of their surplus-value income on consumer goods. The

[1] Karl Marx, *op. cit.*, II, p. 466.

exact relation for capitalist behaviour in Department I was:

$$\text{consumption} = \tfrac{1}{2} \text{ (surplus value)}$$

This is the consumption function for capitalists in Department I. In a consistent theory it should be expected that capitalists in Department II would also behave in a similar fashion, their consumption being a function of their surplus-value income. True, Marx assumed that the capitalists in Department II consumed out of their surplus-value income, but he did not assume that there existed an independent relation between consumption and surplus value for capitalists in Department II. The behaviour of capitalists in the consumer-goods industry was entirely passive in the sense that their consumption was calculated as a residual. This residual consumption was taken to be the difference between total surplus value in Department II and that part of surplus value which was transferred to expenditure on constant and variable capital. The latter expenditure was calculated by Marx so that the reproduction scheme could work smoothly without a glut of the market. Marx did not assume, by any means, that capitalism works smoothly; but he set down in his reproduction schemes the conditions under which capitalism could work smoothly. He argued that if his conditions were not met a crash would occur. One step in a possible method of introducing fluctuations into the model, with recurring crises and recovery, is to make capitalist consumption in Department II also a function of surplus value. We can even simplify the entire system by doing away with the distinction between departments I and II. Let us assume instead that capitalists behave the same way in both departments. Identical behaviour is assumed for workers in these two departments, and it seems reasonable to assume that capitalists should not have different consumption habits according as they produce consumer goods or producer goods. Hence we shall assume that the consumption of capitalists is a function of surplus value.

Denoting the consumption of workers by $R_1$ and the consumption of capitalists by $R_2$ we have the two consumption functions:[1]

$$R_1 = V \qquad \qquad \ldots (3.9)$$

$$R_2 = a_0 + a_1 S, \quad 0 < a_1 < 1 \qquad \ldots (3.10)$$

[1] As a first approximation, we shall assume a linear system.

The total consumption function is given by:

$$R_1 + R_2 = R = a_0 + a_1 S + V \qquad \dots (3.11)$$

In a more general formulation, where the workers' marginal propensity to consume is not unity, we have:

$$R_1 = a_2 + a_3 V, \quad 0 < a_3 < 1 \qquad \dots (3.9')$$

$$R = (a_0 + a_2) + a_1 S + a_3 V, \quad a_3 > a_1 \qquad \dots (3.11')$$

The next step is to derive the demand for the other type of good in the system – investment or producer goods. We shall first derive the demand relation for constant capital (capital used up) according to Marx and then transform the demand for constant capital into investment. Workers buy only consumer goods in the Marxian system, for that is what distinguishes workers from capitalists. The demand for constant capital will be based entirely on the behaviour of capitalists. Again, we rely on the examples of expanded reproduction in order to discover the variables influencing capitalists' demand for constant capital.

In Volume II, Marx assumed that capitalists in Department I (the producer-goods industry) spend from surplus value on constant capital. His relation was:

$$\text{constant capital} = C_0 + k \text{ (surplus value)}, \quad 0 < k < 1$$

where $C_0 =$ the initial level of constant capital and $k =$ a fraction which is the product of the fraction of surplus value to be accumulated in both variable and constant capital and the fraction of total capital represented by constant capital.

The expenditures on constant capital in Department II were like the expenditures by capitalists on consumer goods in that department in the sense that both expenditures were calculated as a residual. The capitalists in Department II did not decide, independently, to accumulate capital but based their decision entirely on the relationship between expenditures in both departments so that the process would run smoothly without a glut of the market. We can again do away with the assumption of a smooth-working capitalist system by supposing that capitalists behave the same way in both departments in so far as the demand for constant capital is concerned. We shall assume that capitalists in both departments demand constant capital as a fraction of surplus value.

There is one condition, implicit in Marx's example, which must be avoided for our model. Marx assumed that whatever capitalists do not spend out of surplus value on consumer goods they spend on constant or variable capital. We shall assume, instead, an independence between the marginal propensity to consume and the marginal propensity to invest. We must point out, however, that Marx made this assumption only to obtain the conditions for a smooth-working system. He did not imply that these conditions held in the real world. Our alternative assumption is one way of achieving the conditions of the real world in the Marxian spirit.

We now have the equation:

$$C = \beta_0 + \beta_1 S \qquad \ldots (3.12)$$

Since we are going to work with the variable $I$ instead of $C$, it will be necessary to carry out a transformation of variables. The transformation involves commonsense technological relations which are constructed by the present author and do not appear in *Capital*.[1]

The variable $C$ represents the amount of fixed capital used up in the production process. The amount of capital used up (depreciation) will depend upon the stock of fixed capital in existence. The capital in existence will, in turn, be made up of the elements of durable capital, plant, and equipment – acquired at various stages of past history. Denoting the capital acquired during the $p$th preceding time period by $x_{-\mathrm{p}}$, we have:

$$C = C(x, x_{-1}, x_{-2}, x_{-3}, \ldots) \qquad \ldots (3.13)$$

or in a linear approximation[2]

$$C = \delta_0 + \delta_1 x + \delta_2 x_{-1} + \delta_3 x_{-2} + \ldots \qquad \ldots (3.14)$$

In statistical work we cannot measure separately the capital purchased during every preceding time period, but we can approximate all these variables with a proxy variable which re-

[1] These transformations are so obvious that it is assumed that anybody wishing to work with $I$ instead of $C$ would use approximately the same transformations.

[2] Since the linear function is an approximation we shall not assume the constant term equal to zero, although logically there should be no constant term in this equation.

presents all the capital accumulated up to the time period under consideration. Instead of (3.14), let us write:

$$C = \delta_0 + \delta_1 x + \delta'_2 Z_{-1} \qquad \ldots (3.14')$$

The stock of existing fixed capital, $Z_{-1}$, can be written in terms of the net investment of all preceding periods as

$$Z_{-1} = \sum_{t=-1}^{-\infty} I_t. \qquad \ldots (3.15)$$

Equation (3.14') at least makes the distinction between new and old capital, but it is not so complete as (3.14), which makes the distinction between capital of all different age-groups. This distinction is useful because the capital in different age groups has different productivities, the newest capital being technologically superior.

It is net investment rather than gross investment which is of primary importance for the particular model of this paper. We can obviously write:

$$x = I + C \qquad \ldots (3.16)$$

Substituting (3.16) into (3.14') we get

$$C = \delta_0 + \delta_1 (I + C) + \delta'_2 Z_{-1} \qquad \ldots (3.17)$$

or

$$C = \frac{\delta_0}{1 - \delta_1} + \frac{\delta_1}{1 - \delta_1} I + \frac{\delta'_2}{1 - \delta_1} Z_{-1}$$

We can now eliminate $C$ between (3.12) and (3.17) to get

$$I = \beta_2 + \beta_3 S + \beta_4 Z_{-1} \qquad \ldots (3.18)$$

This is the final form of our investment function.

There is now lacking one more equation for the completion of the system. Capitalists demand commodities in the form not only of producer and consumer goods but also in the form of labour power. Our equation of the demand for labour power will appear in a disguised form. We shall develop an equation which serves to determine the aggregate amount of variable capital, $V$. But this variable represents the total remuneration paid out by capitalists for labour power. The equation which serves to determine $V$ in our system is the same thing as the demand equation for labour power.

Those familiar with Marx will recall that he regarded the surplus value as transformed into variable and constant capital in his schemes of expanded reproduction. We could have made $C+V$ a function of $S$ instead of making $C$ alone a function of $S$. However, since Marx always assumed a definite relation between $C$ and $V$, we were able to eliminate $V$ in the above relation. He imposed the condition that variable and constant capital be used in the same proportions throughout the production process; hence we were able to develop a relation between $C$ and $S$ not involving $V$. While Marx assumed a definite relation between $C$ and $V$, he also assumed a definite relation between $S$ and $V$. It may appear that we are getting too many equations, but both these relations (that between $C$ and $V$, and that between $S$ and $V$) are not independent. Suppose that total capital is a function of surplus value:

$$C+V = f(S) \qquad \ldots (3.19)$$

and that variable capital is also a function of surplus value:

$$C+V(S) = f(S) \qquad \ldots (3.20)$$

or

$$C = f^*(S)$$

This forms the basis of equation (3.12). It is evident that there must also be a relation between $C$ and $V$, since:

$$S = V^{-1}(V) \qquad \ldots (3.21)$$

and

$$C = f^*(V^{-1}[V]) = f^{**}(V)$$

This simple demonstration shows that a relation between $C$ and $S$ and a relation between $V$ and $S$ imply a relation between $C$ and $V$. The latter relation is not independent of the other two; hence there are not too many equations.[1]

[1] The above demonstration is a method of keeping the system from becoming over-determined. However, it is questionable whether Marx intended the relation between $C$ and $V$ to be dependent on other relations or whether he intended it to be an independent technological phenomenon. From a technological point of

As was seen above in the brief discussion of the theory of the falling rate of profit, the assumption, $S/V =$ constant, led to very important conclusions. In the numerical examples of expanded reproduction, Marx maintained a constant ratio between $S$ and $V$. This assumption implies that labour will receive a constant fraction of net national income. Economists have long been puzzled by the fact that national-income statistics have shown labour's share of total income to be nearly constant over a long time period. There has possibly been some trend in these data which show that labour's share has been gradually increasing. This trend term could be explained by the institutional phenomenon of a growing labour movement in the United States.

The next equation is thus:

$$V = \gamma_1 S \qquad \ldots (3.22)$$

We may introduce the trend by a modification to:

$$V = \gamma_0 + \gamma_1 S + \gamma_2 t \qquad \ldots (3.22')$$

Since $V+S = Y$, it is equivalent to say that $V$ and $S$ are proportional or that $V$ and $Y$ are proportional. In recent years the stability of labour's share has usually been discussed in terms of $V$ and $Y$ rather than $V$ and $S$. As an alternative formulation, we could write:

$$V = \gamma_3 + \gamma_4 Y + \gamma_5 t \qquad \ldots (3.23)$$

The Marxian system is now complete. The entire set of equations is:[1]

$$R = a_0 + a_1 S + a_2 V \qquad \ldots (3.24)$$
$$I = \beta_0 + \beta_1 S + \beta_2 Z_{-1} \qquad \ldots (3.25)$$
$$V = \gamma_0 + \gamma_1 Y + \gamma_2 t \qquad \ldots (3.26)$$
$$Y = S + V \qquad \ldots (3.27)$$
$$Y = R + I \qquad \ldots (3.28)$$
$$\Delta Z = I \qquad \ldots (3.29)$$

---

view, there is no reason why labour and capital should be used in a fixed relation during the entire production process; hence we have not made use of an independent technological relation between $C$ and $V$.

[1] We have renumbered all subscripts on the parameters for purely aesthetic reasons.

Equation (3.24) follows from (3.11′), (3.25) from (3.18), (3.26) from (3.23), (3.27) from (3.7), (3.28) from (3.8), and (3.29) from (3.15). We have, in (3.24)–(3.29), six equations and six endogenous variables $R$, $V$, $S$, $I$, $Z$, $Y$. All variables are measured in 'real' units, and we have been able to complete the system without introducing the quantity of money.

Several observations are called for before we go on to some problems of economic analysis based upon this model. While it is true that this version of the Marxian theory has been developed largely through an examination of Marx's writings and by a slight generalization of his own methods (i.e., a generalization of his numerical examples into functional relationships), the same model can readily be developed from other considerations. By assuming certain behaviour patterns for workers and capitalists, like utility- and profit-maximization, we can obtain the same mathematical model. The reader will also notice that the model (3.24)–(3.29) is very similar to Kalecki's theories. Practically no model implies a unique theoretical basis. Furthermore, we have not utilized Marx's methods to their fullest extent. Only those aspects of Marx's theories are used that are necessary to build a complete system of equations. Many Marxian theories are unrelated to the principle of effective demand, but even some of those parts of his theory that are related to effective demand have been left out. It was necessary to make the latter omission in order to keep from getting an over-determined model. For example, Marx assumed that the wage *rate* would be determined by the value of the means of subsistence of a worker, where the means of subsistence, in turn, depends upon the traditional standard of life in the particular region where the worker lives. But it is easy to show that the model cannot contain this theory of an autonomous wage rate as well as the theory underlying equation (3.26). Suppose that equation (3.26) is accepted as a correct theory. The model then enables us to determine the real wage bill and the level of output. Every system must contain a technological input–output relationship. In the Marxian system, input is given by the employment of labour power and the depreciation of fixed capital, $C$. From our discussion there are enough relations to determine output and $C$; hence the other type of input, employment of labour power, is uniquely determined. Since the real wage bill and employment are known, the real wage rate is also known. There is no room in this system for an autonomously determined wage rate. The strong empirical foundation behind equation (3.26) is an argument for using this Marxian hypothesis rather than the other hypothesis of a given wage rate. It is certain that both hypotheses cannot be used simultaneously within the framework of our model. This example serves to show that the above model is not the only mathematization of *Capital*. There are a variety of models that can be developed from the Marxian theories, and we have chosen one that is plausible, simple, and useful for the analysis of specific problems.

It is interesting to make certain comparisons between the Keynesian and the Marxian models. A simple version of the Keynesian theory – in which the quantity of money and the interest rate do not appear as variables – is a special case of the Marxian model. By substitution from (3.26) and (3.27) into (3.24), it is possible to make consumption a function of income; and, by substitution from (3.26) and (3.27) into (3.25), it is possible to make investment a function of income and the stock of capital. For the short-run theories, Keynes took the stock of capital as given; thus, such a reduced version of the Marxian model comes to the same thing as the simple Keynesian model. The primary advantage of the Marxian model is that it provides more information than does the Keynesian system. In the former model the complete solution always gives the demand for consumer goods, producer goods, and employment, while in some forms[1] of the latter model, the complete solution gives only the demand for consumer goods and the demand for producer goods. The demand for factors of production (employment and producer goods) determines supply; hence the Marxian model has the virtue of always giving the full conditions of demand and supply. This cannot be said, in general, of the Keynesian model.

It is not meant to imply that Marx fully anticipated the Keynesian theory of effective demand. Our model is intended as an extension of the Marxian analysis to a logical conclusion in terms of a theory of effective demand. Actually, Marx laid the

[1] This is true in those forms of the Keynesian theory in which the savings-investment equation alone is used to determine the level of output.

groundwork for a complete equation system to determine the level of income (effective demand) but did not build the complete system. In his discussions of the reproduction schemes in Volume II of *Capital*, Marx set forth some conditions under which there would not be excessive savings in the system, conditions under which all savings are offset. He then showed that these conditions are very complex and that it is not reasonable to assume that they will always be met, hence the crisis. But he did not offer an exact theory to show the quantitative extent to which they will not be met. Keynes' theory also shows the conditions for full employment and argues that they will not always be met, but Keynes went one step further: He provided a general theory to determine the level of employment when it is not one of full employment. The Keynesian model shows how any level of employment is determined. Our procedure in this paper has been to introduce mathematical extensions of the Marxian theory to show how any level of income (or employment) is determined. In case the conditions for full employment – or for no glut of the market in Marx's sense – are not met, our mathematical model shows precisely what level of employment will ensue under the less-than-full-employment conditions.

It should be pointed out that the author has applied various methods of statistical estimation to the Marxian model and has found the estimated parameters to be very reasonable in size. Moreover, the model fits the observed data very closely. Except for small random error, workers and capitalists have, in fact, behaved as the Marxian model says they behave. Lags, government investment, taxes, etc., were introduced in the statistical models in order to depict the real world more exactly. A discussion of the statistical results is too lengthy to be included in this paper, and the conclusions are mentioned only to inform the reader that the model is not purely hypothetical.

### 4. THE STAGNATION THESIS

It has become very popular of late to criticize the stagnation thesis severely and to assert that ours is still a young, vigorous, expanding economy. The critics have been quick to forget the lesson of the thirties and have misunderstood the thesis. Negative though most criticism has been, the spirit of this section is one of constructive criticism, by which some new ideas that support the thesis may be injected into the argument.

Despite the fact that the stagnation thesis grew out of the discussions of Keynesian economics of the past decade, the foundations of the theory are much older, going back to Marx's theory of the falling rate of profit. The critics would have had a much more difficult time finding evidence against a mature-economy doctrine based on the theory of the falling rate of profit than against the doctrine based on such factors as population growth, disappearance of the frontier, and growth of depreciation reserves. They were quick to point out that population growth slowed down and the frontier disappeared long before the decade of the thirties, yet stagnation did not then set in.

The Marxian theory states that, with a constant rate of surplus value $(S/V)$, the rate of profit will vary inversely with capital accumulation. Equation (3.5) shows that the rate of profit is the product of 'the rate of surplus value' and 'one minus the organic composition of capital'. Capital accumulation implies a rising organic composition of capital and, hence, a falling rate of profit from (3.5). The main hypothesis of this theory, the constancy of the rate of surplus value, is known to be valid, as shown by the available data. This theory can easily be applied to the inter-war period. The application runs as follows: After World War I the profit outlook in manufacturing (especially automobile), utilities, and housing appeared to be good and persistent. Capitalists accumulated all during the twenties. They built so many plants and houses and so much equipment that the rate of return on the expanded volume began to fall. The rate of return on the greatly expanded capital structure was so small during the thirties that there was little capital investment and the system was depressed for a decade. It was the capital accumulation of the twenties which led to the fall in the rate of profit and the consequent stagnation of the thirties. The theory does not say that the stagnation or maturity is permanent. It is no contradiction of the theory to observe that housing capital, *relative to the population*, declined during World War II, thus generating a high rate of return on housing capital and a building boom again. Similarly, the present capital expansion in other industries is no contradiction of the theory. However, the theory indicates specifically that the capital expansion will not continue indefinitely. Once a large stock of capital has been accumulated again, the mature-economy doctrine should predict another stagnant period of a decade or more.

In the Marxian model, (3.24)–(3.29), it will be observed that the demand for investment goods depends upon two variables – profits and the stock of capital. The essence of the Marxian theory is that both variables must be in this relation. The dependence on profit is positive, and the dependence on capital is negative. The stock of capital becomes a very serious drag upon the system. Many of the present author's statistical investigations in separate industries, as well as for the economy as a whole, have shown that the stock of fixed capital is negatively related to investment. The more capital there is, other things unchanged, the less is the desire for new capital. The consequences of capital accumulation have never been fully explored. For example, if we drop the capital variable from the Marxian model or if we use the customary forms of the Keynesian model, the multiplier equation for the whole system usually takes the form:

$$Y + a_1 Y_{-1} + a_2 Y_{-2} + \ldots + a_n Y_{-n} = \beta G, \qquad \ldots (4.1)$$

where $Y$ = real income and $G$ = real exogenous investment. If, on the other hand, the variable, $Z_{-1}$ = stock of fixed capital, is introduced in the equation of demand for producer goods, the multiplier equation will have the form:

$$Y + a_1 Y_{-1} + a_2 Y_{-2} + \ldots + a_n Y_{-n} = \beta_1 G + \beta_2 G_{-1} \ldots (4.2)$$

The difference between (4.1) and (4.2) is significant. The values of $\beta$ and $\beta_1$ will be positive, but if capital has a depressing influence on investment, the value of $\beta_2$ will be negative. Both the truncated and the untruncated multipliers from (4.2) will be smaller, the larger is the negative value of $\beta_2$. The depressing influence of capital accumulation operates not only partially in the demand equation for producer goods but also permeates the entire system with a depressing influence. The stimulative shocks given to the system by exogenous investment, such as new industries and government spending, will be cushioned by the depressing influence of capital accumulation.

The reason for introducing the stock of fixed capital in the investment–demand equation of the Marxian system is that in this form the equation fits in so well with the theory of the falling rate of profit. It is also possible to argue that an implied 'theory of the declining marginal efficiency of capital' in the Keynesian theory would call for the introduction of a variable representing capital accumulation in the Keynesian investment schedule. In the past, economists have modified the Keynesian investment function in this way, but only for the long-run theory in which investment is zero. The real world, however, is not one of long-run equilibrium in which investment is zero or one of short-run equilibrium in which the stock of capital is taken as given. The real world falls between these extremes, and the Marxian model of this paper is a representation of the compromise.

## 5. REDISTRIBUTION OF INCOME

No theory has received more vulgarizations than has the theory of the effect on employment of the redistribution of income. The correct results need to be systematized with all assumptions stated explicitly. For simplicity, we shall consider redistribution between only two types of income, wages and non-wages (= profits). One type of vulgarization is to look at wages only as a demand factor and not at wages as a cost factor. The argument is that a redistribution from profits into wages will always increase income and employment.

Many old-fashioned trade-unionists argue that the only way to cure a condition of unemployment is to redistribute income from profits into wages. They see faulty distribution as the principal flaw in the economic system and regard its correction as a sufficient policy to insure smooth working of the social mechanism. Many economists who call themselves Keynesians have also relied very heavily on redistribution of income as a powerful antidepression policy. They have often over-emphasized the demand aspects of wages to the neglect of the cost aspects.

There is another group of economists who look at wages purely as a cost factor and neglect the influence of wages as a demand factor. Most of the supporters of wage cuts as a policy for curing depressions are in this category. They argue that, if wages are cut, capitalists will have lower costs and hence will be able to expand their plants. This argument is wrong not only because it is based on an incorrect analysis of redistribution but also because it does not take into account the possibility that falling wages may generate adverse expectations.

Obviously, the most proper type of model for analysing the effects of redistribution is one that gives full effect to wages as a cost factor and to wages as a demand factor. The Marxian model is very well suited for this purpose. The consumption function distinguishes between wages and profits as separate demand factors, while the investment function – an equation of capitalist behaviour alone – depends on profits, which means that wages enter as a cost factor. If our analysis is limited to the instantaneous effect on output of redistribution of income *within a given period*, we can neglect the influence of capital accumulation as a variable in the investment function. The term $\beta_2 Z_{-1}$, in (3.25), can be incorporated with the constant term because $\beta_2 Z_{-1}$ is predetermined and thus given for any single time period.

The following result can be stated for our model: If the capitalists' marginal propensity to spend (consume and invest) is greater than the workers' marginal propensity to consume, redistribution from profits into wages will decrease income. If the two marginal propensities are the same, income will be unaffected by the redistribution, and if the latter marginal propensity is greater than the former, redistribution from profits into wages will increase the level of income. It is by no means certain, *a priori*, which propensity is greater. Capitalists like to accumulate, and workers like to consume. Only by making accurate quantitative measurements of the propensities can the final result be determined. The author has found that some methods of statistical estimation give one result, and some methods give another. By any method of estimation used thus far, the confidence intervals for the parameters are so large that no definite conclusion can be drawn.

The intuitive explanation of the foregoing propositions is very simple. If a dollar is taken away from a capitalist, he will cut expenditures by the amount of his marginal propensity to spend, and, if this dollar is given to a worker, he will increase expenditures by the amount of his marginal propensity to consume. The quantitative effect on income depends on the extent to which these marginal propensities diverge. The data upon which the statistical models are based show that the marginal propensities are, at least, close together. If we take into account the capitalists' marginal propensity to spend on producer goods as well as the marginal propensity to spend on consumer goods, we find that the total marginal propensity to spend is probably between 0·7 and 0·9. The workers' marginal propensity to spend is also in the same neighbourhood, between 0·8 and 0·9. In the discussion of redistribution, economists often tend to consider only the two groups' marginal propensities to consume, which are, of course, much farther apart.

There are special cases in which unequivocal results can be obtained. Marx has been interpreted has having claimed that the workers spend all their income, i.e. have a marginal propensity to consume equal to unity. If, as seems reasonable, the capitalists have a marginal propensity to spend which is less than unity, it follows by assumption that redistribution from profits into wages will always stimulate production. It can be shown that, for this case in the Marxian model, the increase in income is always greater than twice the amount redistributed. This is not a realistic case, however, because time-series and family-budget data both show that the marginal propensity to consume out of wages is not so great as unity. The budget data show little or no aggregate savings in the low-income classes, but some investigators have wrongly interpreted this to mean that the marginal propensity to consume is unity. The thing to look at is not the aggregate savings in the low-income groups but the slope of the savings or consumption function in this income range. The slope is definitely not unity throughout the range $0–$3,000 income per year. In this income range there are both dissaving and saving, which cancel each other to a large extent and make the total appear small. But the dissaving can always be more or less than the observed amount, and it is not correct to infer that the existence of dissaving means that low-income families consume exactly 100 per cent of every extra dollar of income that they receive.

Another special case in which the effects of redistribution can be more exactly assessed is that of exogenous investment. If it is believed that investment decisions of businessmen are unrelated to variables internal to the system – depending instead on innovations, psychological expectations, legislative decisions, etc. – the only relevant parameters for the redistribution problem are the marginal propensities to consume of workers and capitalists. The data show definitely that the marginal propensity to consume of the former class is greater than that of the latter class; therefore, within the framework of the model of exogenous investment, redistribution from profits into wages will always stimulate income.

There are also special models where redistribution from profits into wages certainly decreases income. For example, there is a tendency on the part of many model-builders to assume that total income (wages plus profits) is the relevant variable in the consumption function. This assumption gives equal weight to wages and profits on the side of demand for consumer goods. If, to this assumption, is added the assumption that investment expenditures depend on profits, the marginal propensity to spend out of profits will be greater than the marginal propensity to consume out of wages, and redistribution will have the above-stated effect.

There is nothing in the uncertainty of the conclusions of this section to contradict either the Marxian or Keynesian theoretical systems. This point must be made clear because many supporters of these theories make more extravagant claims about redistribution than can be justified on the grounds of the theories of employment alone, convincing though these claims may be from the point of view of economic welfare, equity, and justice.

In the Marxian theory, to state matters mildly, there is no hint that redistribution of income is a sufficient policy to insure that capitalism will always provide uninterrupted full production and employment. This is consistent with the findings that the marginal propensity to spend out of profits is not very different from the marginal propensity to spend out of wages, so that the redistribution effect is minimized. If the system is such that the latter marginal propensity exceeds the former, one must conclude that workers are kept so close to physical subsistence that they are forced to spend practically all their income. This is the situation which calls for redistribution from profits into wages as an employment-creating policy. If the former marginal propensity exceeds the latter, the Marxian explanation is that capitalism generates such fears and uncertainties about the future in the minds of the workers that they are forced to save for the 'rainy day'. Precautionary saving of this type is enough to drive their marginal propensity to consume below the marginal propensity to spend out of profits. Under such circumstances, redistribution from profits into wages which does not alleviate the fear of the future[1] will not create employment. In the Marxian theory, redistribution policies which do not alter the mode of production are not adequate to solve the problem of the occurrence of crises.

[1] Social security planning is a type of redistribution which does alleviate the fear of the future.

## SELECTED BIBLIOGRAPHY

ALEXANDER, S. S. 'Mr Keynes and Mr Marx', *Review of Economic Studies*. February 1940.

MEEK, R. L. 'The Place of Keynes in the History of Economic Thought', *Economics and Ideology*. Chapman & Hall, 1967.

ROBINSON, J. 'Marx, Marshall and Keynes', *Collected Economic Papers:* II. Oxford: Blackwell, 1960.

# Keynes versus Marx: The Methodology of Aggregates

*Shigeto Tsuru*

IN THE Foreword to her *An Essay on Marxian Economics*, Mrs Joan Robinson writes: 'Until recently, Marx used to be treated in academic circles with contemptuous silence broken only by an occasional mocking footnote.'[1] Although this may well have been true in the English-speaking world, such a dictum would not apply to many other countries. Nevertheless, it is true that even in those countries where both Marxism and modern economics are equally pursued as academic disciplines, the two schools usually have not been on speaking terms with each other. One school does not understand the language of the other, and the latter would not care to understand the former. It is therefore a great tribute to Keynes that, although he himself treated Marx 'with contemptuous silence, broken only by an occasional footnote', he opened a new vista in modern economics which almost naturally led to a fruitful comparison between his doctrines and those of Karl Marx. As Schumpeter wrote in his obituary essay on Keynes:

> Though Keynes' 'breakdown theory' is quite different from Marx's, it has an important feature in common with the latter: in both theories, the breakdown is motivated by causes inherent to the working of the economic engine, not by the action of factors external to it.[2]

The full implication of this common feature is yet to be explored. But in a slightly narrower vein, the *rapprochement* between the

[1] Joan Robinson, *An Essay on Marxian Economics*, 1949, v. The Foreword was written in September 1941.
[2] J. A. Schumpeter, *Ten Great Economists*, 1951, p. 284.

Reprinted from Kurihara (ed.): *Post-Keynesian Economics*. Rutgers University Press, 1954.

two schools has been progressing mainly in the hands of Mrs Joan Robinson, an undisputed Keynesian, whose interest appears to lie in making Marx a precursor, though imperfect, of 'the modern theory of effective demand.'[1] The similar position was also expressed by Alan Sweezy in the following words:

> Some of Marx's most important insights, ideas he was struggling to express with the inadequate analytical apparatus then available, became thoroughly clear for the first time in terms of the modern analysis [the Keynesian theory of money, income, and employment]. . . . It shows exactly how an inadequacy of investment outlets produces depression and unemployment. Marx sensed the connection but was unable with the tools at his command to work it out in detailed, systematic fashion.[2]

Lately, Mrs Robinson has expanded her foci of comparison and given us many hints which go beyond the problem of effective demand as such.[3] We also have an article by Lawrence R. Klein,[4] which, directing our attention to Marx's theory of the falling rate of profit,[5] attempts to rewrite the Marxian scheme into an econometric model with specific 'behaviour equations'.

Once we set our mind to reading Marx with sympathetic eyes, it is easy enough to find many points of similarities between him and Keynes. For example: the proposition to the effect that investment generates purchases without sales and so promotes boom conditions can be found in both; both repudiated Say's

[1] See Joan Robinson, 'Marx on Unemployment', *Economic Journal*, June–September 1941, p. 248.

[2] *American Economic Review*, March 1942, pp. 138–39 (a book review).

[3] See *An Essay on Marxian Economics*, first published in 1942, reissued in 1947 with slight alterations; *Collected Economic Papers*, 1951, especially Part III; her Introduction to Rosa Luxemburg, *The Accumulation of Capital*, 1951; and *The Rate of Interest and Other Essays*, 1952, especially pp. 90 ff.

[4] 'Theories of Effective Demand and Employment', *Journal of Political Economy*, April 1947. (See p. 138 above.)

[5] He actually says: 'The Marxian theory of the falling rate of profit is one of the first, and probably one of the best, tools for analysing the stagnation theory.' (*Ibid.*, p. 118.) (See p. 154 above.)

Law, though for slightly different reasons; Keynes' dictum that 'it is preferable to regard labour ... as the sole factor of production, operating in a given environment of technique, natural resources, capital equipment, and effective demand,'[1] along with his practice of expressing economic quantities in terms of wage units, is suggestively close to Marx's theory of value; in a sense Marx foreshadows the departure which Keynes made from the orthodox theory of the rate of interest; and above all, both regarded, though with fairly material difference in emphasis, that causes inherent to the working of the system would bring about a change from capitalism into something else.

Before we become over-enthusiastic about the possibilities of establishing points of similarities between Marx and Keynes, however, we must fully acquaint ourselves with certain fundamental differences between the two, the differences which, far from political or ideological, pertain to the methodological aspect of the economic analysis and lurk often behind the formal equivalence of piecemeal propositions. My purpose in this essay is to examine such differences particularly in connection with the use of aggregates in economic analysis.

Modern society, in its economic aspect, presents itself as an interrelation of a tremendously large number of economic units. One kind or another of theoretical consolidation of these units has been practised since the birth of economics as a scientific discipline. Doctrinal survey would reveal how, since Quesnay's time, such consolidation of economic units has undergone an historical evolution.

Products of consolidation usually pertain to society as a whole and are called, in recent economic literature, simply 'aggregates'. The set of aggregates most widely used in modern economic discussion is, of course, the one associated with the economics of John Maynard Keynes. Let us refer to them as 'Keynesian aggregates'.

It is often said that the problem of aggregates is purely definitional and that one set of aggregates, if defined in terms of objective facts, can always be translated into another set. Though this

[1] J. M. Keynes, *The General Theory of Employment, Interest and Money*, 1936, p. 213.

latter proposition is frequently valid,[1] it is hardly true that the problem of aggregates is purely definitional. Consolidation is a way of organizing manifold data; it is the anatomy of the economic organism. It is natural that a specific consolidation, by resulting in a correspondingly specific fixation of our subject matter, may direct attention at certain problems and away from others, and that it may even exercise an influence on the solution arrived at. To give an example, it is sufficient here to recall the terminological climate of Böhm-Bawerkian capital theory, owing to which it was long denied that the elasticity of demand for labour could have a value smaller than one. To ascertain precisely at which point an error creeps in is not, alas for our science, a logical problem *simpliciter*. More than two alternative representations of a certain subject matter can not only be compatible but are often complementary, as are projections of a multidimensional object from different angles. Conflict, however, becomes especially patent when we enter the realm of practice, for there it is necessary to test empirically the relative effectiveness of alternative approaches. What may appear theoretically to be only two sides of a shield finds its counterpart in practice as two opposing policies. A recent, though a relatively minor, example of this kind is the controversy between the cost-adjustment and the effective demand schools of business cycle control. Often, of course, the conflict in practice goes deeper than here, for the fundamental reorganization of society may become involved.

Let us then begin with the Marxian aggregates and state the essentials of this system in such a way that both the contrast and the comparability with the Keynesian aggregates could be brought out in bold relief.

The principle of consolidation which Marx adopted is twofold. On the one hand, he divides all the products into producers' goods and consumers' goods. This is a division from the standpoint of *material use* of the product and actually transcends specific mode of production. That is to say, such a division exists under socialism as well as under capitalism. On the other hand, Marx divides all the products into three components of value, namely, constant capital $(C)$, variable capital $(V)$, and surplus

---

[1] See Shigeto Tsuru, 'On Reproduction Schemes', Appendix to P. M. Sweezy, *The Theory of Capitalist Development*, 1942.

value ($S$). This is a division which is characteristic of capitalism. Constant capital subsumes the cost of raw materials, fuel and depreciation, and is so called because these items are considered to go into the value of the product without changing their value-magnitude. Variable capital refers to capital reserved for payment of wages, and is so called because it is the category which is considered to be the source of all the new value created and thus finds its *raison d'être* only if it is variable. Surplus value is the part which, according to Marx, is a residue out of the new value created over and above the necessary payment for wages. When we apply these two principles of division to the total products of society, we obtain the following six aggregates, in which the subscript 1 refers to the producers's goods sector and the subscript 2 to the consumers' goods sector.

$$C_1 + V_1 + S_1$$
$$C_2 + V_2 + S_2$$

Here in its simplest form is a *tableau* of commodity circulation. It is a *tableau* because these six categories are mutually inter-related. The vertical division into $C$, $V$ and $S$, which may be said to represent the 'cost' structure of each sector, is actually coterminous with the horizontal division into producers' goods and consumers' goods. If we take the simplest case of circular flow and assume that both workers and capitalists consume all of their incomes, both $V$'s and $S$'s, while governed by the specific conditions of value relation, constitute at the same time the demand for consumers' goods. In other words, each of the six categories above constitutes at once (1) an aliquot part of the particular kind of product, i.e., either producers' goods or consumers' goods, (2) a specific item in the cost structure, i.e. either constant capital, variable capital, or surplus value, and finally (3) a demand for either producers' goods or consumers' goods. In this way, the *tableau* becomes a self-contained one in which each item of cost is in itself a demand for the product specific in the tableau. The significance of this circularity becomes obvious if we visualize a situation in the non-capitalist world. Under socialism, for example, it is conceivable that the cost of labour becomes insulated from the demand for consumers' goods by workers. The amount of purchasing power given to specific workers may be governed by principles which are not directly inherent in the cost structure. It is, in fact, one of the most important characteristics of capitalism that what is a cost item constitutes directly a demand for something. Thus the reduction of wage rates, while it may improve the cost-price maladjustment, results *ipso facto* in the shrinkage of effective demand. Marx's *tableau*, though quite simple, brings out this mechanism very explicitly.

Even if we advance a step towards realism and introduce the fact of saving or accumulation, the fundamental character of the *tableau* undergoes no change. Suppose that capitalists save a part of their surplus value and invest it in buying additional producers' goods and labour–power. Then surplus value $(S)$ divides itself into the part reserved for capitalists' consumption $(S_k)$, the part destined to demand producers' goods $(S_c)$, and the part destined to demand the additional labour–power $(S_v)$. And now the *tableau* may be rewritten as follows:

$$C_1 + V_1 + S_{k1} + S_{c1} + S_{v1}$$
$$C_2 + V_2 + S_{k2} + S_{c2} + S_{v2}$$

The manner in which these categories are related to each other can best be brought out by stating the condition of smooth exchange which would enable the system to go on without either overproduction or underconsumption. On the supply side we have:

| | |
|---|---|
| *Producers' goods* | $C_1 + V_1 + S_{k1} + S_{c1} + S_{v1}$ |
| *Consumers' goods* | $C_2 + V_2 + S_{k2} + S_{c2} + S_{v2}$ |

And on the demand side we have:

| | | |
|---|---|---|
| *For producers' goods* | $C_1 + S_{c1}$ | *from the first sector* |
| | $C_2 + S_{c2}$ | *from the second sector* |
| *For consumers' goods* | $V_1 + S_{k1} + S_{v1}$ | *from the first sector* |
| | $V_2 + S_{k2} + S_{v2}$ | *from the second sector* |

In order that the supply and demand for each kind of product be equal, it will be sufficient if the equation

$$V_1 + S_{k1} + S_{v1} = C_2 + S_{c2}$$

is satisfied.[1] What use we can make of this equation we shall touch upon later.

Superficially, the system of Marxian aggregates we have described above could easily be translated into Keynesian terms. Although in many ways the Keynesian aggregates are much more complex than the Marxian, in one respect they are simpler. That is, in the Keynesian system the degree of consolidation is still more thorough than in the case of Marx. Thus, to establish a bridge between the two systems, first of all we add the categories of the two sectors of Marx and obtain: ($C_1 + C_2 = C$, and so on)

$$C + V + S + S_k + S_c + S_v$$

which is the total output, $A$, of Keynes.[2] His $A_1$, or entrepreneurial transactions, can be written as the sum of $C$ and $S_c$. On the other hand, his $G'$, or the net value conservable from what was on hand at the beginning of the period, if we may ignore his $B'$[3] as insignificant, is equal to the sum of $C$ and $V$, while the means of production on hand at the end of the period, his $G$, consists of $C$, $S_c$, $V$ and $S_v$. Labour–power bought is included among the means of production, inasmuch as it is an asset in the sense of renderable service and may be regarded as the limiting case of 'goods in process'.

Equivalent expressions for such terms as user cost, $U$, investment, $I$, income, $Y$, saving, $S$, and consumption, $K$, can easily be derived from the above. In the definitions of Keynes:

$$U = A_1 + G' - G \text{ (ignoring } B')$$
$$I = G - G'$$
$$Y = A - U$$
$$S = A_1 - U$$
$$K = A - A_1$$

[1] Readers can easily satisfy themselves that this is the case by equating the supply side with the demand side for each sector and cancelling the identical terms from both sides.

[2] Cf. J. M. Keynes, *op. cit.*, chapter 6.

[3] B' is the sum which the entrepreneur would have spent on the maintenance and improvement of his capital equipment if he had decided not to use it to produce output.

Translated into Marxian categories:

$$U = C - S_v$$
$$I = S_c + S_v$$
$$Y = V + S + S_v$$
$$S = S_c + S_v$$
$$K = V + S_k + S_v$$

Take for example the equality: $Y = V + S + S_v$ (in which $S = S_k + S_c + S_v$). It appears that the Keynesian $Y$, or national income, subsumes not only the wages-bill $(V)$ and surplus value $(S)$, which two exhaust the 'value added' in the period, but also *additional* expenditure on labour–power $(S_v)$ paid out of the surplus value, and that 'consumption' and 'saving-investment' overlap to the extent of such expenditure. In other words, $S_v$ is registered twice as income and appears to be only once exchanged against goods. There is no mystery, however, once we make explicit the position of the commodity labour–power in the network of circulation. In the strict logic of capitalism, additional labour–power is just as much a part of the net national product as would be, for example, a new robot-machine. Two metamorphoses of $S_v$, therefore, have two distinct counterparts in the form of commodity, once in labour–power and secondly in consumers' goods.

The Keynesian consolidation is explicit as regards the so-called 'service industries' of which labour–power is a constituent, but does not admit labour–power, which is a 'producers' good', into the category of investment goods. The difficulty is overcome, however, by imparting labour–power with a character of 'goods in process'. The minute a new labour–power is purchased, it presumably commences to take part in the process of production; and to the income, disbursed against the labour–power, corresponds the limiting case of 'goods in process' as a part of investment.[1]

[1] The point, which I developed earlier in 'On Reproduction Schemes', Appendix to P. M. Sweezy, *The Theory of Capitalist Development*, 1942, received a number of criticisms, of which C. Bettelheim's 'Revenu national, épargne et investissements chez Marx et chez Keynes', *Revue D'Economie Politique*, 1948, pp. 198–211, was the most prominent. To him, I answered in my 'Accumulation and Consumption in the Reproduction Schema' (in Japanese),

The comparability of this kind, even if perfect, is of course not very significant. In the sections to follow I shall try to indicate some of the more important differences in methodology which should not be lost sight of in using the aggregates of either school. But here we may stretch our comparison a step further and try to see additional possibilities by way of finding formal similarities between the Marxian system and that of modern economics.

For this purpose, let us reproduce the equation

$$V_1 + S_{k1} + S_{v1} = C_2 + S_{c2}$$

which, as the reader will remember, was the condition for the smooth reproduction of an economy which accumulates. Now if we define:[1]

$s$ = the rate of surplus value, or the ratio of $S_1/V_1$ which is assumed to be equal to $S_2/V_2$

$r_2$ = the organic composition of capital, or the ratio of $C_2/V_2$

$h$ = the proportion between the value of variable capital in the second sector and that in the first, or the ratio of $V_2$ over $V_1$. (If the wage rate is the same in both sectors, it indicates the proportion in which the total labour force is divided into the two sectors.)

$x_1$ (or $x_2$) = the ratio of $S_{c_1}$ ($S_{c2}$) over $S_1$ ($S_2$)

we may rewrite this equation as:

$$sx_1 + shx_2 - (1 + s - hr_2) = 0$$

Solving this equation for $h$, we obtain:

$$h = \frac{1 + s - sx_1}{sx_2 + r_2}$$

---

*The Economic Review*, July 1950; and to Mr Osamu Shimomura, who also made a similar point, I answered in 'Discrepancy between Income and Product' (in Japanese), *The Economic Studies Quarterly*, October 1951.

[1] See my article 'Marx's *Tableau Economique* and "Underconsumption" Theory', *Indian Economic Review*, February 1953.

This is an equation which tells us that when there is a balanced growth in the economy the proportion in which the total labour force is divided into two sectors, producers' goods and consumers' goods, namely $h$, is governed in a specific manner by three factors: ($1$) the rate of surplus value, $s$, ($2$) the 'propensity to save' or 'the propensity to invest'[1] in the two sectors, $x_1$ and $x_2$, and ($3$) the organic composition of capital in the consumers' goods sector, $r_2$. From this equation we can say definitely that when the rate of surplus value rises, the proportion of labour force going into the consumers' goods sector has to become smaller than before, that when the 'propensity to invest' rises, assuming that $x_1 = x_2$, the said proportion also has to decline, and that when the organic composition of capital in the second sector rises, the result is the same.

Now it will not be too far-fetched to compare these three factors with the famed three dynamic determinants of Harrod.[2] Our first factor here, the rate of surplus value, or $s$, is roughly a ratio of profit income to wage income; hence its rise corresponds exactly to what Harrod calls 'the shift to profit', his second dynamic determinant. Our second factor, the 'propensity to invest', or $x$'s, is quite similar, with only inconsequential differences, to his first dynamic determinant, 'the propensity to save', although the latter is formulated explicitly as a relation between two contiguous periods. Our third factor, the organic composition of capital in the second sector, or $r_2$, focuses our attention upon the relation which Harrod chooses to call 'the amount of capital used in production', his third dynamic determinant. In terms of these concepts, the reader may remember, Harrod stated that:

(i) Suppose that representative income-receivers save the same proportion of their increment of income as they previously saved of the income of the day before. (ii) Suppose that there is no shift to profit. (iii) Suppose that the productive methods for which the new capital goods were designed are

[1] In the Marxian scheme the ratio of investment to the total of capitalists' income is actually larger than this, for the wages-fund for the additional labour force to be employed is also included in the category of 'investment'.

[2] Cf. R. F. Harrod, *The Trade Cycle*, 1936, pp. 88–101.

the same as those previously employed. On these conditions consumption on the present day will rise in the same proportion as capital goods are increased and by the same amount as that which the new capital goods were designed to provide, and this experience seems to justify the present rate of advance.[1]

Harrod is not speaking in terms of the proportion in which the total labour force is divided into the two sectors. But in both cases, that of Marx and of Harrod, the question implicitly asked is the same; namely, what are the factors which determine the proportion in which the national product is divided between consumers' goods and producers' goods as the economy advances steadily. Since the two men dealt with basically the same problem, it is not at all accidental that the correspondence between them appears to be almost perfect. What Harrod is saying in the above quotation is, in fact, what Marx would say, in our terminology, that $h$ does not change if $s$, $x$'s and $r_2$ remain constant. Harrod, of course, goes further and speculates for those cases where $s$, $x$'s and $r_2$ change. For example, 'if people saved a larger proportion of their increment of income or there were a shift to profit on the same day, . . . so far as these two determinants were concerned, consumption would advance less than the capital goods increased on the given day.'[2] In our terminology, this means that when $s$ and $x$'s rise $h$ has to decline. Harrod's reasoning concerning the case of a rise in 'the amount of capital used in production' is slightly more complicated, but the conclusion comes to the same thing as the one obtained above in connection with the Marxian schema.

Thus the correspondence between the two systems is quite uncanny. But we cannot stop here. We must not fail to note the point of basic contrast between the two as regards the methodological position which the three determinants ($s$, $x$'s and $r_2$) occupy. In Marx's model, they are variables or parameters implicit in the structure of his aggregates, and hence are formulated with explicit reference to the specificity of capitalism. Harrod, on the other hand, by setting these factors apart as forces inde-

[1] *Ibid.*, p. 90.
[2] *Ibid.*, p. 91.

pendent of the system upon which they impinge, is obliged to fall back upon *a-social* generalizations for the explanation of the characteristic behaviour of the determinants. Thus, the propensity to save is a 'fundamental psychological law'. The shift to profit and its positive sign are regarded as due to the joint operation of the laws of diminishing returns and of the diminishing elasticity of demand. And finally, the amount of capital used in production, barring short-run fluctuations, is made dependent upon inventions.

Through the apparent similarities on a certain restricted plane between Marx and Harrod, we immediately see a number of differences which are fairly basic. One of them is the difference in efficacy attributed to what may be called 'parametric adjustments' in the system.

A typical capitalistic process can be visualized as that of a cluster of 'parametric adjustments'. Each economic unit, be it a household or a firm, is independent of each other and, being such an infinitesimal part of the whole, is typically confronted with prices, wages, the rate of interest, etc., over which each economic unit singly has no control. In other words, these quantities (prices, wages, etc.) present themselves to economic units as parameters. For its part, the economic unit has no way of perceiving directly the state of economic conditions relevant to its action *except through* its contact with those parameters. Thus it watches changes in them and adjusts itself to them presumably according to one kind or another of maximization principle. When, e.g. there is an epidemic of cow disease, consumers do not and need not know about it. The number of cattle slaughtered inevitably will decline and the price of beef will rise. Consumers, finding the price of beef relatively dearer, will do this 'parametric adjustment' and shift their demand to chicken or pork. So long as competition is perfect, 'parameters' will reflect changes in data fully and instantaneously and call forth necessary adjustments on the part of economic units. It is in this manner that economic units, each independently enjoying the prerogative of freedom and in spite of the fact that they are separated from relevant economic data by a cloud of 'parameters', are considered to comprise a society in which maximum economic welfare can be maintained even while the objective conditions keep on changing. Therefore, modern economic theory made much of the mechanism of 'parametric adjustments' and has built extremely intricate doctrines around the concepts of elasticities (indicating the manner of response of economic units to parametric changes) and flexibilities (indicating the manner of response of parameters to changes in data).

In the thirties, however, the long-standing confidence in the positive function of 'parameters' gradually waned. For one thing, such phenomena as rigidities of wages, inflexibility of monopoly prices and artificial control of exchange rates, coming to our attention all at once, have shaken our confidence in the presumed harmony in the system.[1] At the same time, certain statistical studies drew the attention of economists anew to the regularities of income effect which seemed to stand out much more clearly than the patterns of 'parametric adjustments'. In the words of Paul Samuelson:

> Among the most striking uniformities yet uncovered in economic data are the relationships between various categories of expenditure and family income.... In fact, so strong are these income effects that it is very difficult to find empirically the influence of price, the variable customarily related to demand by the economic theorist.[2]

In other words, the time was ripe for the emergence and rapid acceptance of the type of aggregative analysis propounded by Keynes in his *General Theory*. And for a while, there arose a sharp division among the ranks of economists between those who would emphasize the income effect and slight the problem of cost-price adjustment *and* those who would give far greater weight to the efficacy of cost-price relationships. Even then, however, the

[1] There is also a more general point which was expressed by N. Kaldor as follows: 'It is now fairly generally recognized ... that the price mechanism, even under the most favourable conditions, can register only some of the gains and losses which result from any particular piece of economic activity; there is a cluster of effects (what the economists call the external economies and diseconomies) which escape the net of price-cost measurement.' Appendix to W. H. Beveridge, *Full Employment in a Free Society*, 1945, p. 401.

[2] Paul A. Samuelson, 'A Statistical Analysis of the Consumption Function', Appendix to Chapter XI of A. H. Hansen, *Fiscal Policy and Business Cycles*, 1941, p. 250.

most ardent of Keynesians would not ignore entirely the relevance of 'parametric adjustments' to many of the analytical
problems. As time went on, the sharp contrast initially drawn
gave way gradually to an attempt at synthesis and then to a tendency to place the crude aggregative analysis in its proper place.

The Marxian approach, on the other hand, is radically different in this regard. Marx himself was keenly aware of the important place which such categories as prices, the rate of interest, etc.,
occupied in the workings of a capitalist system. Thus he
repeatedly brings out the point that commodities, for example,
appear to be an independent entity which naturally seems to
possess the attribute of price to which men passively react. He
does not deny the effectiveness of price categories, nor the process of 'parametric adjustments' which could be analysed in an
objective manner. But he is more concerned with the social
relations among men which are hidden behind what appear to be
natural attributes of things. Marx, of course, regarded the
capitalist system as only one stage in the development of human
societies, and he was especially eager to pin down the historically
specific characteristics of capitalism as distinguished from other
modes of production. Thus for him it was much less important
to analyse the forces which determined the magnitude of value
than to seek the reason why the product of human labour took
the specific form of commodities under a capitalistic system. And
his answer to this question was: 'Only such products can become
commodities with regard to each other as result from different
kinds of labour, each kind being carried on independently and for
the account of private individuals.'[1] In this type of society, the

---

[1] *Capital*, Vol. I (Kerr edition), 1918, p. 49. In similar vein he also
wrote: 'As a general rule, articles of utility become commodities
only because they are products of private individuals or groups of
individuals who carry on their work independently of each other.'
(*Ibid.*, pp. 83–84) Paul Sweezy elaborated on this as follows: 'The
exchange relation as such, apart from any consideration of the
quantities involved, is an expression of the fact that individual
producers, each working in isolation, are in fact working for each
other. . . . What finds expression in the form of exchange value is
therefore the fact that the commodities involved are the products of
human labour in a society based on division of labour in which
producers work privately and independently.' (*The Theory of Capitalist Development*, 1942, p. 27.)

specific manner in which men are socially related to each other cannot be directly grasped but, instead, expresses itself through various quantitative relations among commodities, money, etc., and imparts upon the latter the appearance of being an independent social agent. Marx characterized this deceptive aspect of the commodity society as the 'fetish character of commodities'. In his own words: 'The character of having value, when once impressed upon products, obtains fixity only by reason of their acting and reacting upon each other as quantities of value. These quantities vary continually, independently of the will, foresight and action of the producers. To them, their own social action takes the form of the action of objects, which rule the producers instead of being ruled by them.'[1]

Marx felt it quite natural that what he called 'bourgeois economists', being unable to pierce through this fetishism, were mainly concerned with the quantitative analysis of 'the action of objects' which appeared to rule the producers, for they took it more or less for granted that capitalism was an immutable social relation and did not find it necessary to question the specific characteristic of the system as such. Since this was his major concern, Marx deliberately slighted the quantitative analysis of value and of its fluctuations, but developed his theory largely on the assumption of what Marshall would call 'long-run normal price'. Thus his discussion of *tableau économique*, which appears towards the end of the second volume of *Capital*, is conducted throughout on the assumption that commodities are exchanged strictly at their value or at 'long-run normal price'. In other words, 'parametric adjustments' have no place in the stage of abstraction where Marx took up his aggregative analysis.

It is quite important to emphasize this point because there have been so many attempts to make mechanistic use of the Marx's *tableau* to prove a set of premeditated conclusions. The most visionary of these attempts is that of Henryk Grossmann, who tried to prove, on the basis of Marx's scheme of extended reproduction, the inevitability of breakdown of the capitalistic system.[2] What he did was to produce a general equation, on a

[1] *Ibid.*, p. 86.
[2] See Henryk Grossmann, *Das Akkumulations- und Zusammenbruchsgesetz des kapitalistischen Systems*, 1920. Actually, of course, his

set of rigid assumptions as to the rate of increase in wages-bill and constant capital (approximately, user cost), giving us a number of years which would elapse before capitalists' income would be no longer sufficient to cover the required amount of net investment. Using the same notation we have given earlier and designating by $n$ the number of years before the 'breakdown' comes, we may rewrite Grossmann's equation as follows:[1]

$$ n = \frac{\log\left(\dfrac{s - \dfrac{Sv}{V}}{r_0 \cdot \dfrac{Sc}{C}}\right)}{\log\left(\dfrac{100 + \dfrac{Sc}{C}}{100 + \dfrac{Sv}{V}}\right)} $$

Thus if we assume, with Otto Bauer, that the rate of surplus value is unity throughout, that the organic composition of capital in the initial period is two, that constant capital increases at the annual rate of 10 per cent (i.e. $S_c/C = \dfrac{10}{100}$), and that wages-bill increases at the rate of 5 per cent (i.e. $S_v/V = \dfrac{5}{100}$), then $n = 33 \cdot 5$; that is to say, after approximately thirty-four years capitalists' income would become insufficient to meet the required rate of accumulation.

---

theorizing was a specific product of the contemporary controversy and perhaps should not be criticized out of that context. He was originally trying to challenge Otto Bauer by carrying out to the logical conclusion the set of assumptions which Bauer employed in criticizing Rosa Luxemburg. As such, Grossmann's critique of Bauer contained an element of truth. In fact, however, Grossmann raised to the point of absurdity the common mechanistic error of a whole train of economists starting with Tugan-Baranowsky who made Marx's *tableau* serve a purpose for which it was never intended.

[1] $r_0$ stands for the organic composition of capital for the economy as a whole in the initial period.

This reasoning illustrates most strikingly the case of complete abstraction of 'parametric adjustments'. It is in the essence of price mechanism to register various tensions and disequilibria within the system, thus calling forth appropriate 'parametric adjustments' on the part of economic units (firms and households). Convulsive movement of the economy, which we call business cycles, is nothing but an expression of such an adjustment process; and Marx would have considered absurd the extension of his logic of abstract *tableau économique* to a theory of breakdown without first going through many steps of concretization which certainly would have included the matter of 'parametric adjustments'. In other words, it must be strictly borne in mind that Marx's scheme of reproduction, or the framework within which his aggregative analysis is conducted, is highly abstract and does not permit indiscriminate attempts at manipulation.

The caricature which Grossmann made out of Marx's reproduction scheme is the culmination of a series of controversies conducted in terms of an all too mechanistic use of the categories in Marx's *tableau*. If one ignores parametric adjustments of any sort and assumes, as Rosa Luxemburg does, that the propensity to save is always 50 per cent in both the producers' goods and the consumers' goods sectors, it will be easy enough to show, by giving appropriate arithmetic examples, that effective demand will become insufficient to absorb all the final goods produced. Rosa Luxemburg's insight in seeing this problem of effective demand is certainly not itself sterile, as Mrs Robinson has pointed out.[1] But the use which Luxemburg made of the Marxian *tableau* in 'proving' the point is quite arbitrary and actually oversteps the limits which Marx himself carefully imposed upon the *tableau*. Thus it was not difficult for Otto Bauer to 'prove' the possibility of smooth reproduction on the very assumptions which Luxemburg employed, namely (1) that the propensity to invest is the same in both sectors, and (2) that the organic composition of capital rises as time goes on (or the capital-output ratio rises as time goes on).[2] So long as we confine

[1] See Joan Robinson, 'Introduction to Rosa Luxemburg', *The Accumulation of Capital*, 1951.

[2] Otto Bauer, 'Die Akkumulation des Kapitals', *Die Neue Zeit*, Vol. 31, No. 1, 1913.

ourselves within the logic of Marx's *tableau*, smooth reproduction is possible, as we have seen earlier, if the equation

$$sx_1 + shx_2 - (1 + s - hr_2) = 0$$

is satisfied. Luxemburg's problem boils down to the question of whether this equation can be satisfied when $x_1 = x_2$ and $s$ and $r_2$ rise with time. It will be easy enough to show that there is nothing in the logic of Marx's *tableau* to indicate that the steady growth will be upset by these assumptions.

In other words, it will not be correct to make too much use of the *tableau* in the form Marx left us. If we wish to address ourselves to a kind of problem with which modern economics concerns itself, Marx's reproduction scheme in itself does not give us an answer. The Marxian system must be further extended by an incorporation of a theory of 'parametric adjustments' in a manner consistent with the basic framework of the Marxian theory.[1]

One of the significant differences in the methodological character of aggregates between Marx and Keynes lies in the direction in which *abstraction* is carried out. Marx's intention was to represent, as simply as possible, the specific interrelation of aggregates which is characteristic of capitalism, whereas Keynesian aggregates do not necessarily concern themselves with the specificity of capitalism. They are designed primarily to assist in accounting for the level of total employment under the simple assumption that it is proportional to the net national product. A similar purpose, with differing assumptions, once gave rise to such concepts as 'wage-fund' and 'subsistence-fund' (Böhm-Bawerk). These concepts made us focus upon that aggregative quantity which controlled the demand for labour in capitalist society. Keynes has reoriented our attention to the

[1] An interesting attempt was once made by Professor Kei Shibata in this direction. See a series of articles (in English) he published in *Kyoto University Economic Review* in the first half of 1930s, or, in a more complete form, in his two-volume work: *Theoretical Economics* (in Japanese), 1935, 1936. See also my criticism of a part of his theory in 'Marx's Theory of the Falling Tendency of the Rate of Profit' (in English), *The Economic Review*, July 1951.

other side of the shield, so to speak, namely, to the simplest functional relation between the demand for various types of goods and the level of total economic activity ... a relation which appears to transcend the specificity of capitalism. Thus his first task was to carry through certain abstractional operations which would cut through complex appearances and to distil such aggregative quantities as might be independent of the capitalistic accounting method. The result is the Keynesian concept of national income which has only one dimension, that of being *consumable sooner or later*. The part which is consumed during a given period is called 'consumption', and the remainder in whatever physical form it may be, is called 'investment'. Conceptually, this set of aggregates is perfectly unambiguous. To any type of society, be it primitive-tribal or socialistic, we may apply them and refer to the ratios between them by means of such terms as 'the propensity to consume', 'the propensity to invest', etc. The Keynesian aggregates gain this simple unambiguity by sacrificing certain distinctions which other systems of aggregates may be capable of making. In particular, they are indifferent to what Marx would call 'the metamorphosis in the realm of commodity circulation'. For example, $x$ amount of consumers' goods can either be assumed to have been sold or unsold and national income is in no way affected. For $Y = A - U$. And $y$ amount of producers' goods can be assumed to have been either sold or unsold and investment is in no way affected. For $I = G - G'$. Again, $z$ amount of export could just as well have been left unsold and remained in the warehouse of disappointed sellers, and national income would have remained the same.

In fact, the contrast between Marx and Keynes can be brought out most sharply in connection with the definition of investment. The definition of investment from the Keynesian standpoint is given by Samuelson as follows: 'The importance of investment consists in the fact that it involves disbursal of income to the factors of production while not at the same time bringing to the market goods which must be currently sold'.[1] Thus, from this point of view, the accumulation of inventories

[1] P. A. Samuelson, 'The Theory of Pump-priming Re-examined', *American Economic Review*, September 1940.

has the same function as the construction of new plant and equipment because such accumulation no less than the latter 'involves
disbursal of income to the factors of production while not at the
same time bringing to the market goods which must be currently
sold'. Export surplus has also the similar function. So does the
government deficit. In other words, the Keynesian investment
is defined mainly from the standpoint of its multiplier aspect and
subsumes all kinds of economic acts which may be quite dis-
similar to each other with respect to their productivity aspect.
As such, it is no doubt a very convenient concept for the short-
run analysis, especially since it is a highly operational concept
and lends itself to relatively easy statistical measurement. But
once we try to apply it to a slightly longer-run analysis of
dynamic character, its shortcomings become immediately
apparent. The failure to take note of this limitation has led Mr
Hicks, for example, to construct a highly unrealistic theory of
trade cycle with the concept of 'autonomous investment' which,
like pyramid-building, absorbs savings without adding to productive capacity. Nowadays, of course, such unrealism is no
longer tolerated by many; and we have a number of doctrines
of economic dynamics, even in the camp of what may be regarded as the Keynesian school, which give a prominent place to
the productivity aspect of investment activities. Domar's $\sigma$ effect
is one such example.[1] But when we try to incorporate the
productivity effect of investment into our theory, we immediately realize that we must re-examine the concept of investment
itself and make it theoretically a much more abstract concept
than when we use it in the multiplier analysis. Pyramid building,
for example, has to be deducted from it. When we do this, we
come closer to the concept of accumulation in the Marxian
*tableau* which is throughout expressed in terms of value and is
placed in the schema in such a way as to produce the *dual* effect
of both creating effective demand and adding to the productive
capacity. The original concept of investment in the Keynesian
aggregates is indifferent to the differing effects on productivity
or to occurrences of short-run character other than those affect-
ing effective demand.

[1] E. D. Domar, 'Expansion and Employment', *American Economic Review*, March 1947, p. 46.

Apparent indifference to distinctions of this kind does not mean, however, that the Keynesian system is altogether blind to them. Here lurks an important difference between Keynes' method of abstraction and that of Marx; and it is worth our brief examination. As Marx proceeds with his model, the indifference to certain distinctions on a given level of abstraction means the absence of these distinctions in the model itself at that level. For Keynes, *the very strength of his abstraction lies in the fact that the reality in its entire complexity is contained in it though only in one-dimensional projection.* Concretization of the system for Marx is typically the process of successive approximation. For Keynes, it is to change the angle of projection. Thus whatever distinctions to which the Keynesian aggregates *appear* to be indifferent are in fact contained in them implicitly and make themselves explicit on another plane of projection. For example, instead of distinguishing in *aggregates* between investment financed out of dishoarding and investment financed out of current saving, Keynesians would call both of them simply investment when projected on the plane of aggregates but would take care of the distinction on another plane as between diminutions in liquidity-preference and increases in the marginal efficiency schedule of investment.

In short, in point of contrast, aggregates themselves are neutral in the Keynesian system to the specificity of capitalism, viz., reduced to the simplest common denominator, as it were, for all types of society. The special relationships among aggregates which are characteristic of capitalism are squeezed implicitly into the form of functions; the consumption function, the liquidity-function, the marginal efficiency schedule of investment, etc. And by the use of such terms as 'propensity' and 'preference' the impression is created, if only unwittingly, that these relations among aggregates are analogous to personal reactions on the conscious level and therefore are direct, and as if they too were independent of the particular system of economy which they are used to analyse.

However, to say, for example, that the consumption function is a relation between aggregates analogous to personal reactions on the conscious level is not exactly correct. It is realized that, *theoretically speaking*, aggregate relations in modern economics are essentially *derived* relations, that is to say, deduced from household or firm relations.[1] But this fact creates a fresh theoretical problem. In the case of economic problems related to microeconomic units, the principle of maximization (whether of utility or of profit) helps us to derive a meaningful theorem, thus enabling us 'to determine the nature of the changes in our unknown variables resulting from a designated change in one or more parameters'.[2] A large part of the body of economic doctrines today is dependent on the use of some kind of extremum position in arriving at a *theoretical* conclusion. The aggregate relation such as a consumption function, on the other hand, has first been established as an empirical relation based upon statistical observations and has no claim for theoretical stability except as it is continually supported by facts. The failure of economic model-building in 1945 illustrates this methodological character of aggregate relations. Thus although Keynesians make much use of macro-economics, they have to fall back upon microeconomics for giving *ultimate theoretical* foundation to macroeconomic theorems. It is for this reason that Duesenberry states that 'aggregate relations which can be deduced from household or firm relations I shall call *fundamental* aggregate relations'.[3] Thus the theoretical basis of Keynesian aggregates reduces itself finally to those relations between scarce means and alternative uses which form the foundation of modern theoretical economics and which actually transcend any specific characteristic of capitalist mode of production.

The Marxian aggregates, on the other hand, are not operational as the Keynesian one. The former appear midway in Marx's theoretical journey from the most abstract discussion of value to the more concrete elucidation of crises and other typically capitalistic phenomena. Thus such concepts as the rate of surplus value and the organic composition of capital which can be expressed directly, as relations between aggregates, are not necessarily susceptible of statistical treatment. In the form presented in Marx's *tableau*, aggregate relations cannot be subjected to empirical testing. They are theoretically pure concepts. For

---

[1] See James S. Duesenberry, *Income, Saving, and the Theory of Consumer Behaviour*, 1949, p. 72.

[2] P. A. Samuelson, *Foundations of Economic Analysis*, 1947, p. 7.

[3] Duesenberry, *op. cit.*, p. 72. Italics added.

example, the reproduction scheme as discussed in the second volume of *Capital* is constructed on the basis of the following assumptions: that all the products are exchanged at value (i.e. long run normal price); that there are only two classes of people, capitalists and workers; that workers consume all of their income; that there are sufficiently large numbers of capitalists in one field to permit perfect competition to take place; that it is a closed economy; that there are only two kinds of commodities, the producers' good and the consumers' good and the period of turnover of capital is the same in both sectors; that there is no change in technical coefficients; that capital does not move between the two sectors, that is to say, the saving of the capitalists in the first sector is invested only in the first sector, and similarly for the second; that there is no durable capital equipment whose useful life extends beyond one period; that there are no inventories; that money functions only as a means of circulation; and that wages are paid in advance of the sale of the products to whose production the workers contribute. In other words, the Marxian aggregates depict the bone structure, as it were, of the capitalistic circular flow as seen through X-ray, whereas the Keynesian aggregates show us the delineation of our subject matter as projected on one dimensional plane.

The fact, however, that the Marxian aggregates are theoretical does not imply that it is possible to manipulate the elements of the *tableau* to prove any particular theorem which is not already implicit in the structure of the *tableau* itself. In this sense, the Marxian aggregates by themselves do not claim to possess much deductive value. They are rather to serve for illustrative purposes, pointing up to us the nature of interdependence among various categories in the social circulation of a capitalist economy. And it is quite significant that in serving this purpose, the *tableau* is divided into two sectors of the producers' goods and the consumers' goods. This is not the same thing as the distinction between investment and consumption. This latter distinction is a division of *net* national product, whereas the former is a division of *gross* product of the society. In fact, the difference between Marx and Keynes in this respect is much more significant than is commonly supposed.

The Keynesians have made the concept of national income (or net national product) the pivot of their aggregative analysis and worked out a set of nice theoretical relations such as the multi-plier, acceleration, etc., with the aid of this concept. And the rationale of using the net concept in economic analysis seems to be further reinforced by the fact that it corresponds also to the index of welfare magnitude. National income has long been a measure of economic welfare, and as such, even Marxians would not object very much. But the question is whether it is equally efficacious as *a tool in the economic analysis* of a capitalist society. To formulate our problem in terms of net concepts is as if to study the functioning of a certain organic body in terms of flows of energy which go in and come out of that body. Since this approach does not probe into the workings of internal structure of the body, it will not be possible to 'tag' a particular output as coming out of a particular input. What we do is to watch at the point of spigot, so to speak, what flows in and out of the body, and relate these flows to each other. Thus any relation between aggregates, such as consumption to income, has to be regarded only in terms of 'a flow during a period coincident with the flow of income during the same period'.[1] The method has undoubted merits. It enables us to formulate macro-economic relations in the simplest possible manner and at the same time gives us a strategic category in the form of money flow. But at the same time it makes us close our eyes to the functioning of the internal structure itself, which, far from being solely technical, possesses specifically economic characteristics under capitalism. It has the capacity, e.g. of 'making mills to make more mills' for a time. It can distend itself or shrink without necessarily registering cor-responding changes in net flows. The Marxian *tableau*, on the other hand, focuses our attention, again in the simplest possible manner, to the logic of this internal structure under capitalism by incorporating the value relation of $C$ plus $V$ plus $S$ into the *tableau*. This method corresponds to the basic understanding of Marx that under capitalism production is not for the purpose of ultimate consumption but for the continuous maximization of profit. The contrast in this respect is more material than it appears on the surface. Although Keynesians do say that 'ex-penditure creates income and thus employment,' they will not

[1] A. P. Lerner, 'Saving Equals Investment', *Quarterly Journal of Economics*, February 1938.

say that 'expenditure' provides the *motivating force* of production and further production. Marx would say, however, that the competition of capital striving towards the maximization of profit provides in itself a motive force for accumulation and technical progress; and such an orientation, which dispenses with either the acceleration principle or a special theory of investment function, is directly reflected in the construction of the Marxian *tableau*.

It was already pointed out earlier that the *tableau* form of aggregates enables us to follow through the so-called dual aspect of investment, i.e. the aspect of creating effective demand and that of increasing productive capacity. It is possible for Keynesians to say that 'if investment today, however large, is equal to that of yesterday, national income of today will be just equal and not any larger than that of yesterday'.[1] But it will be impossible for Marxians to visualize a case of 'extended reproduction' in equilibrium, i.e. the case of an economy which accumulates at all, without a corresponding increase in net national product. Investment in the Marxian *tableau* is traced in its dual aspect to its proper destination in a manner consistent with certain significant constraints which are specified within the *tableau*. Furthermore, since the tableau makes explicit the relation between $C$ and $S_c$ (or roughly, between 'user cost' and the net addition to capital), our attention can easily be directed to the position which replacement (or depreciation) occupies in the mechanism of social circulation. It is only in the recent period that this problem has come to be discussed as an integral part of the mechanism of a growing economy.

In parts I may have drawn too sharp a distinction between the treatment of aggregates by Marx and that by Keynes. Most of these points of difference were in fact sharp at the time when Keynes first brought out his theory of effective demand. Since that time many refinements and improvements have been added to the original scheme of simple Keynesian aggregates. Some of them have been actually in the direction of narrowing the difference between Marx and Keynes on this matter. Dissatisfaction with the analysis conducted solely in *net* concepts is a most

[1] E. D. Domar, 'Expansion and Employment', *American Economic Review*, March 1947, p. 40.

notable example. I suspect that in future the reproduction scheme of Marx will draw the attention of a larger number of academic economists than in the thirties. But there is one last fundamental difference in methodology which still divides the modern school of economics and the Marxian. The point may be illustrated from Mr Harrod's methodological dicta in his *Trade Cycle*. So far as we can gather from his scattered remarks in that book, his methodology may be paraphrased as follows: we go as far as we can by means of *a priori* method, the principal tool of which is introspection; and if *a priori* yields no more, we revert to observed facts and see what actually does happen. When, however, he reverts to observation, it is in order to look for an answer to a specific question which introspection alone is incapable of solving. It is characteristic of him to say, for example:

> The shift to profit has been shown ... to depend on two factors. ... It would be rash to say much *a priori* about the operation of either of these laws [the law of diminishing returns and the law of diminishing elasticity of demand] ... But experience is that there usually is a shift to profit in a pronounced upward movement.[1]

And this is enough for him in order to assert that there is a shift to profit. But, as Schumpeter would say, 'this is a problem to be solved, not a datum to be accepted'.[2] The problem of social science only begins, to say the least, at the point where introspection leaves off.

What is conspicuous in Harrod is his extreme reluctance to recognize the existence of objective laws of *social* relations. It is more than a playful dictum, we may venture to guess, when he says: 'We are reluctant to suppose that man's course of endeavour can be governed by something so superficial and artificial as his own banking system'.[3] If, however, society, as a subject matter of scientific endeavour, is a complex of relations qualitatively distinctive on its own level and not simply an amalgam of individuals who compose it or of atomic matter to which all existence may be reduced, it will be wisdom in

[1] Harrod, *op. cit.*, p. 92.
[2] J. A. Schumpeter, *Business Cycles*, 1939, p. 188.
[3] Harrod, *op. cit.*, p. 4.

methodology to presume that social relations are governed by objective laws which are not reducible to psychological and physical laws and which are beyond the reach of introspection, however discerning it may be. A theoretical edifice in social science built upon such a presumption is evidently under a handicap in developing its 'analytical apparatus' if by the latter is meant an apparatus to account for the phenomena of a particular society in terms of anything but the specific laws pertaining to that society. Marx's major concern was precisely the elucidation of the specific laws pertaining to a capitalist society, and his aggregates are tools of analysis for that purpose designed primarily to lay bare the social circulation of capital.

## SELECTED BIBLIOGRAPHY

BARAN, P. 'National Economic Planning' in Haley (ed.) *A Survey of Contemporary Economics*. Homewood, Illinois: Richard D. Irwin Inc., 1952.

DOBB, M. 'Full Employment and Capitalism', *On Economic Theory and Socialism*. London: Routledge, Kegan Paul, 1955.

ROBINSON, J. 'Kalecki and Keynes', *Collected Economic Papers*: III. Oxford: Blackwell, 1965.

ROLL, E. 'The Decline of Liberal Economics', *Modern Quarterly* (London): Vol. I, No. 1, 1938.

WARD, E. F. 'Marx and Keynes', *Economic Record*. April 1939.

# 3. Marx and Modern Economics

# *Das Kapital* for the Modern Man[1]

*Martin Bronfenbrenner*

## APOLOGIA

THERE are translations aplenty of *Das Kapital* into academic economics, more or less predigested, desiccated and vulgarized. Some translations have been Marxist in intent, some hostile, and some like this one, eclectic. Since the present essay represents an *n*th attempt, its only *raison d'être* is an immodest hope that 'I can do it better' than ($n$-1) eminent predecessors.

Several improvements are attempted. (1) We shall concentrate on the macro-economics (aggregative economics, income and employment theory) of *Capital*, rather than the micro-economics (valuation and pricing of individual commodities). (2) We shall stress Marx's merits, not always recognized, in anticipating analyses and ideas which we academics only derived (however independently) fifty years after his death. (3) We shall try to show that the Marxian system is easily transformable into a balanced Walrasian general-equilibrium one. In an algebraic restatement, the number of its equations equals the number of its unknowns; this is *prima facie* evidence that both circularity and inconsistency have been avoided.

We shall aim, until the closing section, to be expository rather than critical, and to further mutual understanding, as opposed to mutual recrimination, between 'bourgeois' and Marxian economists. We neither know, nor greatly care, whether or not this constitutes 'ideological coexistence'.

[1] My principal debts in preparing this essay are to Dr Paul Sweezy of *Monthly Review* and Prof. Murray Wolfson of Oregon State University. Responsibility for remaining errors is, of course, my own.

Reprinted from *Science and Society*, Autumn 1965.

## OVERVIEW

To whatever incomplete extent Marx's theoretical economic system is separable from the remainder of his social philosophy, it may be regarded as a system of moving equilibrium at less than full employment. In this respect it anticipates Keynes. It also goes beyond Keynes, in deriving an employment position which deteriorates over time.

Take any (percentage) level of unemployment you desire. In the Marxian model of capitalism, if we interpret it correctly, this level will eventually become impossible to maintain. That is to say, we will eventually become unable to find any rate of profit which will simultaneously be *high* anough to avoid a liquidity or hoarding 'crisis' (depression) from the capitalist side, and *low* enough to permit the output of the system to be 'realized' or purchased, primarily by the workers, without an over-production or realization 'crisis' and a further increase in unemployment (decrease in the value of output). This is the dilemma which drives the system to stagnation and eventual breakdown. It involves *both* the 'falling rate of profit' *and* the 'tendency to over-production'; we need not put primary emphasis on either one to the exclusion of the other, as many Marxists have felt compelled to do. This dilemma is at once an economic 'contradiction of capitalism' and the 'law of motion' of the capitalist economy.

## LABOUR THEORY OF VALUE: EQUATION SYSTEMS I–II

To demonstrate all this, and not merely state it, we can begin by measuring the system's total output and total input in whatever units we choose. In the tradition of English classical economics, Marx chooses 'value' as his scale of measurement. His unit of value is the hour of 'socially necessary labour' of a general or unskilled sort. This usage is quite comparable to the 'wage-units', 'efficiency-units', and 'units of productive power' of contemporary academic economists.

Neither Marx nor his predecessors ever succeeded in showing that actual prices of individual commodities were strictly proportional to their values per unit. George Stigler speaks of

Ricardo, Marx's major creditor, as holding a '93 Per Cent Labour Theory of Value' in this sense. When we deal with economic aggregates, however, it is not necessary that values of individual commodities correspond to prices in any simple pattern. In macro-economics, no 'great contradiction' results when they do not so correspond. The so-called 'transformation problem' between values and prices vanishes into insignificance at the aggregate level. Few matters of significance to the evolution of the capitalist system depend upon it. We need neither be concerned with the weaknesses of the labour theory of value as a theory of relative prices, nor propound significant criticism of the Marxian structure by dwelling upon these weaknesses.

Marx, we have said, divides the economy into Department I, producing capital goods, and Department II, producing consumer goods. Let the total value produced in Department I be $W_1$ (from the German *Wert*). It is measured in labour-hours, and should not be confused with the value or price of a unit of homogeneous capital. Marx also subdivides $W_1$ into three parts. One part, $C_1$, or constant capital, represents the value of raw materials and of the depreciation of fixed capital instruments involved in producing $W_1$.[1] The second part, $V_1$, or variable capital, represents the value of the direct labour–power consumed in production, i.e. the value represented by the wages of blue-collar or production workers. (Marx places great importance on the distinction between $V_1$ and the value of labour itself, which in Department I might be the total of $W_1$). The variable capital $V_1$, the value of workmen's wages, while measured in labour hours, is less than the number of hours that workers actually work. The difference is $S_1$, or Surplus Value (in German, $M_1$ or *Mehrwert*). It represents the value, still in labour-hours, of all payments made to the white-collar salariat and the owners of property, whom Marx sees united by common membership in the capitalist, or bourgeois, class of society. The sum $(S_1 + V_1)$ approximates what academic economists call the *value added* of Department I, measured, however, in labour hours.

[1] Marx seems himself to have worked with a time period long enough for all capital instruments to depreciate, so that $C_1$, for example, equals the total value of constant capital. The present procedure is offered as a simplification rather than a translation.

Everything we have said about Department I applies equally well to Department II (producing consumer goods), except that the relevant subscript is 2 instead of 1.

If individual commodity prices are not proportional to their values, Marx has said in a pregnant hint, this makes no difference so long as the sum of all the values created by society is the same as the sum of all the prices. (By the sum of all the prices we must mean the sum of all [price times quantity] pairs, converted into value units). Let us denote by $p_1$ and $p_2$ not the average price in each Department but the average *ratio* of price to value in each sector. Now the Marxian condition, that the sum of values equal the sum of prices, takes on an algebraic form:

$$W_1 + W_2 = p_1 W_1 + p_2 W_2$$

Having just introduced a little algebra, we can state all the results of this section to date in a group of three equations expressing the barest outlines of the Marxian labour theory of value. We shall refer to this group of three equations, all definitional, as System I:

$$W_1 = C_1 + V_1 + S_1 \qquad \textit{System I}$$
$$W_2 = C_2 + V_2 + S_2 \qquad \textit{(3 Equations)}$$
$$W_1 + W_2 = p_1 W_1 + p_2 W_2$$

Our model economy would, however, be out of equilibrium unless the average working day and week, the wage rate and the rate of profit were the same in the two Departments. If the working time and wage rate (both measured in hours of labour) were not the same, workers would move from the long-hour and/or low-wage Department to the short-hour and/or high-wage one, changing the relative sizes of $W_1$, $W_2$, and their respective components.

In competitive equilibrium, the working week will be the same in both Departments (say 50 hours), and the common weekly wage for ordinary labour will suffice to buy, say, 30 hours of value. The difference, or 20 hours, is in Marxian terms the surplus value resulting from the week's work, whereas the 30 hours value the worker can buy is the value of his labour power, or variable capital. Expressing the surplus value $S$ as a percentage of the variable capital $V$, we obtain a rate of surplus value, sometimes called the rate of exploitation, of 20/30 or $66\frac{2}{3}$ per cent. The Marxian symbol for the rate of surplus value is $S'$ in English ($M'$ in German). It equals $S/V$, and tends to equality between Departments – per man-day, man-week, or man-month, as well as in total.[1]

If capital, here interpreted as including administrative and white-collar labour, earns different rates of return between Departments, it is too free to move. When capitalists shift capital between Departments, they tend to lower specialized wages and equipment prices in the Department from which they are leaving, and raise them in the Department to which they are moving. In competitive equilibrium, capital earns the same rate of profit in both Departments, and there is no incentive for it to move. This common rate of profit, which Marx calls $P'$, has as its numerator, like $S'$, the total of surplus values, or $S$. Its denominator is, however, total cost, which includes constant capital charges $C$ as well as wages $V$. (No elements of surplus value, or $S$, are included in cost.) In equilibrium, as we have said, $P'$ as well as $S'$ tends to equality as between Departments.

---

[1] By the same token, the wage *rate* or value of labour power, which, measured in labour hours, we may call $w$, is equal to a proper fraction (less than unity):

$$w = \frac{V_1}{V_1 + S_1}$$

in Department I, and similarly in Department II. Also, since $S' = (S_1/V_1) = (S_2/V_2)$:

$$= \frac{1}{1 + S'} \quad \text{or, alternatively, } S' = \frac{1 - w}{w}$$

In our numerical example (50 hours' work for 30 hours' value), $w = 0\cdot6$, which is consistent with our value of $S'$ ($66\frac{2}{3}$ per cent). It would have been possible to derive $w$ first, since it must be equal in both departments, and then use the right-hand equation immediately above to obtain $S'$.

If we were to add the wage rate $w$ to the list of unknowns in the text, as has been suggested by several friendly critics, either of the two equations above should also be added to System II, with no material disturbance to the remainder of the argument. (It would be illegitimate to add *both* these equations, since they are not independent of each other!) (Added May 1966.)

But now we are in trouble. Translated into symbols, the rate of surplus value $S'$ equals $S/V$ as we have seen, while the rate of profit $P'$ equals $\dfrac{S}{C+V}$. Dividing both numerator and denominator by $V$, $P'$ becomes $S' / [1 + C/V]$. So much is clear, but if $S'$ must be the same in each Department to avoid mass transfer of labour, how can $P'$ also be the same and avoid mass transfer of capital? Apparently the $C/V$ term, which Marx calls the 'organic composition' of capital, must also be the same in each Department, but in the real world, it apparently is not – and when production processes differ, why should it be?

This apparent inconsistency at a less aggregative level was called by the Austrian economist Böhm-Bawerk the 'great contradiction' of the Marxian system. If we understand Marx correctly, however, he escapes the trap with the aid of his price-value ratios $p_1$ and $p_2$. These are adjusted in the market-place to bring about a common equilibrium profit rate in each Department. More specifically, the Department with the higher 'organic composition' $C/V$ also has the higher average ratio $p$ of the price to the value of its output.

To express these results we turn again to elementary algebra. A new group of four equations, which we call System II, equates the rates of both surplus value and profit in the two Departments of the Marxian system. Two of these equations relate to the rate of surplus value, the other two to the rate of profit.

$$S' = \frac{S_1}{V_1} = \frac{S_2}{V_2}$$

*System II*
*(4 Equations)*

$$P' = \frac{S_1 p_1}{C_1 + V_1} = \frac{S_2 p_2}{C_2 + V_2}$$

The second pair of equations may also be written, after dividing numerator and denominator by the appropriate $V$ term and equating values of $S'$ in the Departments as per the first pair:

$$P' = \frac{S' p_1}{1 + (C_1/V_1)} = \frac{S' p_2}{1 + (C_2/V_2)}$$

This justifies our statement of a higher price-value rate compensating for a higher organic composition of capital as between departments (not, be it noted, over time).

## SUPPLY AND DEMAND: EQUATION SYSTEM III

However whole-heartedly Marxists may attack the supply-and-demand formula as a superficial substitute for a theory of either price or value, Marx never lost sight of supply and demand as a necessary condition for economic equilibrium. Indeed, Engels devoted the major part of the second volume of *Capital* to exploring from Marx's manuscripts the ramifications of supply and demand within his system.

Consider first Department I (capital goods). Total supply we already know from System I. It equals $(C_1 + V_1 + S_1)$. Demand we do not have. One component is $(C_1 + C_2)$, representing the replacement of constant capital used up in the process of production. If there is no more, we have what Marx calls 'simple reproduction', which is equivalent to the 'stationary state' of the English classical economists. In simple reproduction, or the stationary state, we should have as an equilibrium condition for Department I:

$$C_1 + V_1 + S_1 = C_1 + C_2, \text{ or simply } V_1 + S_1 = C_2$$

But the more general case is 'expanded reproduction', or what academics prefer to call economic growth. Under expanded reproduction, a certain positive proportion of surplus value is also spent in Department I, increasing the productive capacity of the community. Marx works through many numerical examples, which this writer finds tedious, showing how his model economy can enjoy equilibrium growth at various levels of this proportion, and with $C/V$ either constant or variable. Let us side-step these difficulties by an algebraic generalization, namely, by introducing a growth coefficient $g$ to represent the proportion of surplus value spent in Department I. (If workers also invest invariable capital in Department I, the coefficient $g$, related here to surplus value alone, is somewhat larger than the percentage of capitalist saving proper.) In any event, the demand side of Department I under extended reproduction has two components instead of one. The equilibrium condition takes the form:

$$C_1 + V_1 + S_1 = C_1 + C_2 + g(S_1 + S_2)$$

This simplifies to: *System III*

$$V_1 + (1-g)\, S_1 = C_2 + gS_2 \qquad (1\ \textit{Equation})$$

which is indeed our third equation system. In the special case of simple reproduction $g$ is zero and System III reduces to the simpler equality:

$$V_1 + S_1 = C_2$$

The case of a declining economy, where capital is not replaced as it wears out or is used up, we may treat as involving a negative $g$. But the careful reader will inquire: What about Department II, and what about consumer goods? In raising this question he is in good company; such eminent Marxist theoreticians as Rosa Luxemburg have doubted that expanded reproduction is possible at all in the Marxian model, without the dumping of 'surplus' consumption goods abroad. It turns out, however, that the supply-demand equilibrium condition for Department II is the identical one derived already from Department I. Only the 'supply' and 'demand' terms are transposed. Equilibrium on one market implies equilibrium on the other. The two equilibrium equations are not independent of each other. It would be positively fallacious to include both of them in our system.

Let us examine first simple reproduction. Supply is $(C_2 + V_2 + S_2)$, by analogy with our argument for Department I. Demand comprises everything but constant capital. Both workers and capitalists consume all their net incomes and we have:

$$C_2 + V_2 + S_2 = V_1 + V_2 + S_1 + S_2, \text{ or } C_2 = V_1 + S_1$$

as before, with the left and right sides of the equation reversed.

The same result holds in expanded reproduction, where the proportion of surplus value spent for the products of Department II falls from unity to $(1-g)$. In this more general case:

$$C_2 + V_2 + S_2 = V_1 + V_2 + (1-g)\, (S_1 + S_2)$$
$$C_2 + gS_2 = V_1 + (1-g)\, S_1$$

which is precisely our System III.[1] Under equilibrium conditions at least, Marx was apparently right and Rosa Luxemburg apparently wrong.

### TECHNICAL REQUIREMENTS: EQUATION SYSTEM IV

We now pause for a preliminary count of unknowns and equations. Our unknowns are, for each Department, the set $W$, $C$, $V$, $S$, and $p$, or ten in all. In addition, we do not know the system-wide rates of surplus value and of profit $P'$, $S'$, and we have introduced an unknown net investment or economic growth coefficient $g$ as a proportion of surplus value. This gives us a total of thirteen unknowns. Offsetting them, we have three equations in System I, four in System II, and one in System III, or eight equations in all. The system is still indeterminate; the reasoning is either circular or incomplete.

Whether or not Marx was aware of a formal circularity problem in his model of capitalism, he seems to have taken steps to solve it. The devices he uses are primarily technological. In this respect, Marx not only emphasizes the primacy of productive relations, but anticipates both the input–output analysis of Wassily Leontief and the technocratic institutionalism of Thorstein Veblen and his disciple, Clarence Ayres.

Three technological relations comprise the equation system we denote by IV. The first two relations we have mentioned already in passing. Within each Department, the organic composition of capital $C/V$ is a constant, which we may call $k$. The constant is technologically determined by the 'state of the arts'

---

[1] A similar result holds when all variables are expressed in terms of price. The key equation is now:

$$p_1[V + (1-g)S_1] = p_2(C_2 + gS_2)$$

derivable from either

$$p_1(C_1 + V_1 + S_1) = (p_1 C_1 + p_2 C_2) + g(p_1 S_1 + p_2 S_2)$$

or

$$p_2(C_2 + V_2 + S_2) = (p_1 V_1 p_1 + p_2 V_2) + (1-g)(p_1 S_1 + p_2 S_2)$$

I am grateful to Mr Y. Kosai (Economic Planning Agency, Japanese Government) for pointing this out to me.

at any point in time. In particular, it is independent of price-value ratios $p_1$ and $p_2$, as it must be if the labour theory of value is not to be jeopardized or compromised.

Less clearly expressed is a third ratio, which we call $h$, between the total values, $W_1$ and $W_2$, produced by the two Departments. Being set technologically (so much capital required for so much consumption goods), this ratio is independent not only of relative prices but also of interest rates, time preferences, and the other technical apparatus of academic economics. Marx's model of the capitalist world does not permit 'mills to make more mills forever' at any set whatever of prices or interest rates. (Rosa Luxemburg's apprehensions on this point may have been unnecessary.)

We have indicated already the algebraic forms for our fourth equation system. Each equation involves a technical constant, which is, however, taken as given, so that no unknowns are added to the economic system proper. Three more equations, however, do not yet close the gap between equations and unknowns. With the three equations of System IV, we now have 11 equations in all; but there are 13 unknowns:

$$C_1/V_1 = k_1 \qquad C_2/V_2 = k_2 \qquad \textit{System IV}$$
$$\overline{W_1/W_2 = h} \qquad\qquad\qquad (\textit{3 Equations})$$

## GROWTH AND UNEMPLOYMENT FUNCTIONS: EQUATION SYSTEM V

In common with most theoretical economists of his time, Marx appears to have scorned the general functional notation $x = f(y, z)$. If one cannot be more precise than this about what his functional relations look like, their use seems like an easy, lazy fudge. This viewpoint has much to recommend it even today.

For equilibrium closure of his analysis of capitalism, Marx seems to have had conscious or unconscious recourse to at least two general functional relationships. Neither of these are explained at all clearly or succinctly by either Marx or Engels. Rather than employing general functional notation, furthermore, Marx preferred embedding relations in literary context and numerical illustrations, when he could not specify some precise and simple algebraic form for them.

One of the relations which seem necessary to close the Marxian system is a growth function, by which the coefficient $g$ of System III is determined. (The grain of truth in Rosa Luxemburg's strictures is that this coefficient must *not* be taken as given *a priori*.) In the present translation of Marx, which may of course be far too free, we are making $g$ dependent on the profit rate, on the technical input-output coefficient $h$, and on total consumption $W_2$. In functional notation, without specifying the relation further:

$$g = g\ (P',\, h,\, W_2)$$

with all derivatives positive. A higher rate of profit, a higher input–output coefficient, or a greater volume of final consumption may each serve to raise the equilibrium value of the growth coefficient $g$.

It is possible that, had some such function as this been spelled out for Rosa Luxemburg, the numerical paradigms of the second volume of *Capital* might have seemed less arbitrary and circular, and her particular brand of ultra-Marxian over-production–under-consumption thesis might not have been required.

Another function (actually a definition plus a function) is required to relate the Marxian system to the rate of unemployment. Although an equilibrium system, the Marxian model anticipates Keynes and his followers not only by introducing growth under the guise of extended reproduction, but also by denying full employment as an attribute of equilibrium. (It is unemployment, not rising population, which Marx sees as holding wages down.) We have said nothing thus far about Marx's 'reserve army of the unemployed', either openly unemployed or in the status we now call 'disguised unemployment'. If employment (measured by value of variable capital rather than numbers of persons employed) is $(V_1 + V_2)$, but maximum total availability of labour is $V$, a simple unemployment ratio, which we shall call U, is given by:

$$U = \frac{V - (V_1 + V_2)}{V} = 1 - \frac{V_1 + V_2}{V}$$

It should be noted that this expression adds a new unknown, $U$ (the unemployment ratio) to the Marxian system, since it is determined together with the remainder of that system. The term $V$, total variable capital available, is however to be taken as demographically given.

We interpret Marx as relating the unemployment ratio $U$ primarily to $S'$, the rate of surplus value, although it also depends upon such 'givens' as the organic compositions of capital in each Department. Eclectics might also add other variables (population, wage rates, capital stocks, etc.) which affect $V$, $V_1$, or $V_2$ immediately. Some simple relation between unemployment and exploitation and/or profit seems, however, to be assumed not only by Marxists but by other over-production, under-consumption, or maldistribution theories of business depression. John A. Hobson and the Fabian Socialists in England, the New Deal in the United States, and trade unionism throughout the capitalist world, have used similar arguments. Marx himself does not use the vague function which we write below, but it appears implicit in much of his thinking. Once again, a forthright statement might have satisfied even Rosa Luxemburg:

$$U = U(S')$$

Naturally, the relation is a direct one. Given the organic composition of capital, unemployment rises as the rate of surplus value rises, and falls as the rate of surplus value falls.

This hypothesis may be interpreted in either or both of two ways. An interpretation from the demand side of the labour market is, that high rates of surplus value raise prices relative to mass purchasing power, and therefore lower output and employment. This interpretation runs from $S'$ to $U$. The other interpretation, also important in Marx, is that capitalists can wring a higher rate of surplus value out of the proletariat when the reserve army of the unemployed is high than when it is low. This supply-side interpretation approaches a bargaining theory of wages, and involves causation running from $U$ to $S'$.

Before taking leave of the unemployment function, we can restate it in an inverse form (consistent with causation running from $U$ to $S'$), by making the unemployment rate the independent variable:

$$S' = U^{-1}(U)$$

The relation is still direct, with $S'$ and $U$ rising and falling together at any point in time.

This 'inverse function' complication will come in handy in the next section, when we treat such dynamic aspects of the Marxian scheme as the falling rate of profit and the principle of increasing misery. Marx himself employs no such mathematical tricks, but the inverse function seems to be implied by some of his conclusions. At any rate, we do not believe it inconsistent with anything Marx said, or a distortion of his meaning.

Summarizing the results of this section: we have added three equations to our translation of the Marxian system. At the same time we have added a new unknown, the unemployment rate. The number of independent equations (now 14 in all) has increased to equality with the number of unknowns, also 14. The system is *prima facie* a consistent, or general-equilibrium, one.

$$g = g \ (P', h, W_2)$$
$$U = 1 - \frac{V_1 + V_2}{V} \qquad \begin{array}{l} \textit{System V} \\ (\textit{3 Equations}) \end{array}$$
$$U = U \ (S')$$

## DYNAMIC IMPLICATIONS

Equilibrium system or not, logically consistent or not, Marx's economic statics exercises no great charismatic appeal in either its original form or in translation. Its appeal arises from Marx's dynamic extensions of the system, his 'laws of motion of capitalism'. It is to these that we now turn.

Marx maintains that as capitalism progresses and capital accumulates, the rate of profit on capital tends to decline, misery tends to increase, chronic shortage of purchasing power tends to impede the 'realization' of values, 'crises' increase in frequency and severity, and the system eventually breaks down. It is these conclusions that we attempt to reformulate, and in some cases reinterpret. (We omit the *international* aspects of the system, as added by, e.g. Lenin's *Imperialism*, and limit ourselves to the 'closed economy'.)

The key equations with which to begin equate the rates of profit in the two Departments. We have developed them in System II as:

$$P' = \frac{S_1 p_1}{C_1 + V_1} = \frac{S_2 p_2}{C_2 + V_2} \text{ or } P' = \frac{S' p_1}{1 + (C_1/V_1)} = \frac{S' p_2}{1 + (C_2/V_2)}$$

Since each $C/V$ is a technologically-determined organic composition of capital, $k$, we have:

$$P' = \frac{S' p_1}{1 + k_1} = \frac{S' p_2}{1 + k_2}$$

which implies that:

$$\frac{1 + k_1}{p_1} = \frac{1 + k_2}{p_2}$$

We may call this common value $1 + k$, defining $k$ as the organic composition of capital in the two Departments combined, i.e., in the economy as a whole. Substituting $1 + k$ in our expression for the rate of profit, we obtain:

$$P' = \frac{S'}{1 + k}$$

An alternative expression can use the inverse form of the unemployment function, as developed in System V, namely:

$$S' = U^{-1}(U)$$

to give us:

$$P' = \frac{U^{-1}(U)}{1 + k}$$

Now for the dynamics. Capitalists save, invest, and accumulate capital. The accumulation of capital 'embodies' within it, to use the modern Cambridge terminology of Kaldor and Mrs Robinson, technological improvements of a labour-saving sort. The combination of capital accumulation and technological improvement means that the organic composition of capital increases over time. If there were no technical progress, the organic composition $k$ would remain constant indefinitely, barring changes in the interdepartmental coefficient $h$, which are themselves hard to envisage without technical progress of some kind.

If $k$ rises over time, then $S'$ must rise and/or $P'$ must fall. Furthermore, if our conjectural unemployment function represents Marx's view correctly, $U$ must rise if $S'$ rises, either as effect or as cause of the rise in $S'$. A plausible interpretation of Marxian dynamics would have all these things happen in varying degrees. The downward trend in $P'$ is, of course, the falling rate of profit, sometimes called 'Marx's Law', although Marx was himself far more modest than his disciples in admitting of exceptions to the generalizations. (See particularly *Capital*, Vol. III, Ch. 14.) The upward trends in $S'$ and $U$ may constitute part or all of what Marx means by 'increasing misery', although this is by no means certain. (The meaning of the term to Marx himself seems to have varied quite substantially from period to period in the twenty-five years he pondered the problem.)

To Marx's English predecessors, the falling rate of profit implied nothing more than the eventual cessation of accumulation and the peaceful replacement of growth by stationary conditions, as capitalists reduced their net saving and investment. To Marx it implies a far greater malady for capitalism. If $P'$ falls below a certain minimal but positive rate $P''$, capitalists will reduce their saving and investment by more than they increase their consumption expenditures. In other words, they will neither reinvest nor consume the entire surplus value which they receive. They will instead seek to hold increased amounts of liquid (monetary) assets, i.e. to hoard. The higher their incomes, the more they will seek to hoard. (Readers of Keynesian economics can find the doctrines of liquidity preference and the liquidity trap presaged in *Capital*!) When capitalists do not spend their surplus value in either Department I or Department II, our supply-and-demand equation of System IV no longer holds, and equilibrium breaks down. Instead of $g$ per cent of $S$ being spent in Department I and $(1-g)$ per cent in Department II, a gap develops (the post-Keynesian 'deflationary gap') between $S$ and the sum of the expenditure coefficients from $S$ in the two Departments. The entire static system goes out of equilibrium at the initial level of $U$, and restores it, if at all, at some *lower* level of income, employment, and surplus value. This relapse, whether temporary or permanent, can be called a 'liquidation' or 'hoarding' crisis. Those Marxist writers who, like Maurice Dobb, see in the falling rate of profit the 'greater vehicle' of capitalist breakdown anticipate such crises in increasing number and severity. More generally, Marxist writers see in the falling rate of profit the nemesis of reformist trade union or government policies. If, for example, collective bargaining or wage-and-hour legislation succeeds in raising wages at the expense of profits, will this not merely accelerate the decline in the rate of profit and hasten the collapse of capitalism?

At another extreme, let us suppose the formation of a giant nation-wide cartel, *Interessengemeinschaft*, *Zaibatsu*, *or* 'One Big Union of the Vested Interests', dedicated to maintaining or increasing the rate of profit, presumably by raising the rate of surplus value to compensate for the rising organic composition of capital. This could foil the falling rate of profit, but, in the Marxian system, only at the price of a crisis of another sort. The total value ($W_1 + W_2$), or $W$, which could be actually collected or realized under such a scheme, could be produced by an increasingly smaller proportion of the labour force as the rate of surplus value rose. (We are again relying on our unemployment function, which is only quasi-Marxian.) As unemployment rose, we should have a realization, over-production, or maldistribution crisis.[1] Writers who, like Rosa Luxemburg and Paul Sweezy, see in tendencies towards over-production the main thrust of the Marxist model of capitalist decline, naturally anticipate such crises in increasing number and severity.

Our own interpretation, a minority but not an original one, would combine both of these one-sided views in dilemma, or Scylla-Charybdis, form. At any constant rate of surplus value (and consequently, any constant level of unemployment), the secular rise in the organic composition of capital means a fall in the rate of profit, which will eventually reach the critical minimum $I''$ and set off a *liquidation* crisis. Alternatively, holding the rate of profit constant will result in rising levels of surplus value and unemployment, and increasingly severe *realization* crises. Actual events and policies may fluctuate between these extremes and produce crises of both types. In any case, the system is doomed in the sense that no level of unemployment, however large, can be set up and held indefinitely as a maximum.

Marx's argument, in this interpretation, can be illustrated by

---

[1] Marxists object to the implications of the term 'under-consumption', as implying that consumers are somehow at fault for not buying more than they can afford.

the diagram on page 222 in which the horizontal axis represents time, and the vertical axis the profit rate $P'$. The critical minimum profit rate $P''$ is drawn as a horizontal line; Marx does not specify its movement over time, but its time-rate of change, if not zero, is presumably small. The area below the $P''$ line involves conditions of liquidation crisis. A family of downward-sloping curves labelled (0, 4, 8, . . ., 20) indicate the course over time of the maximum profit rates consistent with the several unemployment rates indicated by the numerical indices. They trace the function:

$$P' = \frac{U^{-1}(U)}{1 + k}$$

over time, as $k$ rises, for different values of $U$ Their negative inclination illustrates Marx's Law. The area above and to the right of each line involves a realization crisis as measured from that base unemployment level. The wavy line corresponds to a possible course of affairs, moving from crisis to crisis at increasing unemployment.

The dilemma arises in that as the organic composition of capital rises, all the

$$\frac{U^{-1}(U)}{1+k}$$

curves cross the horizontal $P''$ line from above. To the right of each intersection, there is perpetual crisis (depression, stagnation, unemployment higher than indicated by the intersecting curve). Once the curve has crossed the $P''$ line, liquidation crisis can be avoided only at the cost of realization crisis, and vice versa. Since each curve eventually crosses the $P''$ line, no level of employment can be held, however low; eventually, unemployment must rise even higher. This is stagnationism, in a form more general and acute than any propounded by Keynes, by Hansen, or by Schumpeter!

If we choose to define or forecast some level of unemployment as the maximum supportable without revolution (say, a 20 per cent rate), the intersection of the curve labelled 20 with the $P''$ line indicates the outer limit of capitalist survival. In the diagram, it is labelled $Z$ (from the German *Zusammenbruch* meaning

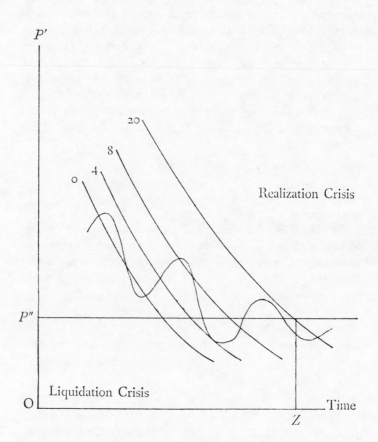

breakdown), but Marx did not identify it in so misleadingly (?) precise a manner.

A HASTY CRITIQUE

This writer has never considered himself a Marxist, but an imperfectly inconsistent eclectic, with non-Marxian elements dominating his private brand of eclecticism. In developing here what is intended as a sympathetic exposition and interpretation of Marxism, how did he resist conversion?

Lacking either time, space, or intent for anything like another full-dress *Marx-Kritik*, we may sample from our doubts under the heads of omission and commission.

The omissions are the most significant. This is not to fault Marx for making them a century or more ago, but rather his disciples for leaving them uncorrected in the interim. The Marxian system (as outlined and vulgarized here) has no Government, hence no public revenue, expenditure, and debt policy. It has no monetary system, and hence no monetary policy. The treatment of innovation seems sketchy and fragmentary, particularly with regard to capital-saving rather than labour-saving innovations. The impact of population growth is sketchier and yet more fragmentary. Somewhat the same criticisms hold for that unfinished masterpiece, *Capital*. (The elaborate discussion of money and credit in Vol. III, Part V, for example, is not up to Marx's standard, particularly in its treatment of paper money and 'fictitious value'.) Marx cannot be blamed for anticipating only partially monetary and fiscal policy developments which came generations after his manuscripts were written. It is however unfortunate that his followers have been more vituperative than analytical or convincing, in filling the gaps he left behind.

The besetting weakness of the Marxian system, omissions apart, is to this writer what many another critic considers a pillar of strength. This is its structuralism, which is to say, its tendency to take important relations as technically determined behind the back of the price system, leaving that latter with few functions beyond equating profit rates in industries with different organic compositions of capital. In this respect the labour theory of value remains an incubus even in the aggregate. It would be formally easy to transform such important coefficients as $h$ (the ratio of $W_1$ to $W_2$) and the several $k$ (organic compositions of capital) into unknowns, dependent in part on relative prices, wages, and interest rates, as contemporary orthodoxy usually does. Unfortunately for the labour theory of value, such changes would whittle away at it by stressing the deviations of prices from values. It is not surprising that Marxists do not choose this path.

The inclusion of most white-collar and managerial labour in surplus value, and the use of total surplus value as a numerator determining the rates of exploitation and of profit, made better sociological sense in Marx's time than it now does in developed countries. The white-collars and the managers were in those times predominantly capitalists; if not actual capitalists, future capitalists, or relatives of capitalists by blood, marriage, or adoption. Payments to these people could naturally be regarded as redivisions of property income rather than separate categories, so that equalizing rates of surplus value and profit (as Marx defined them) was an intelligible and defensible procedure. In the second half of the following century the facts seem somewhat different, and revisions may be in order.

It is clear that Marx excluded direct consumer services from his system. They are neither embodied in physical commodities, nor do they contribute at all directly to their production. Therefore Marx, like the English classical economists, denied that they had value. A number of micro-economic conundrums arise from this denial: How can the piano have value, when the pianist's services do not? These conundrums are not our concern here. The relevant question pertains to the flow of expenditures between sectors – demand and supply, as in System III. We know that income earned in commodity production is partially spent for consumer services, and vice versa. An implicit assumption of the Marxian system seems to be that flows in and out of consumer services are always in balance, so that the omission of the non-value-producing consumer service sector makes no difference. This is not always the case, in economies whose consumer-service sectors are growing or declining as proportions of the commodity-producing ones.

We close what threatens to become a series of quibbles and debating points with one elementary, but potentially important, example of the quandary to which certain of the difficulties seem to lead. This example concerns population growth, in its effects upon the unemployment rate and upon the organic composition of capital in Marx's dynamics. Marx apparently, and plausibly, assumed population growing with sufficient speed to avoid any complications from the side of an inadequate full-employment position $V$. But if over-all labour shortage should occur, whether from family planning, epidemics, nuclear fall-out, or mass emigration, how would his dynamics work out? (This problem has already disturbed at least one economist, Anatol Murad, sympathetic to Marxism.) Clearly, such a fall in $V$ would lower the unemployment rate $U$. Any fall in $U$ would lower $S'$ and therefore $P'$. It might bring on a liquidation crisis by lowering

$P'$ below $P''$ (Figure I). But it would not be the type indicated by $Z$ in Figure I, because $U$ would not be high. What *would*, indeed, happen in such a case? Would labour shortage simply move the breakdown point $Z$ ahead in time, and to a lower level of $U$? (Murad thinks so, if I follow his argument.) Would the 'equilibrium' value of $U$ turn negative, destroying the usefulness of equilibrium conditions which were only *prima facie*, after all, neither necessary nor sufficient? Would the equilibrium value of $g$ perhaps turn negative, meaning an economy declining instead of growing, but with no collapse at all? The writer cannot determine, with the aid of the Marxian system as he understands it.

Within conventional bourgeois economic models, such population effects would be met mainly by accelerated rise in the capital–labour ratio, even without the spur of innovation. In the same way, redundance of population or of investment would lead (over wide ranges, and over long periods) to corrective changes in capital–labour ratios by the movement of relative prices, without any necessity for technical change. But Marxian structuralism, like any other brand of structuralism, rules out such expedients – reasonably, perhaps, in the short period, but less so over the longer term.

CONCLUSION

The year 1967 marks the centennial of the first German edition of the first volume of *Capital*. At this anniversary, communication between Marxist and bourgeois economists still seems more difficult than the morning after the volume's publication. On the Western side of the several curtains separating the Socialist and capitalist worlds, the present essay is only one of several relatively brief, dispassionate, and up-to-date expositions of the Marxian system in terms intelligible to academic economists, and with controversy muted if not precisely minimized. The results have not been stupendous, and the Marxian dilemmas are not taken sufficiently seriously by many academic economists, but a good beginning has been made, dating (in English) from Dobb's *Political Economy and Capitalism* (1937) and Sweezy's *Theory of Capitalist Development* (1942). Is it Utopian to hope for similarly dispassionate expositions of Western economics on the Eastern sides of the curtains – either original expositions or translations of Western teaching materials? Once again we neither know, nor greatly care, whether or not this would constitute 'ideological coexistence'.

## SELECTED BIBLIOGRAPHY

ADELMAN, IRMA. *Theories of Economic Growth and Development.* Stanford University Press, 1962.

BRONFENBRENNER, M. 'The Marxian Macro-Economic Model: Extension From Two Departments', Reprint No. 237. Graduate School of Industrial Administration, Carnegie Institute of Technology, Pittsburgh, Pa.

# Technical Change and Marxian Economics

*Mark Blaug*

MARXIAN economics claims to provide an analysis of 'the laws of motion of capitalism'. Orthodox economics in recent decades has devoted much attention to explaining the hitherto successful performance of the capitalist system so as to discover what light past trends may shed on future prospects. For the first time in a century of debate between Marxian and orthodox economics the nature of the central issue is not in dispute. In the past, fruitful discussion was impeded by fundamental differences in approach: the two schools of thought were simply interested in different things. This is no longer true, and the recent flurry of articles on Marx suggests that there is still something to be learned from the Marxian theory of economic development. Its persistent emphasis upon technical change as an inherent feature of the process of capital accumulation provides a healthy antidote to the static bias of received doctrine. Even Marx's mistakes are extraordinarily instructive. But the one great merit of the Marxian system – a merit which supplies the rationale of this paper – is that criticism of it leads one to consider all the difficulties which have so far stood in the way of a satisfactory theory of technical change. The central point I wish to make is that Marxian economics, despite its prescient insights into the nature of technological progress, contains no systematic theory of the factor-saving character of technical improvements. It is for this reason, and not because of any logical errors, that it failed correctly to predict the evolution of capitalism.

I

The basic axiom of Marxian economics is the proposition that surplus value (profit plus interest plus rent) is unearned income, in the strict Marshallian sense of the phrase; for Marx, capital

Reprinted from *Kyklos*, Vol. III, 1960.

has no supply price and property income is purely a function of the private ownership of the means of production. Since the argument proceeds in the context of a perfectly competitive economy, we might think that the individual entrepreneur – whose contribution to total output is too small to influence price – would expand output in the effort to reap more surplus value, until wages are bid up so as to reduce the surplus to zero. What is it that holds wages down? Having abandoned the Malthusian theory of population, Marx could not assume that population growth would preserve wage rates at the subsistence level. Instead, he postulated the existence of 'the industrial reserve army' of the unemployed, providing unceasing competition for vacancies. Booms deplete the reserve army and slumps replenish it, but secular growth at full employment levels is conceptually impossible, according to Marx. Unemployment arises initially from inappropriate factor endowments combined with limited possibilities of factor-substitution: full capacity use of the capital stock is insufficient to absorb the available labour supply. When this ceases to be true at some levels of the capital stock, further accumulation must involve a sufficient flow of labour-saving innovations so as to produce chronic unemployment. Thus, the Marxian conception of mature capitalism is predicated upon a bias towards labour-saving technical change.

It is not difficult to demonstrate that if the underlying production functions show either diminishing or constant returns to scale, a persistent labour-saving slant in technological progress must lead to a rise in capital requirements per unit of output. And, unless the property share of output rises proportionately, this will cause the rate of profit to fall. Marx's Law of the falling rate of profit is, in fact, based upon exactly this kind of reasoning.

The argument is in principle very simple. Since most of Marxian economics thrive under a cloud of terminological confusion, the first step in translating Marx is to agree upon a set of definitions. Writing small letters for flows and capital letters for stocks, Marx's 'constant capital' $c$ is defined as the sum of depreciation charges on fixed capital and inputs of raw materials. Adding the wages of production workers $v$, Marx's 'variable capital', we get the flow of outlays $k$. Dividing the components of $k$ by the appropriate rates of turnover, we get the stock of capital invested $K$. $K = C + V$, where $C$ stands for the value of the stock of durable equipment and inventories of raw materials and $V$ stands for working capital required to meet weekly payrolls. Following Marx, surplus value $s$ is defined on a flow basis as the excess of gross revenue over variable and fixed costs. For the economy as a whole this amounts to the excess of net national product over the wages bill. The rate of surplus value $s'$ is $s/v$. The rate of profit $p'$, as Marx defined it, is $s/k$; on a stock basis it is $s/K$[1].

Marx himself never explicitly defined the so-called 'organic composition of capital'. What he had in mind, however, is clearly the ratio of embodied labour to current labour or of machine costs to labour costs: $C/v$[2]. When multiplied by the wage rate, and ignoring $V$ as negligibly small, this becomes the amount of capital per man, i.e. $K/v \cdot v/L = K/L$. At all times Marx shuffled freely between stock and flow definitions without warning the reader. His expression for $p'$ is actually the share of profits in the turnover of capital; it is equal to profits per unit of capital on the assumption that the whole of capital turns over once a year. Marx was aware of variations in the turnover rates of $v$ and $c$ and to that extent he recognized the distinction between stocks and flows.[3] Still, he put no stress upon the point and it soon dropped out of sight in the Marxist literature.

So much for definitions. The rate of profit $p'$ varies inversely with 'the organic composition of capital' $Q$ and directly with the ratio of surplus to wages.[4] Taking into account variations in wages per man, $p'$ may be said to vary inversely with the capital/

[1] The expression $s/K$ is still not the rate of profit as conventionally understood; this is given by $\bar{s}/K$, where $\bar{s}$ stands for non-labour income minus administrative overhead, sales and advertising expenses, rents and indirect business taxes. Marx himself includes administrative and sales expenditures in the numerator of the expression $s/v$ but excludes salaried personnel from the denominator.

[2] Some commentators interpret him to mean the capital/output ratio which seems far-fetched or the ratio $c/K$ which varies through time in much the same way as $c/v$.

[3] See *Capital* (Chicago, 1909), II, Ch. 16; III, Ch. 4.

[4] Marx writes the gross profit rate as $s/(c+v)$, which is identically equal to $s'/(q+1)$, where $q = c/v$. Strictly speaking, this should be amended to $p' = s'/Q$ where $Q = q \cdot t$, $t$ being a weighted average of the durabilities of $c$ and $v$.

labour ratio and directly with the amount of surplus per man, i.e.

$$p' = \frac{s}{v} \cdot \frac{v}{L} \Big/ \frac{K}{v} \cdot \frac{v}{L}$$

As far as Marx was concerned this established the law that the rate of return on capital must fall with the increased mechanization of industry. Having concluded that the wage rate rises little, if at all, in the course of capital accumulation while technical change constantly raises the stock of equipment per worker, he thought it obvious that the organic composition of capital must show a steady upward trend. It is true that this will not lower $p'$ if the rate at which $s'$ is rising exceeds that of $Q$. And as mechanization raises the productivity of labour it can hardly fail to raise $s'$. Marx realized that there was some functional connection between $Q$ and $s'$, but, after satisfying himself that $s'$ could rise only within 'certain impassable limits', he assumed it to be constant. He did recognize the influence of autonomous increases in $s'$, which he handled under the label of 'absolute and relative surplus value', but these too he dismissed with more justification as having definite physical limits.[1]

The constancy of $s'$ was only a simplifying assumption but, as both Sweezy and Robinson have pointed out, it was a particularly clumsy simplification for the Marxian system. Since wages and profits exhaust total income, a constant $s'$ for the economy as a whole implies constant relative shares. This means that real wages rise as fast as the average productivity of labour, i.e.,

$$s' = \frac{s}{v} = \frac{s}{o} \Big/ \frac{v}{L} \cdot \frac{L}{o}$$

But not only did Marx frequently imply that labour's share would decline but it is the function of 'the reserve army' to keep wages at subsistence. However loosely interpreted, this presumably means that wages do not rise as fast as the average productivity of labour. And so long as this is true, every increase in output per man raises $s'$. *A fortiori*, if real wages are

[1] For references to Marx's writings on this point, see H. D. Dickinson, 'The Falling Rate of Profit in Marxian Economics', *Review of Economic Studies*, February 1957, p. 123 n.

constant, $s'$ will rise sharply as $K/L$ increases. Thus, the tendency for $p'$ to fall is indeterminate: it all depends on the nature of the explicit function $s' = f(Q)$. Marx's attempt to demonstrate the existence of an upper bound to this function involved him in a horrible confusion between physical-productivity and value-productivity.[1] On his own terms, the only relevant question is whether productivity is likely to increase faster in the wage-goods industries than in other sectors. If so, this will mean a fall in the value of the Marxian measuring rod of labour-hours with the result that $p'$ will tend to rise. The law of the falling rate of profit, therefore, calls for some denial of this effect, be it on logical or on empirical grounds.

It is possible, however, to make out a case for Marx's Law on orthodox grounds. Assume that the aggregate production function shows constant return to scale, the obvious assumption for the Marxian two-factor case. By the properties of the function, output rises for every increase in capital per man along the given function but less than proportionate to the increase in capital. As the capital/output ratio rises, the increase in capital will entail a fall in $p'$ even though $s' = f(Q)$.[2] Innovations as such are not enough to upset this conclusion. If technical change does not work to reduce capital per unit of output, $p'$ will nevertheless fall. This is because the capital-absorbing effects of the inno-vational process governs the degree to which wages rise as capital increases. If wages rose as fast as output per man, relative shares would be unaffected and the rising capital/output ratio alone would lead directly to a fall in $p'$. In the Marxian system labour's share is alleged to fall through time; therefore, a rising capital/output ratio here does not necessarily imply a falling $p'$. But this is only to say that the Marxian Law of the falling rate of profit is predicated upon a very rapidly rising capital/output ratio, which implies in turn that technical change is heavily slanted towards labour-saving improvements. For the claim

[1] *Capital*, III, p. 290.
[2] This rather obvious point is proved indirectly in Dickinson's recent paper, *op. cit.* By itself it provides no support for Marx's Law since Marx denies that capital can increase without technical change. Dickinson's defence of Marx's argument, however, abstracts from innovations.

that capital per man rises faster than profits per man, or in Marxian terms that $Q$ rises faster than $s'$, is tantamount to claiming that the capital/output ratio rises faster than the property share in output:

$$p' = \frac{s'}{Q} = \frac{s}{L} / \frac{K}{L};$$

dividing through by $L/o$, we get

$$p' = \frac{s}{o} / \frac{K}{o}.$$

The fact that the aggregate capital/output ratio has remained practically unchanged in advanced economies over the last seventy-five years is fatal to the Marxist schema. Together with the observed long-run stability in relative shares, it leads directly to the conclusion that profits per man have risen as fast as capital per man and hence that $p'$ has not declined. In the American case, the rate of return to privately owned physical capital has in fact shown a slight tendency to fall in the twentieth century. But the reason for this is not that technical change has been excessively labour-saving; on the contrary, the evidence suggests a mild capital-saving bias in the American economy over the last four decades.[1]

The facts make it unnecessary to consider the deeper contradictions in Marx's argument. After all, a labour-saving slant in technical change implies that the rise in man-hour productivity is concentrated in the finishing stages of production: all cost-reducing improvements in the capital goods industries are capital-saving for the economy as a whole. Hence, the prices of consumer goods fall faster than machine prices. In terms of the labour theory of value, this means that the value of $v$ declines faster than the value of $c$ or $s$, so that it is not at all certain that $Q$ or $s'$ will increase. The Marxian Law of the falling rate of profit, even when accepted on its own grounds, is caught up in a bewildering mesh of opposing forces whose outcome is not deducible from elements supplied by the theory.

[1] For a discussion of the evidence, see W. Fellner, *Trends and Cycles in Economic Activity* (New York, 1956), pp. 246–57.

II

Given the weaknesses of Marx's argument, it is hardly surprising that his predictions failed to materialize. Even Marxists have now conceded the point. A recent book by an American Marxist for the first time submits the law of the falling rate of profit to a statistical test.[1] Using census data for American manufacturing over the period 1849 to 1939, the author, J. M. Gillman, starts out by accepting Marx's categories on a flow basis. The results are very disquieting: although $q$ showed a fairly strong tendency to rise until the turn of the century, the trend-value through 1919–39 was constant. Since $s'$ rose persistently, the trend in $s/k$ was decidedly upward over the whole of the ninety-year period.

When the ratios are converted to a stock basis, however, the data breaks clearly into two historical phases.[2] Until 1919 capitalism in manufacture behaved very nearly as Marx had predicted: $Q$ rose significantly and $s'$ did not increase sufficiently to prevent $p'$ from falling. Then something went wrong. The organic composition of capital stabilized in the 1920s at levels reached in 1919 and fluctuated counter-cyclically in the 1930s; it fell all through World War II and had risen little by 1950. If the decade of the 1930s is excluded, there is in fact some indication of a secular decline in $Q$. In addition neither $s'$ nor $p'$ showed any definite trend.[3]

---

[1] J. M. Gillman, *The Falling Rate of Profit* (London, 1956).

[2] In the absence of data on the rate of turnover of raw materials before 1922, and neglecting $V$ as too small to matter, $K$ is calculated on fixed capital only, i.e. the value of plant and equipment estimated at their reproduction cost in current prices net of depreciation.

[3] Since production workers declined as a fraction of the total labour force in manufacturing, Gillman infers that the rate of net profit $\bar{s}/K$ did fall very slightly over the years 1910–50 (*Ibid.*, p. 98). But in fact the regression line estimated by the method of least squares shows no trend component whatever on the 5 per cent level of significance. The same negative results are shown by Mann's non-parametric ranking test for trend which makes no assumption about the mathematical properties of the trend line or about the character of the population distribution.

Gillman has nothing to say about the average productivity of capital. But his findings are complemented by studies of the capital/output ratio in American manufacturing: measured in current prices, it rose through 1880–1909 and then fell continuously until 1948. When capital and output are estimated in 1929 prices, the peak is reached in 1919. Furthermore, the downtrend since 1919 holds both for the ratio of fixed capital and of working capital to output.[1]

Thus, Marxists and orthodox economists do not disagree about the facts. Not so long ago some Marxists were predicting an even sharper tendency towards labour-saving technical change,[2] but Gillman adduces evidence of the increasing importance of capital-saving innovations.[3] This is where agreement ends, however. Gillman seems to regard capital-saving improvements as novel manifestations of a complex technology which Marx could not have foreseen. Apparently, labour-saving innovations are induced by rising real wages eating into profit margins but capital-saving innovations just happen, for technical reasons, to occur only in late-stage capitalism. Capital-saving innovations play the same role in Gillman's book as trade union pressures in the works of other Marxists: they enter into the analysis as exogenous variables which reconcile the theory with reality.

Ironically enough, Gillman here adopts an attitude which not so long ago was widely shared by most orthodox economists but, as we shall see, not by Marx himself. A brief digression will help to place the matter in perspective. Economic development was traditionally said to involve continuous capital deepening in the sense of increased capital requirements per unit of output; capital-saving innovations were regarded as only becoming im-

[1] D. Creamer, *Capital and Output Trends in Manufacturing Industry* (NBER, Occasional Papers 41, 1954). The fall in the capital/output ratio since 1919 is all the more remarkable if it were true, as Marxists allege, that late-stage capitalism reveals a chronic tendency towards under-utilization of capacity. As the denominator is usually measured, a fall in the utilization of capacity should, everything else being the same, increase the capital/output ratio.

[2] P. M. Sweezy, *The Theory of Capitalist Development* (New York, 1942), p. 276.

[3] *Op. cit.*, pp. 74–9.

portant when an economy was already richly endowed with capital. The temptation to draw unwarranted conclusions from the historical increase in capital per man proved irresistible:[1] technical innovations lighten human toil by substituting mechanical power for hand labour; therefore, technological progress as such is necessarily labour-displacing and, in the absence of sufficient capital-widening, will lead to chronic unemployment. The constant preoccupation with the problem of technological unemployment, out of all proportion to its actual importance, testifies to the hold of this line of thought. Implicitly, it will be noticed, technical change was being discussed as if it consisted mainly of inventions in the narrow sense of the term rather than of any change, for whatever reason, in the technical horizon of producers.[2]

With hindsight it is hard to believe that anyone could ever have doubted that capital-saving improvements are as normal a feature of technical change as labour-saving innovations. It is difficult now to appreciate how quickly and how recently economists have changed their minds on this question. In 1937 Joan Robinson declared that:

It appears obvious that the development of human methods of production, from the purely hand-to-mouth technique of the ape, has been mainly in the direction of increasing 'roundaboutness', and the discovery of short cuts, such as wireless, are exceptions to the general line of advance.

But in 1956 she concluded:

There is no reason to expect technical progress to be exactly neutral in any one economy, but equally there is no

[1] This ignores the fact that changes in the capital to labour ratio over time reflect not merely technical change or even factor-substitution without technical change, but also autonomous changes in the supply of savings and in the growth of population.

[2] See e.g. J. R. Hicks, *The Theory of Wages* (London, 1932), pp. 123–5, and the comments by G. F. Bloom, 'A Note on Hicks' Theory of Invention', *American Economic Review*, March 1946; for recent version of Hicks' argument, see K. W. Rothschild, *The Theory of Wages* (New York, 1954), pp. 117–19.

reason to expect a systematic bias one way or the other. Capital-using innovations raise the cost of machines in terms of commodities and give entrepreneurs an extra motive to find ways to cheapen them. Capital-saving innovations tend to produce scarcity of labour in the consumption sector and give entrepreneurs an extra motive to increase productivity. Each type of bias tends to get itself compensated by the other.[1]

Capital-saving innovations fall into two classes, those that save fixed capital and those that save working capital. Apart from cheaper and better machines, any improvement that widens the scope of auxiliary instruments, reduces floor space, or lengthens the physical life of a plant, belongs to the first class of innovations. Economies of working capital, on the other hand, release operating funds by reducing the stock of goods which must be carried for given output. Typically, they take the form of lower freight charges, faster handling of materials, reductions in delivery-time, and fuel savings through recovery and use of waste-products. Put this way it would be surprising indeed if capital saving innovations had not proved important even in the earlier phases of capitalist development. A good many of the crucial inventions of the Industrial Revolution on balance released rather than absorbed capital: the smelting of iron with coal, Cort's puddling and rolling process, chlorine bleaching, Watt's vacuum engine, Neilson's hot blast, Woolf's compound engine, not to speak of the transport revolution associated with the names of Macadam and Bridgewater.[2] The canal era, or for that matter the replacement of the stage-coach by railroads, certainly drew heavily on capital resources. But its effect in reducing the prices of coal, timber, and iron in which the cost

[1] J. Robinson, *Essays in the Theory of Employment* (London, 1937), p. 135; *The Accumulation of Capital* (London, 1956), p. 170.

[2] For the most part, the economic history of the period has been written with other questions in mind. But see the works of T. S. Ashton, *The Industrial Revolution* (London, 1948), pp. 91–2; *An Economic History of England: The Eighteenth Century* (London, 1955), pp. 90, 100, 108–13. No historian has done more to attract attention to the importance of capital-saving improvements in the eighteenth century.

of carriage weighed heavily, was such that it is doubtful whether it raised capital requirements per ton-mile of freight carried.[1]

Capital-saving innovations *may* involve such revolutionary inventions as explosives for mining, radio, telegraphy and aeroplanes, but they need not. Frequently, they consist of minor but not necessarily routine improvements in technique and for that reason they tend to escape recognition. Indeed, awareness of the very existence of capital-saving innovations came late in the history of economic thought. Even the classical economists realized that time-saving improvements raise the rate of profit by increasing the turnover rate of capital funds; when railways were first introduced, their advantages in economizing working capital were thoroughly canvassed.[2] But such ideas were not systematized and economies of fixed capital were never seriously contemplated. Sidgwick in 1883 seems to have been the first to hint at the general concept of a capital-saving innovation; Taussig and J. B. Clark made references to it in their writings. But none of them doubted that technical change had been overwhelmingly labour-saving in the past.[3] The growing influence of the Austrian theory of capital around the turn of the century, emphasizing as it did capital formation which increases the durability of plant and equipment, further encouraged the belief that capital deepens as it grows.[4]

[1] W. T. Jackmann, *The Development of Transportation in Modern England* (Cambridge, 1916), I, pp. 404–51; II, pp. 724–9.

[2] *Ibid.*, II, pp. 490, 543–4.

[3] For page references to the neo-classical authors see A. Gourvitch, *A Survey of Economic Theory on Technological Change and Employment* (Works Project Administration, Philadelphia, 1940), pp. 93–5.

[4] Böhm-Bawerk maintained that while some inventions do reduce roundaboutness, the capital so released tends to be applied to lengthening the period of production elsewhere. Only if the innovation is both capital-saving and product-replacing will the average period of production be shortened. This he dismissed as exceptional, citing the secular increase in physical capital per head as presumptive evidence of the greater frequency of time-increasing inventions: 'Industrial experience will verify two propositions ... first, that with the larger capitalistic equipment, the product per unit of labour increases; and, second, that this increase in product does not go on

Marx, on the other hand, was not only aware of capital-saving changes but spoke of them as the product of automatic market forces. 'Capitalist production,' he writes, 'enforces economies in the employment of constant capital' which tend 'to check the fall in the rate of profit.' 'This shows once more,' he concluded, 'that the same causes which bring about a tendency of the rate of profit to fall, also check the realization of this tendency.'[1] Chapter five of the third volume of *Capital*, written by Engels in the early 1890s, elaborates upon the tendency of certain inventions to shorten the time of production, thus raising profits by saving goods in the pipelines. This contention is richly illustrated with examples drawn from British industry. Engels notes that 'the revolution in the means of communication in the last fifty years . . .' have more than doubled or trebled 'the productive capacity of the capital engaged in world commerce'. These comments, however, were merely suggestive and even as such they were confined to innovations which save working capital; neither Marx nor Engels considered the effects of technological progress concentrated in the capital goods industries. In the final analysis, Marx too remained a victim of the myth of a labour-saving bias in technical change.

### III

Technological progress acts to offset diminishing returns to the faster growing factor. When innovational investment is insufficient to offset diminishing returns it is possible that both profits and wage rates decline as capital per man increases. But if technical change is strongly biased it would require a very low level of innovating activity to produce the perverse result of unfavourable trends in both profit and wage rates. Viewed in this light, the Marxian view of capital accumulation seems almost deliberately paradoxical. Marx draws no distinction be-

*pari passu* with the addition of capitalistic equipment.' 'The Positive Theory of Capital and its Critics', *Quarterly Journal of Economics*, January 1896, p. 150. It is worth noting that Wicksell's famous discussion of the effect of inventions upon wages in the *Lectures on Political Economy* does not consider the possibility of capital-saving improvements.

[1] *Capital*, III, pp. 103 and 277.

tween movements along production functions and shifts in the production functions themselves: capital cannot be invested without altering the state of the arts. Hence, there is no question in the Marxian system of insufficient offsets to diminishing returns. At the same time, Marx assumed that innovations would be heavily slanted in the labour-saving direction. Yet, he concluded that capital accumulation will depress the rate of profit without necessarily raising real wages per man. The mechanism that is supposed to produce this result is entirely independent of any third factor receiving an increasing residual. It is solely due to what Marx liked to call 'the passion for accumulation'. An excessive rate of capital formation lowers the profit rate while the innovations embodied in the increments of capital hold down wage rates by being largely labour-saving.

The Marxian situation is theoretically possible.[1] Events have not turned out that way, but is there any reason to think they could have done so? If a given rate of accumulation depresses the yield of capital (say, by hastening the rate of obsolescence or driving down the prices of finished goods), what prevents the system from settling down to a slower rate of growth? After all, if capitalists accumulate wealth for reasons of prestige and status irrespective of the rate of profit, so long as it is positive, and this is what Marx implies, a rate of accumulation so rapid as to depress the rate of return must defeat itself.[2] Putting this aside, it is still true that if capital is being incessantly invested in labour-saving improvements, the capital/output ratio must rise. This means a higher share of depreciation and interest charges in total costs with consequent pressures to affect economies in the use of capital. Likewise, 'the passion for accumulation'

---

[1] See W. Fellner, 'Marxian Hypotheses and Observable Trends Under Capitalism: A "Modernized" Interpretation', *Economic Journal*, March 1957; but see the elliptical comments of P. A. Samuelson, 'Wages and Interest: A Modern Dissection of Marxian Economic Models', *American Economic Review*, December 1957, pp. 893–4.

[2] In other words, the demand for capital is *less* elastic in the long run than in the short run: all savings come out of profits and the capital stock is used to capacity; hence, a lower profit rate depresses savings not because it affects the willingness to save and invest but because it affects the ability to do so.

should lead to a chronic excess demand for capital; consequent difficulties in obtaining finance, expressing itself in an upward sloping supply curve of funds available to the firm, should be enough to induce capital-saving innovations. No matter how we look at it, the investment-demand function must be of a very peculiar shape to sustain the Marxian case.

Under perfect competition innovations as such cannot *for long* lower both profit and wage rates. Any sharp trend in factor-returns will generate a stabilizing shift in technical change. This is not to imply that innovations can be said to have a unique effect upon rates of return to productive agents: without knowledge of the underlying production functions nothing specific can be inferred.[1] Nevertheless, if technical progress is plentiful and yet produces a fall in the rate of return to capital it does suggest that the factor-saving slant of innovations is out of line with relative factor scarcities. In an economy in which capital is the scarcer factor, a persistent bias towards labour-saving improvements must erode the profits which each individual producer expects to reap from an improvement; this is the case Marx had in mind. When labour is the scarcer factor, as in advanced Western economies, a bias towards capital-saving improvements likewise works to reduce the yield of capital. The reason that technical change has not exhibited either bias to any marked degree is that the long-term pattern of innovations is the outcome of successive adjustments to differential rates of growth in the factor supplies as reflected in relative prices. Producers in a perfectly competitive market face infinitely elastic supply

---

[1] Innovations may be conveniently classified in terms of their effect upon relative shares (see Fellner, *op. cit.*, pp. 212–13). A capital-saving innovation raises labour's share and, of course, tends to lower the capital/output ratio; the effect upon the rate of profit, however, depends upon which of the two consequences predominate. A spate of capital-saving innovations occurring together will engender commodity-substitution towards capital intensive goods which fall in relative price; this stimulates the demand for capital and, the capital/output ratio may actually rise. Indeed, to predict the effect of an innovation upon rates of return and upon relative shares it would be necessary to know the elasticity of demand for every product and the elasticity of supply of every factor-input in addition to the changes in the marginal rates of substitution of factors.

curves in factor markets; hence, the perfectly competitive market seems to provide no signal to induce the 'appropriate' factor-saving innovation. But the factor-supply curves do shift through time and there is nothing in the static theory of the competitive firm which leads us to deny that firms will learn to adapt themselves to a persistent trend in the shifting of factor-supply curves. Producers simply become conditioned by experience to avoid disappointment by choosing improvements which save the relatively scarcer factor. This process of adjustment damps down sharp cumulative changes in factor returns and thus works to stabilize the relative shares.[1]

It is not necessary to assume that factor-prices have a *conscious* redirecting effect on firms: the familiar 'realistic' objections to marginal productivity theory are irrelevant in this context. The argument rests essentially on competitive survival, regardless of the nature of individual motivation and foresight.[2] Firms adopting, say, capital-using devices in the light of falling wage rates and rising interest charges will not prove viable. The successor innovator will be saving capital and absorbing labour and the economist looking on will find the system as a whole adapting technical change to relative factor scarcities.

This response mechanism is not likely to operate very smoothly, as the existence of business cycles will testify. At the crude aggregative level adopted here, objections crowd in from every direction. Technical constraints may not permit enough substitution of other factors for labour to prevent a rise in total labour costs as wages rise; when labour costs bulk larger in total costs than do capital charges, the effect of a change in wages is not symmetrical with the effect of a change in the rate of interest. Moreover, scarcity of capital is not adequately reflected by the rate of interest owing to the practice of capital rationing.

In addition, indivisibility of capital in some industries may

[1] See *ibid.*, pp. 220–2. Professor Fellner notes that under conditions of monopsony, in which the firm necessarily affects the price of the input it purchases, producers are made directly aware of relative factor scarcities by the respective gaps between average and marginal factor costs.

[2] See A. A. Alchian, 'Uncertainty, Evolution and Economic Theory', *Journal of Political Economy*, June 1950.

cause capacity to be installed far ahead of the market. Such industries may be impervious, for relatively long periods of time, to changes in wages and interest rates. Capital-saving improvements are often the result of external economies generated by the growth of social overhead facilities. Since external economies are not reflected in the price system, improvements so originated form an important exception to the theory of market-induced innovations. Then too, it has been tacitly assumed up to this point that all innovations are cost-reducing. What of product-replacing or demand-creating innovations for which there is no basis of comparison with previous cost-outlays? These are certainly as significant nowadays as process-improvements and yet little can as yet be said about them. Variations in the level of inventive efforts raise further questions but we need go no further to make the point. Nevertheless, these reservations do not destroy the notion that the innovational process as a whole is the outcome of responses to market pressures: rational optimizing behaviour precludes the possibility of any pronounced bias in technical change over long periods of time.

IV

The idea of an adjustment-mechanism governing the innovational process goes back to Marx. But Marxian economics provides only a truncated theory of factor-saving innovations. Changes in factor-prices are said to affect the choice of new techniques but capital-saving innovations are not treated on the same footing as labour-saving innovations. Yet Marx recognized that a falling rate of profit will induce entrepreneurs to economize upon fixed and working capital. The failure to consider the consequences of such tendencies is the fatal weakness of the Marxian theory of capital accumulation. It results in a theory of economic growth in which investment-prospects dry up not because there have been too few labour-saving improvements but because there have been too many. This conclusion is hard to justify in any competitive economy and has certainly proved to be irrelevant to the experiences of developed capitalist countries. Marx erred in not envisaging the possibility that labour might become the relative scarcer factor. It is only fair to say that this was in fact a common error of all nineteenth-century economic thought. It matters more for Marx, however, because he alone claimed to predict the historical evolution of capitalism.


## SELECTED BIBLIOGRAPHY

DICKINSON, H. D. 'The Falling Rate of Profit in Marxian Economics', *Review of Economic Studies*. February 1957.

GILLMAN, J. M. *The Falling Rate of Profit*. London: Dobson, 1957.

MEEK, R. L. 'The Falling Rate of Profit', *Economics and Ideology*. London: Chapman & Hall, 1967.

# Karl Marx and the Accumulation of Capital

*J. Steindl*

## I. GENERAL OBSERVATIONS

THE REMARKS which follow should not be taken, as a study in economic doctrine, an exhaustive appreciation, and perhaps not even as a correct interpretation, but rather only as a sequence of ideas stimulated by Marx's work. Two broad considerations which have not invariably inspired the literature on Marx are to be given due weight. The work of Marx deals seriously with problems which more than one generation of economists – for the greater part – have neglected and ignored. Its greatness has only begun to be recognized, willingly or unwillingly, wittingly or unwittingly, in modern economics. His method of looking at the economy as a whole, analysing the relation of aggregates, and building models, has become an essential part of modern economics. His problems, unemployment, technical progress, under-consumption, concentration of capital, are the problems which occupy at least the more realistic economists of today.

At the same time, economics is not made in the brain alone, not even in a very exceptional one. How Marx himself felt about this can be seen from his never tiring appeal to empirical data and information. But the data at his disposal were defective for his own time. Since then much more information has been collected, referring to his own time and to the time which passed since he wrote. This information is still defective. In fact, economists have constantly to exercise their judgment in relation to the given information which is always inadequate. This involves errors of judgment. The rule of the game, as we conceive it, is to judge on the best available evidence, and to revise judgment when new evidence becomes available. This is hardly in contradiction to the teaching of Marx. In fact the essence of

Originally appeared as Chapter XIV of *Maturity and Stagnation in the American Economy*. Oxford: Blackwell, 1952.

Marxian thinking implies that economics cannot be fixed to a rigid pattern established on the basis of the limited experience available at a certain historical date. The work of Marx is unfinished in more than one sense, and it could not be otherwise. It is not surprising that Marx committed errors of judgment in the light of today's evidence. Regrettably enough, the writers who stand up for Marx sometimes cling with peculiar stubbornness just to these errors of judgment, as if *they* were the essence, and not his approach, his method, his problems.

## 2. THE LAW OF ACCUMULATION

In her critical appreciation of Marx Mrs Robinson concludes that his work contains really no solution of the problem how the product is divided between wage-earners and capitalists. '... as soon as the rigid subsistence level theory is abandoned, it provides no definite answer to the central question – what determines the division of the total product between capital and labour?'[1]

This conclusion is somewhat too negative. The subsistence-level theory is, if we look at it closely, much less rigid and much more complicated than it appears. It calls for a detailed analysis of its logic and its assumptions, part of which may be invalid without necessarily destroying the usefulness of the whole of the argument. Such an analysis is attempted in the following.

The 'subsistence-theory' is at first introduced by Marx in a rather formal way. 'The value of labour–power' (labour–power is what the worker sells and the capitalist buys for a wage) 'is determined by the value of the necessaries of life habitually required by the average worker'.[2] This is a formal statement, satisfying the general rule that commodities have a 'value' corresponding to their production cost in hours of labour, a rule which is here extended to the 'commodity' called labour–power. We are still in the sphere of definition here. The theory

---

[1] J. Robinson, *An Essay on Marxian Economics*, pp. 39–40.

[2] *Das Kapital*. Volksausgave besorgt vom Marx–Engels–Lenin Institut. I. Band XV., p. 544. *Capital* (Everyman), p. 563. (The quotations given in the text are partly the author's own free translation from the German.)

becomes more concrete by the additional statement that the *price* of *labour–power* (that is, the wage) in the long run should tend to approximate to its *value*,[1] but even then it remains still rather formal on account of the very cautious definition of the 'subsistence-level', which is *historically* determined.

Marx becomes, however, quite concrete when he analyses the effects of increasing productivity on real wages. There is no possible doubt whatever that he expected the *relative share of labour* in the product to *decline* with increasing productivity. Even though real wages may rise, he says 'they never rise proportionately to the increase in the productivity of labour'.[2] It should be noted that, time and again, Marx considers and admits the possibility of an *absolute* increase in real wages. This is clear from the passages in which he argues that his absolute increase in real wages does not change the fundamental relations of capitalism. 'An increase in the price of labour–power in consequence of the accumulation of capital means in fact only that the golden chain which the workers have forged by their own work has become so long and heavy that it can be stretched a little more loosely.'[3] And in another place there is the comparison of the small hut and the palace: they may both grow, but if the *relative* discrepancy in size and convenience of the hut and the palace remains or even grows, the owner of the hut remains, in a very relevant sense, as poor as ever, or becomes even poorer. 'Even though the consumption of the worker has risen, the social satisfaction which it grants has diminished in comparison with the greater enjoyments of the capitalist in which the worker has no part, and in relation to the stage of development reached by society in general.'[4]

Marx thus did not deny that the increase in productivity may raise the level of real wages. What he most definitely expected, however, was a diminution of the *relative share* of labour in the product, taking place as a result of the historical process of increasing productivity which is bound up with the develop-

---

[1] *Das Kapital* I. XV.

[2] *Das Kapital* I. XXII, p. 635. Everyman ed., p. 665.

[3] *Das Kapital* I. XXIII, p. 649–50. Everyman, p. 682.

[4] Lohnarbeit und Kapital (Verlag Neuer Weg GM BH 1946), p. 30. Selected Works (Lawrence & Wishart), p. 269.

ment of capitalism. Only in this very qualified sense can we speak of a 'subsistence-level theory'.

This broad expectation of Marx is, however, a result rather than a starting point of his analysis. How exactly did he arrive at this result? The skeleton of his theory is contained in Chapter XXIII of Volume I. We can best start by considering the basic difference between Marx and other writers who held that real wages are in some sense tied to a subsistence level. These other writers, in particular Malthus, and later Lassalle, based their view on the 'law of population': an increase in real wages above subsistence level, they held, would lead to an increase in population which, owing to the decreasing returns to land, would lower the real wage again until it reached the 'equilibrium' – the subsistence level. Now it is perfectly clear that this is not the reasoning on which Marx based his own conclusions. In fact some of his most venomous attacks are directed against the law of Malthus. He perceived in the reasoning in question – probably rightly – the hidden intention of offering a general apology for all the ills of capitalism, by making out that poverty was a law of nature.[1] He did not believe (any more than we do now!) that an improved standard of life has a positive effect on the rate of population increase; as far as fertility is concerned the effect is more likely to be negative.[2] He did not believe in the law of decreasing returns on land as a historical, long-term law. And he finally makes the very appropriate point against Malthus' Law that its mechanism is much too slow to have practical importance.[3]

If this is not the reason for expecting real wages to remain behind as compared with the increase in productivity, what then is it? What is the specific Marxian theory of real wages?

In Chapter XXIII Marx puts the question squarely before us and analyses it.[4] Is an increase in real wages possible? What are its consequences? Yes, he says, an increase is possible, *if it does not interfere with the continuation of the process of accumulation.* If, on the other hand, it *does* interfere with the continued

[1] Critique of the Gotha Programme. Selected Works, Vol. II, p. 573. See also Engels' letter, *ibid.*, p. 589.

[2] *Das Kapital* I. XXIII, p. 678. Everyman, p. 711.

[3] *Das Kapital* I. XXIII, p. 672. Everyman, p. 704.

[4] *Das Kapital* I. XXIII, p. 651. Everyman, p. 683.

accumulation, then the accumulation is temporarily reduced, and this leads to greater unemployment, and this again brings about a pressure on real wages, which are thus in the long run brought back to a sort of equilibrium level.

This is the starting point of the analysis. It is to be noted that *a certain long-run rate of accumulation* has to be assumed as given here: 'The magnitude of accumulation is the independent variable, that of the wage is the dependent one, not the other way round.'[1] It follows then that the real wages in the long run must be *limited* in such a way as to leave over, out of the net product, enough for the capitalist to enable him (after allowing for his own consumption) to accumulate at the given long-term rate. 'The . . . law of capitalist accumulation says in fact only that *by its nature* accumulation excludes any decrease in the degree of exploitation, or any rise in the price of labour, such as could endanger seriously the steady reproduction of capital and its reproduction on a continuously expanding scale.'[2] In other words, the real wage must be low enough to enable the capitalists not only to reproduce their capital (to leave over a sufficient amount for depreciation) but also to enlarge it steadily. Again *a certain* (proportionate) *rate* of this enlargement has to be assumed, although this is not explicit in the last quotation.

We can see that Marx, after all, *has* a theory of the determination of real wages. It is based on the implicit assumption of a somehow given long-term rate of accumulation. This is in no way an illegitimate assumption. The question how this trend rate of accumulation is determined, can be left open (as Marx does leave it) as long as we may assume that it is to a large part determined by factors acting in the past. The assumption, of course, in no way implies that the trend rate of accumulation is constant, but only that it changes relatively slowly. In a modern interpretation, we would say that it is to a large extent deter-

[1] *Das Kapital* I, p. 652. Everyman, p. 684. It is clear from the context that this sentence refers to the long-run (trend) rate of accumulation, and the (average) long-run level of real wages.

[2] *Das Kapital* I, p. 652. Everyman, p. 684. To the 'degree of exploitation' corresponds, in modern literature, the concept of 'relative share of labour in the net product'. Reproduction on an expanding scale means simply positive net accumulation of capital 'Kapital verhältnis' is here rendered as 'capital'.

mined by the trend of capital accumulation in the past, which conveys a certain momentum to the present trend rate of accumulation, while other modifying factors act on it as well.[1]

What is the *mechanism* by which the long-run level of real wages is adjusted to the requirements of the given trend rate of accumulation? According to Marx the *actual* level of real wages deviates in the short run from the 'equilibrium level' which is compatible with the given trend rate of accumulation. These deviations lead to fluctuations of the *actual* rate of accumulation round the given trend level. (These are, in fact, identified by Marx with the trade cycle, although he gives also another, entirely unconnected explanation of the trade cycle – the re-investment theory). We can see that for the *short run* Marx postulates a relation which is completely contrary to that prevailing in the *long run*: namely that the real wage is the primary factor, and the rate of accumulation is determined by it. Real wages, in the short run, are determined by the degree of unemployment; the rate of capital accumulation, in turn, is determined by what is left over to the capitalist out of the net product at the given real wage.

The mechanism, then, works as follows: when real wages rise above the 'equilibrium' level, the rate of accumulation falls below its trend level: accumulation is slowed down. This leads to an increase in the degree of unemployment. The greater unemployment depresses the level of real wages; their fall leads to an increase in capital accumulation, which now rises above its trend level. At this stage we must suppose the fall in unemployment to raise the real wages again above their 'equilibrium' level, etc.

We are still far from a full explanation of the mechanism. But it should be stressed at this stage, that the *short run* relations are of completely different type from the long run relation postulated initially by Marx. Without disentangling the two it is impossible to get a clear understanding of Marx.

As we have seen, the mechanism depends on the influence of

[1] It may be suggested that all this means reading more into Marx's Chapter XXIII than there is. And that Marx only meant real wages must be such as to permit of *some* positive capital accumulation. without thinking of a certain rate of it. The further analysis will show that the more specific interpretation makes sense.

unemployment on real wages. We disregard for the moment the question whether this connection is realistic. To get the concept clear: what influences real wages according to Marx is the proportionate unemployment – the ratio of unemployed to employed.[1] The real wage is a function of the degree of unemployment. The question immediately arises whether we have to imagine this function to remain constant in the long run. Marx does not say anything about it. It would be plausible that, for example with the development of trade union strength, the real wage which corresponds to a certain relative unemployment might rise. We must leave the question open, but for simplification of the discussion we shall for the time being have to assume that the function remains constant.

If that is the case, it would seem that the above mechanism cannot work with every arbitrarily assumed trend rate of accumulation, but that the latter must bear a certain relation to the rate of population increase. To take the simplest case dealt with by Marx: the productivity of labour, the length of the working day and the intensity of labour are constant. The organic composition of capital (the ratio of capital invested to the wage bill) is also constant, and so is the division of the capitalist's share in saving and consumption. Then a constant proportionate rate of accumulation would require that the division of the product and therefore the real wage remains constant. But if the long-run average of the real wage is to remain unaltered, the relative unemployment – again, on the average – must also remain constant. It follows then that the proportionate rate of accumulation must be the same as the rate of population growth! And it would appear that the growth of population is the final datum in the system!

This impression is at once thoroughly corrected by Marx. First of all, it is not the growth of population which is relevant, but the growth of the industrial labour force. This is itself largely influenced by the process of accumulation. In a developing capitalist system, the rate of accumulation can easily exceed the growth of population, because the very process of accumulation will lead to dispossession of small proprietors, and bring new recruits into the army of industrial workers.

[1] *Das Kapital* I, XXIII, p. 671. Everyman, pp. 703–4.

Moreover, there is another even more important factor: *technological progress*. This implies that capital can grow at a greater rate than the labour force. Capital accumulation is in this way freed from the limitations of the available labour. Marx shows again that the process of technological improvements is itself influenced by the pace of accumulation of capital: if this exceeds the growth of the labour force, and relative unemployment therefore declines, a tendency for real wages to rise will set in. This brings about an endeavour on the side of capitalists to introduce labour-saving innovations. The accumulation of capital therefore creates by itself the relative abundance of labour necessary for its own continuation.

There is one special point to be cleared up in this context: a continuing process of technological progress, according to the above, would presuppose that the level of real wages is permanently higher than it would be otherwise. The corollary of this is a permanent decrease in the relative amount of unemployment; the industrial reserve army would thus have to be permanently smaller in a system with technical progress, because this is the very condition for the progress being kept going. But Marx, on the contrary, in one passage even maintains that relative unemployment will (or at least may) be *increased* owing to technological progress.[1] We are led to the conclusion that Marx did not think of technological progress as entirely regulated by the level of real wages. Once the process of innovations has started, it acquires its own momentum, becomes independent of the actual conditions of scarcity or abundance of labour, and sets free even more workers than necessary for the undisturbed continuation of the growth of capital.

It is now clear that the growth of population is not a primary force in the dynamic process envisaged by Marx: if the population growth does not keep pace with the growth of capital, the necessary labour is provided by dispropriation of small owners or by technological progress. The accumulation of capital remains the primary motive force. This is explicitly confirmed by Marx when he talks of 'the law which always keeps the relative surplus population or industrial reserve army in equilibrium with the extent and energy of accumulation'.[2] Now we are able

[1] *Das Kapital* I, XXIII, p. 679. Everyman, p. 712.
[2] *Das Kapital* I, XXIII, p. 680. Everyman, p. 714.

to vindicate the earlier statement, that the rate of capital accumulation *in the long run analysis* is the primary factor, which is
assumed as given: the real wages are determined by it. It is of
the utmost importance to disentangle this fundamental long-run
relation from the short-run analysis, in which, as we have seen
the connection is the other way round.

And now back to the original question: how does Marx arrive
at the conclusion that the relative share of labour in the net
product is bound to fall with the development of capitalism and
the progress of technology?

We shall show that this conclusion is entirely dependent on
the assumed increase in the 'organic composition of capital'. In
the process of technological improvements two things have to
be distinguished: the one is the increase in productivity, which
displaces labour, the other is the increase in the ratio of capital
invested to net product, or to wage bill. (What Marx calls
'organic composition of capital' corresponds to the ratio of
capital invested to wage bill; but in the following discussion we
prefer to work with the ratio of capital invested to net product.)

On a superficial reading it would seem that the productivity
effect of technical progress is alone sufficient for Marx to demonstrate the necessity for a constant pressure on real wages which
prevents them from sharing proportionately in the increase of
the net product. Take, however, a simple model: assume that
technological progress proceeds, involving a continuous increase
in net real output per worker employed, and that the ratio of
capital invested to net output remains constant. Net output and
capital invested therefore grow at the same rate, and this rate is,
on our assumptions, greater than the rate of growth of the labour
force employed (because net output per worker increases). Thus,
if we assume *a given trend rate of growth of capital*, the rate of
growth of employment must fall short of it; the difference will
be simply determined by the increase in productivity per unit
of time. This is the simple demonstration of the displacement
effect of technological progress, and it is based solely on the
assumption of a given trend rate of accumulation.[1]

[1] It may be argued that technical progress itself stimulates the
rate of accumulation, in so far as innovations raise the prospective
rate of profit for the firms which first introduce them (M. Kalecki,

The displacement of labour will first of all act so as to make it possible for capital accumulation, in the heyday of capitalism, to proceed much quicker than the growth of population. As has been said already, the technical progress acquires momentum and is carried on even though the industrial reserve army is more than abundant, thus producing increasing relative unemployment.

Marx argues that this displacement, by increasing the competition among workers and weakening their bargaining position, will press on real wages, thus preventing labour from sharing proportionately in the increase in real income per head. It can easily be seen, however, that this cannot be the whole argument. The increasing share of capital in the net product would necessarily have to go hand in hand with an increasing rate of accumulation – as long as the ratio of capital invested to net product is constant.[1] The increased rate of growth of capital – contradicting the initial assumption – would counteract the displacement, and destroy the validity of the whole argument.

It is thus essential to assume an increase in the ratio of capital invested to net product. If this is done, then the share of capital in the net product not only can, but must, increase *in order to permit the continuation of the given rate of accumulation.* We arrive at the final conclusion that Marx's prediction with regard to the course of real wages is in the last resort dependent on one crucial assumption: the increase in the ratio of capital to net output.

Marx has put this assumption in a slightly different form: his organic composition of capital, or ratio of constant to variable capital, seems to correspond really to the ratio of capital invested to the wage bill.[2] In this form the assumption is really not strict enough, because an increasing ratio of capital to wage bill need not imply an increasing ratio to net product (if the share of

---

The Trend, in *Studies in Economic Dynamics*). But technical progress is not necessarily of this type (as Kalecki points out). An example is the situation in the 1930s when a stimulating effect on investment was not at all apparent, while technical progress nevertheless expressed itself in a very marked increase in productivity.

[1] We are assuming, for simplicity's sake, that the division of capitalists' share in consumption and accumulation is constant.

[2] *Das Kapital* I. XXIII, p. 643. Everyman, p. 675.

wages in the product declines). But in spite of this awkwardness of definition – to which we come back in another context – the sense which Marx wanted to convey is almost certainly correctly interpreted in our formulation.

It is not without interest to note that the famous conclusion of Marx with regard to the secular development of the share of labour is dependent on this particular assumption. Modify this assumption, and the conclusion is different. It so happens that – as far as our evidence goes – both the assumption and the conclusion are not valid for the modern period of capitalism (that is, in America for example, since about 1900). The ratio of net business capital to national product does not seem to have increased at all since the first decade of the century. The data, it is true, are not at all reliable. But Marx certainly expected *very marked* changes, such as could not fail to show themselves even in fairly inaccurate statistics. Changes of this order of magnitude can be with some confidence excluded, as far as concerns the period covered by the data.

That the share of labour in the product does not show any marked tendency to fall in the later stages of capitalism has been shown by various statisticians. To take the case of American manufacturing industries: the share of wages in value added did not show any *spectacular* decline between 1899 and 1939 and, moreover, most of the decline occurred after 1923. The number of workers employed per unit of output decreased from 1899 to 1937 by 50 per cent (1·8 per cent per annum), that is, the cost in working days of a given output was halved.[1] In comparison with this increase in productivity, the decline in the share of wages in value added from 44 per cent in 1899 to 41 per cent in 1937 and 38 per cent in 1939 is certainly much smaller (only about 15 per cent). By and large it is true to say that the expectation of a *marked* fall in the share of labour is not realized in the 'mature' stage of capitalism. But it may have been quite different in earlier stages, especially in the period of hectic development during the 'industrial revolution'.

That the concrete conclusion of Marx is not applicable to the whole of the history of capitalism does not, however, necessarily

---

[1] S. Fabricant, *Employment in Manufacturing*.

reflect on his entire analysis. This has still to be examined on its own merits.

From the point of view of modern theory we run up against a formidable difficulty here. Keynesians have never had much use for this part of Marx's reasoning (the 'law of accumulation' contained in Chapter XXIII), because it assumes, at least for the short run mechanism, a dependence of real wages on the degree of unemployment. This assumption might perhaps be applicable in an open system. In a closed system, however, most economists would nowadays think it unrealistic. The degree of unemployment may well influence *money wages* here (although this relation is subject to considerable long-run changes, money wages becoming more resistant against the pressure of unemployment as trade union organization develops). But a general rise or fall in money wages would not necessarily and regularly affect the share of profits, because it is the capitalists who decide the 'mark-up' which is added on to wage costs in order to arrive at the price; it is quite plausible, at the least, that this percentage mark-up remains unaffected by changes in the general level of money wages. The best support for this modern view is the fact that the share of wages in the course of the trade cycle does not develop according to the pattern expected by Marx. The percentage gross profit margins show no cyclical dependence at all in American manufacturing as a whole,[1] even though money wages did rise in the boom and fall in the slump. The share of wages in the *net* income produced in manufacturing depends indeed on the cycle, but in a way quite contrary to Marx: it falls in the upswing and increases in the downswing.[2]

But the worst about the short-run analysis of Marx is this. By assuming that the degree of unemployment influences not only *gross profit margins*, but also net profits, and thus the *rate of profit*, he has run counter to the best established truth of Keynesian economics: namely that a given amount of profits can only materialize (assuming capitalists alone to be net savers) if there is a corresponding amount of net investment and capitalists' consumption. Marx assumed that the upward pressure of

[1] M. Kalecki, *Studies in Economic Dynamics*, p. 23.

[2] Kuznets, *National Income and its Composition*, 1919–38. Vol. I. Table 74, p. 358.

wages in the boom reduces the rate of profit and therefore discourages accumulation; and that the lowering of wages in the depression raises the profit rate and therefore gives a stimulus to accumulation. This is, of course, straightforward 'classical economics', a faulty reasoning from which Marx did not manage to detach himself completely, and which most other economists got rid of only in the comparatively recent past. The increase in wages could never reduce profits as long as investment (and capitalists' consumption) remain high; a fall in wages could never increase profits, unless investment first increased. In Marxian terms, we should say that surplus value (profits) in order to be obtained, must not only be 'produced' but also 'realized'.[1] And the realization, as the Marxian reproduction schemes show, can only take place if there is a corresponding amount of investment and capitalists' consumption.

The short-run analysis of Marx is therefore a relic of views which Marx would probably have completely discarded had he had the time to develop the under-consumption approach which is implicit in the later parts of his work.[2] But does the failure of the short-run analysis invalidate his long-run theory? This, as we have seen, is of a very different kind. Its basic idea shows a remarkable family resemblance to the type of thought which Keynesians apply to the short run: capital accumulation (investment) is here the primary motive force. Other factors are adjusted so as to make the given rate of capital accumulation possible. In the Keynesian short run theory, these 'other factors' are incomes, which rise or fall so as to provide just enough saving to finance the investment. In the Marxian long-run analysis the adjustment concerns the distribution of income between workers and capitalists (of which the former save nothing and the latter quite a lot): this distribution of incomes in the long run is adjusted in such a way as to provide just the necessary saving to finance the given trend rate of accumulation.

When Marx comes to demonstrate how this long-run adjustment works, he does however apparently rely on the unacceptable elements of his short-run analysis. His basic reasoning, as

---

[1] *Das Kapital* III, p. 272.

[2] See P. Sweezy, *The Theory of Capitalist Development*, Chapter X, 2, p. 162 *seq.*

we have seen, is this: the capitalists always manage to create enough unemployment (through technical progress) to keep real wages low enough to make the given rate of accumulation possible. The influence of unemployment on the distribution of the net product seems to be an unavoidable condition!

It is, however, possible to base the long-run theory of Marx on a different and firmer foundation. The alternative line of reasoning can be found in certain parts of Marx's own work, although he has never made it quite explicit.

When he discusses the question of real wages and of the distribution of the product, Marx says that it should be influenced by two factors: competition between workers, and competition between capitalists.[1] In the version analysed above, it is the competition between workers which does all the tricks. This version is not satisfactory. But what about the competition between capitalists? Is there a possible version which makes use of this idea?

It might look somewhat like this. Imagine there is a given trend rate of growth of capital. If the percentage gross profit margin is arbitrarily determined, then the requisite level of the rate of profit, which enables the capitalists to accumulate at the given rate, will be obtained by an adjustment of the degree of utilization of capacity.[2] If the gross profit margin is relatively low, for example, then the degree of utilization will be high. This high utilization, on the average over a longer period, might lead to a slackening of the competitive struggle between capitalists, who are always to a greater or lesser degree trying to push each other out by price-cutting. Owing to the lessening of the intensity of this struggle for markets, gross profit margins will increase. If, on the other hand, the gross profit margin is relatively high, then the degree of utilization must be low, that is, excess capacity will be great. This should lead to an intensified competition between capitalists, who are now more than usually intent on pushing each other out by price cutting. This will lead to a reduction of gross profit margins.

[1] Lohnarbeit und Kapital, p. 23. Selected Works, p. 262.
[2] This works only as long as it does not involve full use of capacity; in this case the gross profit margins even in the short run could not be assumed any more independently of the rate of investment (Kalecki).

It is by no means fantastic to suggest that Marx has actually thought on these lines or at least come very near to it. A passage in *Wage Labour and Capital* (an early work) shows it fairly clearly. In this passage Marx tries to explain how capital accumulation affects real wages. In dealing with the same question in *Kapital* (Vol. I) he would argue that accumulation might increase the demand for labour, and by reducing unemployment, might raise real wages, although this conclusion is considerably qualified by taking into account the displacement owing to technical progress. This is, then, the version of 'competition between workers'. In the passage in *Wage Labour and Capital* we get a glimpse of the alternative version:

'*How does the growth of productive capital affect wages?*'

'If on the whole the productive capital of bourgeois society grows, then *a more varied* accumulation of labour takes place. The capitals grow in number and extent. *The increase* in capitals increases the *competition among capitalists*.'[1]

And in the following passages Marx proceeds to describe this competition among capitalists as a struggle, in which some (those who have acquired cost advantages through introduction of new methods) endeavour to throw out others. He shows, further, that this struggle for markets can be carried out only by price cutting, and that it affects therefore the cost-price relation, the gross profit margin.

The result of this competitive struggle, according to Marx, is that the *increase* in (gross) *profit margins* acquired by certain capitalists, thanks to the introduction of new methods which cheapen production, *is counteracted*, and the level of profit margins is therefore reduced again.[2]

The idea of 'competition between capitalists' as a factor influencing the distribution of the product is clearly visible in these passages. It is clearly said that this competition is bound up with the process of concentration, the driving out of capitals which are in some sense 'surplus capital', in order to make room for the growth of the remaining capital.

The idea, it is true, has never been followed up by Marx. We

---

[1] Lohnarbeit und Kapital, p. 35. Selected Works, Vol. 1, p. 274 (Italics by Marx).

[2] See also *Kapital* I, X, p. 331–4. *Capital*, p. 330–3.

get a glimpse of a theory *in statu nascendi* but we are left with a great intellectual difficulty. The competition between capitalists is regulated by the relative abundance of capital. If there are more 'capitals', then they push each other harder for there is apparently some sort of restricted room in which they have to operate. But the long-run growth of capital, we know, does at the same time create the markets: the greater the investment, the capital accumulation, the greater the effective demand, the market. How can the growth of capitals then lead to greater competition of capitalists?

The riddle is only solved, if we think of the 'growth of capital' in the context of this sentence as a *potential*, not an *actual* one. The *actual* trend rate of growth of capital is determined by factors acting in the past, and it is this actual rate of growth which (given the capitalists' propensity to save) determines the growth of the market. This is therefore given. But if the gross profit margin rises, there is a *potential* growth of capital which cannot materialize and which expresses itself in reduced utilization: in this specific sense there is then a relative abundance of capital, which does not find sufficient room to operate. In Marxian terms: if the rate of exploitation rises, then there is more surplus value 'produced'. But without an increase in capital accumulation, this increased surplus value cannot be *realized* (as can be seen from the reproduction schemes). It is this *unrealized surplus value*, this merely *potential* accumulation, which brings about the competitive struggle between capitalists, and thus reduces again the rate of exploitation.

It is quite another story that the whole mechanism of competition between capitalists, as described by Marx, is not an absolute law of capitalism, equally valid at all times. Its importance, on the contrary, changes in the course of historical development. The growth of oligopoly in the 'mature' stage of capitalism restricts the validity of this mechanism of competition more and more, because oligopolists are less keen to push each other out. It requires consequently a modification of the analysis, if the later stages of capitalism are to be dealt with realistically. To this we shall soon come back.

### 3. THE DECLINING RATE OF PROFIT

It is an inherent law of capitalism, according to Marx, that the rate of profit should have a tendency to decline. This tendency depends entirely on one assumption, the rise in *organic composition of capital*. This can best be defined, in accounting terms, as the ratio of capital invested to the wage bill. Marx shows, in the first stage, that if, in relation to a given wage bill, capitalists' profits do not rise, but the invested capital does increase, then the rate of profit falls. In the subsequent pages, Marx fully admits that the profits made in relation to a given wage bill can rise (and even will rise) with the increase in productivity in the course of development of capitalism. He nevertheless asserts fairly definitely that this rise in the share of capitalists cannot hold up the tendency for the rate of profit to fall.

Critics have pointed out that Marx has not given any logical proof to justify his position. Strictly speaking this is true. The ratio of capital invested to the wage bill can theoretically rise without limits, but so can the ratio of profits to the wage bill. It is not without interest, however, to point out that Marx could have obtained a logical proof without difficulty if he had chosen a different concept of the 'organic composition'. If, instead of his definition, we take the *ratio of capital invested to the net product*, then the matter becomes immediately obvious: this ratio can, theoretically, still increase without limits. The ratio of profits in the net product, however, can rise only by a certain maximum factor: assuming for example that it was originally 50 per cent, it could at best only be doubled. As the rate of profit is the ratio of profits in the net product divided by the ratio of capital to the net product, the proposition follows: with the increase of capital in relation to a given net product, the profit rate must necessarily decline sooner or later.

With Marx this reasoning must have been at the back of his mind and explains the tenacity of his conviction. It becomes clear only in the following quotation (which is badly worded, and like the whole part of the work shows all the signs of being a mere sketchy draft):

'In so far as the development of productivity diminishes the portion of labour which is paid, it increases the surplus value, because it increases its rate; in so far, however, as it reduces the *total quantity of labour employed by a given capital,* it reduces the factor by which you have to multiply the rate of surplus value, in order to obtain its mass. Two workers who work twelve hours each cannot, even if they could live on nothing and therefore did not have to work for themselves at all, produce the same mass of surplus value as 24 workers who work only 2 hours each. In this respect, then, the compensation of a diminished number of workers by an increased rate of exploitation of labour has certain limits beyond which it cannot go; it can therefore retard the fall of the profit rate, but it cannot stop it.'[1]

The concrete example given has only one interpretation: a given amount of capital[2] employs at first 24 workers (who presumably work twelve hours a day) and produce each 2 hours surplus value a day. After a fundamental change in technical methods, the same amount of capital employs only 2 workers; even if these 2 workers, working 12 hours a day, require no payment at all, and thus produce 12 hours surplus value a day, their total mass of surplus value – 24 hours – is less than the mass of surplus value produced formerly for the same capital, namely 48 hours.

It is obvious that Marx has inadvertently changed his definitions here: for the rate of surplus value, in the above passage, we have to read 'ratio of unpaid labour time to total labour time' (as opposed to his usual definition: ratio of unpaid to paid labour time). And instead of the usual 'organic composition of capital' (ratio of capital invested to paid labour) we are plainly referred to the ratio of capital invested to the *total* hours of living labour used together with this capital. It follows then logically that an increase in capital in relation to labour employed cannot be compensated beyond a certain point by an increase in the amount of unpaid labour per worker.

Thus for the logic of the argument. The empirical hypothesis on which it is built is not as realistic as Marx doubtless expected. In mature capitalism the ratio of capital to net product quite

---

[1] *Das Kapital* III, 15, p. 275–6. *Capital,* Vol. III (Kerr), p. 290 (Italics by myself.)

[2] This is measured, of course, in terms of *labour hours* used up in its production ('frozen labour').

probably does not increase at all. This is partly because the ratio of *net* capital (which is what matters for the computation of the rate of profit) is not only influenced by the technique of production, and the relative cheapness of capital goods, but also by the *age structure*. But even apart from that there seem to be new tendencies in the development of the technical structure which operate in a direction quite opposite to the increase in 'organic composition': in certain cases, at least, the tendency to employ less (gross) capital in proportion to a given output has been demonstrated.[1] Whatever the uncertainty and doubt about the evidence concerning the development of the capital/output ratio, one conclusion seems safe: the increase, if any, cannot have been of the order of magnitude required to make the law practically relevant. This applies fully to the modern stage of capitalism. But even for the earlier stages it is doubtful whether the increase in the capital/output ratio was of such an order of magnitude as to be important in this context.

The chief question about the law of the declining rate of profit, however, is this: do we have to conceive of this tendency as an *actual* fall in the rate of profit, which *in fact* takes place as a consequence of the change in capital-structure? If the law is understood that way, then it is in contradiction to the best modern economics (and with that also to the whole under-consumption approach which, as Sweezy showed, is contained in the work of Marx itself). The amount of profits realized is entirely determined by the amount which capitalists invest and consume (assuming that wage earners do not save, but only capitalists save). As long as the sum of capitalists' consumption and investment, as a ratio of their capital, does not decrease, the rate of profit *can never decrease*. The consequence of a steadily increasing ratio of capital to (planned) output, under these circumstances, will be simply this: the degree of utilization will continuously rise, and the system will finally plunge headlong into inflation. Needless to say, in peacetime capitalism there has never been any sign of that.

The alternative interpretation of the law of the declining rate

[1] D. Weintraub, 'Effects of Current and Prospective Technological Developments upon Capital Formation'. *American Economic Review*, 1939.

of profit is this: we may conceive it as a *potential* tendency, which is never realized, but may none the less be important. We should say then that the capitalists do not, in fact, carry out certain possible changes in the capital structure, because they would lead to a decline in the rate of profit. By thus refraining from making production more capital-intensive, they do of course invest less than they otherwise might, and this is obviously of practical consequence.

It has been demonstrated that individual capitalists, when they consider the introduction of new methods which cheapen production, but raise the ratio of capital to output, may find that the use of these methods would involve a reduction in their rate of profit. This result is the more likely, the greater their net profit margin is to start with.[1] (In a popular fashion this may be expressed simply as follows: if the net profit or the surplus value happens to be a small proportion of the output or value produced, say 10 per cent, there is more room for the proportionate increase in this fraction, than there is if the proportion is, say, 50 per cent to start with. An increase in the ratio of capital to output with constant profit rate is relatively easier in the first case than in the second. A doubling of this capital/output ratio, for example, in the first case would require an increase of the share of net profit in the output to 20 per cent to leave the rate of profit unchanged. In the second case the same result could hardly be achieved at all, because the profit would have to swallow up the whole product.)

The law of the declining rate of profit may therefore be of great practical relevance for the individual capitalist, as long as he considers at all capital-intensive methods of cheapening production. It is true to say that a decline of the rate of profit on this account may easily prevent him from adopting such methods. This is, firstly, because he will not invest at all at a rate of profit below a certain level. And secondly, because there may be other possibilities for investment which do not involve a decline in the profit rate; he may, for example, use technical methods of cheapening production which do not involve greater relative use of capital, or he may concentrate on cheapening

[1] Cf. *Big and Small Business*. Economic Problems of the Size of Firms. Chapter III.

purchase or distribution by large-scale methods, or use all his means to acquire quasi-monopolistic positions, etc.

How far the law of the declining profit rate, in the sense just explained, has operated in the course of capitalist history to restrict the adoption of capital-intensive methods which would theoretically have been available, it is hard to judge. The problem might be relevant for the question of the mature economy, if it could be shown that 'capital-intensification' had been of great importance in earlier stages of capitalism. But it may be thought that other more obvious factors are of much greater importance for the problems of economic maturity.

## 4. UNDER-CONSUMPTION AND THE CRISIS OF CAPITALISM

Marx foresaw that, in one way or another, but for reasons inevitably bound up with its own inherent development, capitalism would function less and less well as it developed. Its disadvantages would grow and more and more outweigh its positive achievements (which Marx never denied). The troubles, or illnesses, which it would develop would finally lead, or at least contribute, to its downfall.

What precisely the nature of these troubles are, and why they should inevitably develop, Marx did not satisfactorily explain. He had various ideas on this score, but they remained in an unfinished state. P. Sweezy has admirably shown that there are two main alternative explanations of the 'capitalist crisis' in Marx, the law of the declining rate of profit and the under-consumption approach. What Sweezy has to say on this subject makes it superfluous to add anything more here.[1] Briefly speaking he regards the first approach – via the 'declining rate of profit' – as not promising, and sees in the second – the under-consumption approach – the basis from which a satisfactory explanation could be developed. His reasons for this view are only too convincing.

Sweezy has also attempted to construct himself the rough outlines of a logically consistent explanation of the capitalist crisis, based on the under-consumption idea. It is this explanation which calls for comment.

[1] Cf. *The Theory of Capitalist Development*, Chapter X.

His basic assumptions can be easily seen from the rigid mathematical demonstration of the argument.[1] In his simple model the national income is defined as the sum of (1) wages (which are equal to workers' consumption), (2) capitalists' consumption, and (3) investment. It is assumed that while the national income rises steadily, both wages and capitalists' consumption increase less quickly than investment. The consequence is that investment in relation to total consumption must rise continuously.

This result is based on the following reasons: the first reason is that capitalists will tend to accumulate a greater and greater proportion of their surplus, and consume a correspondingly lesser and lesser proportion (Sweezy, *op. cit.*, p. 181). The second reason is logically confused.[2] The third reason is not stated

---

[1] Sweezy, *op. cit.* Appendix to Chapter X, p. 186, *seq.*

[2] Sweezy introduces here an exceedingly puzzling distinction between *investment* and *accumulation*: 'accumulation' is the part of the surplus value which is not consumed by the capitalists. *A part of accumulation* is laid out by the capitalist in the purchase of additional raw materials and capital goods and therefore adds to the stock of constant capital (machines, buildings, inventories). This is called 'investment'. The other part of accumulation is laid out in additional wages (and therefore consumed by the workers). This part, according to Sweezy, is not 'investment', although it is 'accumulation', and Sweezy blames the Keynesians for not appreciating this distinction.

The reproach is hardly fair, because Sweezy's distinction is illogical. It implies that some part of his national income flow is *wages*, and at the same time is also *surplus value* (profits) *in the same period*; that some part of the value created *in a given year* is unpaid labour and at the same time also paid labour! No doubt, this unfortunate terminology has its roots in Marx. In fact, it is nothing but a relic of that weird old monster, the wages fund doctrine, which Marx killed in a brilliant attack, only to permit its ghost to muddle up his terminology! There is no reason nowadays, even for a Marxist, to preserve the remains of that fossil out of mere piety.

The assumption in which Sweezy uses the distinction is this: that 'investment' increases in proportion to total 'accumulation'. Together with the first assumption, that accumulation rises as a proportion of surplus value, this should lead to the result that investment rises in proportion to national income (according to the

explicitly, although one has the feeling that it is somehow present in the background. In any case it is a *necessary* reason: namely that surplus value is rising, or at least constant as a proportion of the national income.

Disregarding the second reason, we find that the first and the third yield the result in a perfectly natural way: if we define the sum of investment and capitalists' consumption (contrary to Sweezy, but correctly) as *profits*, or *surplus value*, and assume (*a*) that investment as a proportion of surplus value increases, and (*b*) that the surplus value as a proportion of national income *does not decrease*, then it follows at once that investment increases in proportion to national income and total consumption. Sweezy does not choose to put the argument that way, but it is in point of fact a reasonable interpretation of his algebraically defined assumption.

The further hypothesis which is needed to complete the model is this: if consumption increases by a given amount, then the capital stock must increase by a given and constant amount, assuming full utilization. This amounts to the same as the well-known 'acceleration principle'.

On the basis of these assumptions Sweezy is able to demonstrate 'under-consumption' in the case of a constant or declining rate of increase of national income. The gist of this demonstration might perhaps be rendered verbally as follows: as long as the national income rises at a constant rate, or a declining one, the capital stock should also rise at a constant rate, or even only at a declining rate, to assure full utilization. But a continuous rise in national income involves a rise in surplus value, and *a fortiori* a rise in the rate of investment. Now a rise in the rate of investment, of course, implies that the capital stock will not grow in a linear fashion, but *at an increasing rate:* which clearly cannot be reconciled with the requirement of full utilization.

---

argument in the text, p. 181). It does not yield this result, however, unless we assume something about the proportion of surplus value in the national income! The text (p. 181) gives almost the impression that Sweezy did assume surplus value to rise in proportion to national income ('making as much profit as possible'), but he does not state it explicitly. Once we make this assumption of increasing or even constant surplus value in relation to wages, the whole of the argument about accumulation and investment becomes superfluous!

The argument shows that a discrepancy between consumption and the production capacity must necessarily arise, a discrepancy which most probably would show itself in under-utilization of capacity.

The demonstration of Sweezy, as he himself stresses, does not necessarily hold in the case where the national income rises at an increasing rate. It should be possible, however, to prove it also for the case of a constant logarithmic growth of the capital stock, and thus make it yield a more widely applicable conclusion.

As the theory stands, there is, however, a snag in it. It presupposes a secular increase in the ratio of investment to consumption. The evidence of Kuznets' data does not confirm this assumption, and it is almost certainly not realistic. It is also very unlikely that capitalists' saving as a ratio of their income actually increased in the later stages of capitalist development. It is again unlikely that capitalists' income in relation to wages actually increased. The decrease in the rate of growth of capital in the mature economy and the concomitant decrease in the rate of profit tend to bring about a decline in the share of profits in incomes, and a decline in the share of capitalists' savings in profits.

To take account of the realities of the situation the under-consumption theory needs a different re-interpretation. If we think of it, the tendency for the capitalists' share in the product to increase does, after all, exist *potentially*. It is a consequence of the growth of oligopoly. The expression of this tendency can only be an *increase in the gross profit margins*. That means that the actual share of *net* incomes of capitalists need not increase at all. The increased gross profit margins may be compensated by a reduced degree of utilization, so that there is not a shift of actual income from wages to profits, but a shift of potential income of workers to wastage in excess capacity.

This could be very easily represented in Marxian terms. We should have to say that as a consequence of the rise of oligopoly, the rate of *surplus value produced* tends to increase: the rate of exploitation rises. But as Marx explained, producing surplus value does not necessarily mean realizing it, and the realization depends on the existence of a sufficient market. We should now say that surplus value can be realized only to the extent to which there is a corresponding amount of investment and capitalists' consumption. If this amount does not increase, then the rise in the rate of surplus value *produced* will not lead to any increase in surplus value *realized*, but only to excess capacity.

This has been described already above in connection with the 'law of accumulation'. It was shown there that the excess capacity might lead to an intensified competition between capitalists, and that should tend to bring the rate of 'surplus value produced' down again. To this a modification has to be added now: with the growth of oligopoly, the competition between capitalists works less and less well, and the excess capacity can persist long without leading to the forcible ejection of superfluous capital. The excess capacity remaining, it exerts then a depressing influence on the investment decisions of capitalists, and the rate of growth of capital slows down.

We can see that the appearance of a *'surplus value produced'* which is not correspondingly *'realized'* is capable of fulfilling the function of an under-consumption theory. It is not open to objections on realistic grounds. It can be perfectly well reconciled with the fact that 'surplus value realized', or net profits, actually decline as a ratio of wages. It does not even require that surplus value produced, which we might tentatively identify with the gross profit margin, should continuously rise: because the mechanism of competition between capitalists, which tends to reduce this margin, may still be working, although with much delay. It is then possible that, as the decline in capital accumulation is set in motion and proceeds, the pressure of excess capacity will bring about subsequently some reduction in gross profit margins, but this reduction will be sluggish, just enough perhaps to prevent a continuous rise in excess capacity, but not enough to eliminate the excess capacity created at the outset by the original rise in profit margins.

We may, then, observe a constancy or even fall of gross profit margins in a mature economy, and nevertheless, with the decline in the growth of capital, the gross profit margins may all the time be too high to permit a 'normal' utilization of capacity. There will therefore all the time be under-consumption, expressed solely in an abnormal degree of excess capacity which will continuously react on capital accumulation in an adverse way.

The details of this theory do not need to be gone into here, as they have been discussed in earlier sections of this book. It is of interest, however, to show that this theory can be organically developed out of the underconsumption approach of Marx. It requires a few additional concepts and hypotheses, especially the effect of excess capacity on accumulation, but basically it rests on the idea of a production of surplus value which is not realized, and this happens to be the way in which Marx literally formulated the underconsumption approach.

## SELECTED BIBLIOGRAPHY

BARAN, P. *The Political Economy of Growth.* Monthly Review, 1957.

COONTZ, S. *Productive Labour and Effective Demand.* London: Routledge, Kegan Paul, 1965.

FELLNER, W. J. 'Marxian Hypotheses and Observable Trends under Capitalism: A "Modernized" Interpretation', *Economic Journal.* March, 1957.

KALDOR, N. 'Capitalist Evolution in the Light of Keynesian Economics', *Essays on Economic Stability and Growth.* London: Duckworth, 1960.

MATTICK, P. 'Value Theory and Capital Accumulation', *Science and Society:* Vol. XXIII, No. 1, 1959.

# Social Imbalance and the Marxian System[1]

*James F. Becker*

> 'It is true: I earn my living
> But, believe me, it is only an accident.
> Nothing that I do entitles me to eat my fill.'

BERTOLD BRECHT

AMONG THE principal theoretical systems of contemporary economics, Marx's is still to be numbered. True, it is not preferred by the majority, yet there are men of talent and integrity who rely upon it and whose work is not readily dismissed. Nor do most Western economists find the system flexible and viable; yet economists elsewhere swear by it and presumably not all of them are blind. In addition, there is a certain logical overlapping of Marxian conceptions and laws with neo-classical categories, as with the theories of income and employment and input–output relationships.[2] When, therefore, there is some new phenomenon that we wish to explain, or some old one that we wish to explain anew, it may be well to approach Marx's system pragmatically and without preconceptions as to its explanatory powers. How far can we push its categories and premises before they fail us? Where does the theory fall short of our requirements? We must 'look and see'.

We wish to test its explanatory faculties on the phenomenon of social imbalance, by which we mean an observable tendency to secular distortion in the allocation of social resources. This definition of social imbalance is peculiar in two respects. First, it implies that imbalance is something more than a simple mis-

[1] The author is grateful for criticism and clarification offered by Frederick Schiller.

[2] On the formal similarities of Marx's theory to the theory of income and employment see Lawrence Klein, 'Theories of Effective Demand and Employment' in: *Journal of Political Economy*, April 1947, p. 118. (See p. 152 in this volume.) On the relationship of input–output analysis to Marx's theories of simple and extended reproduction, see Oskar Lange, *Introduction to Econometrics*, Pergamon Press, New York, 1959, Ch. III, 'The Theory of Programming', pp. 206–29.

Reprinted from *Kyklos*, Vol. XV, 1962.

allocation of resources. It is one thing to make the static assertion that there is a resource misallocation; it is another to assume
that there are secular forces that not only produce but intensify
the degree of misallocation. Neo-classical competitive theory
admits a static conception of imbalance, defining and to some
extent describing a 'resource misallocation'. Moreover, a
Pigovian analysis of the nature of secondary and indirect costs
and benefits can be invoked in order to explain discrepancies
between observed allocations and an ideal equality between
marginal social costs and revenues. To date, however, the orthodox analysis does not concede a chronic tendency away from an
ideal allocational equilibrium, just as, at one time, it did not
concede a tendency to less than full employment equilibrium.
But what of the Marxian theory? Can it predict an increasing
degree of resource misallocation?

Second, our definition does not specify the standards with
reference to which one justifies talk of distortion, although it
assumes that they are definable and relevant. This is as it should
be. Any definitional statement must be broad enough to allow
for the fact that those who seek to explain such a phenomenon
may bring quite different moral or aesthetic standards to bear
upon the issue. One thinks of Malthus, De Quincey, Marx,
Hobson, Veblen, and others, all of whom testify to the possibility of more or less powerful secular forces of allocational dis-
order under capitalism. It is probably fair to say that all would
understand what is meant by the assertion that there is some
observable tendency to secular distortion, though they might
disagree both as to its character and causes.

Marx would undoubtedly have said yes to the question of
whether or not there is an eccentric and chronic bias in capitalist
allocations:

'The capitalist mode of production, while on the one hand,
enforcing economy in each individual business, on the other
hand, begets by its anarchical system of competition, the most
outrageous squandering of labour–power and of the social
means of production, not to mention the creation of a vast
number of employments, at present indispensable, but in
themselves superfluous.'[1]

[1] *Capital*, Vol. I, Moscow, 1959, p. 530.

On what theoretical grounds does he assert that there is progressive social squandering, and do these grounds suffice for such claims? Before coming directly to our reconstruction of the Marxian account, it may be well to describe the focal point of endeavour still more precisely.

An attempt has recently been made to deal with the question of social imbalance in Marxian terms. Employing Marxian categories, Joseph Gillman has devised an ingenious test for the Marxian law of the falling rate of profit for manufacturing industries (roughly, the realm of material productivity in the Marxian value scheme).[1] Using Census Bureau and other conventional data, Gillman discloses a rising proportion of unproductive to total expenses in this sector, especially from 1919 to 1939. These relatively increasing 'expenses of circulation' – 'unproductive' expenses which the 'productive' capitalist must assume in order to circulate or sell his product, for example expenses of advertising, administration, and the support of essentially sales-promotive activities of government – cause the 'general' rate of profit to fall when they are incorporated into the Marxian profit formula.

Traditionally, the Marxian profit formula is written:

$$P = \frac{S}{C+V} \text{ or } P = \frac{S/V}{C/(V+1)}$$

Gillman argues most cogently, if not conclusively, that both Marxian theory and the facts of recent economic history justify a rewriting of the Marxian formula in the form, $P = S-U/C+V+U$, i.e. the rate of profit is equal to surplus value minus unproductive expenses of circulation divided by the sum of constant and variable capital and these same unproductive expenses. To repeat, the expenses of circulation, $U$, are expenditures which are required for the 'realization' of surplus value in the form of profits by the capitalist. Gillman's revised formula simply asserts that these 'unproductive' expenses of circulation are of importance relative to the rate of profit, on the one side, and the capitalist's investments in constant and variable capital on the other. From the capitalist's point of view, the 'investment' in unproductive expenses of circulation may be quite as necessary

[1] *The Falling Rate of Profit*, Dennis Dobson, London, 1957.

to the realization of a profit as his investment in productive constant and variable capitals – hence $U$ in the denominator. Yet these very expenditures constitute a drain on productive labour, i.e. they represent an allocation of constant and variable capitals into unproductive lines – hence the $U$ in the numerator.[1]

The augmented profit formula merely exposes another of the contradictions of capitalism. In order to expand sales, capitalists are led to increase their $U$-outlays. This has the unfortunate effect of causing the general rate of profit to fall. This decline intensifies unproductive efforts to enlarge sales and revenues, and so on. The tendency in mature capitalism for resources to be allocated progressively into unproductive lines is simply a by-product of the struggle of individual capitalists to get around the decline in the general rate of profit.

This is Gillman's argument and he contends that the empirical data reveal a relative increase in unproductive allocations since the time of the First World War. *Whether or not* one takes his data as indicating an unmistakable trend, the *explanation* of imbalance is still at issue. Does the Marxian explanation suffice, or is $U$ an 'unexplained' variable within the Marxian system? Is $U$ merely a *deus ex machina* dragged into the Marxian profit formula in order to salvage it from disconfirmation by the data? This latter, it must be noted, is also a possibility, for on Gillman's own showing the traditional profit formula fails to predict a falling general rate of profit when put to the statistical test for the period after 1919. If – as so many do – we see signs of

[1] For the purpose of statistical testing, Gillman modifies still further the formula for the general rate of profit in order to make available United States data accord with Marxian categories. Thus the difficulties of measuring constant capital consumed in production, as required by the traditional formula, lead him to pose the question: what is the equivalent of the traditional formula when we can only measure $C$ on the basis of capital *invested* in, rather than *consumed* in, the process of production? He finds that the modified testing formula must be $P = S-U/C'$, where $C'$ is the *stock* of invested constant capital, i.e. the value of plant and equipment (net of depreciation) plus value of the materials inventory. This is the formula that he utilizes in tracing the decline in the general rate of profit from 1919 to 1939 on annual data. Prior to 1919, he discovers, the general rate of profit declines without allowing for an increasing $U$. Cf. Gillman, *ibid.*, p. 45, n. 2, and *passim*.

imbalance, how do we explain them? How far can we rely upon Marx?

Except in very general terms, Marx did not explicitly predict a secular unproductive bias in the composing of the national output, yet it is hard to believe that a lop-sided evolution of the economy would have caused him any surprise. His two basic categories of productive and unproductive labour, derived, of course, from the classical economics, provide a general basis for such an expectation, and it is from this that he draws an operational line between labour engaged in material, industrial production, including transportation, and all other labour, whether engaged in commercial, financial or distributive enterprises. All labour engaged in circulation, aimed at the realization by sale of the value of commodities of productive labour, falls into the unproductive category:

> 'The general law is that all costs of circulation which arise only from changes in the forms of commodities do not add to their value. They are merely expenses incurred in the realization of the value or in its conversion from one form into another ... They must be replaced from the surplus product and constitute, as far as the entire capitalist class is concerned, a deduction from the surplus-value of surplus product, just as the time a labourer needs for the purchase of his means of subsistence is lost time.'[1]

Within this general class of unproductive expenses ($U$), Marx identifies a sub-class of expenses which are economically quite necessary, such as the expense of supporting the labourer while he purchases his means of subsistence. Call this class $U'$. $U'$ will

---

[1] *Capital*, Moscow, 1959, Vol. II, p. 149. All expenses of circulation are drawn from 'merchant's capital' which includes expenses of wholesaling and retailing ('commercial capital') and finance ('money-dealing capital'). Marx admits the essentiality of some portion of these: 'They are necessary, these unproductive expenses of social wealth. They are the cost of preserving the social product ...' *ibid.*, p. 145.

include all unproductive but necessary expenses of circulation aimed at the realization of use values, and on this basis he places some portion of what he calls 'merchant's capital', capital engaged in commerce, credit and finance, into the $U'$ sub-class.

Within the class $U$ there is another sub-class, a category of sheer waste, $W$, which can be subdivided into two segments. The first compartment (call it $W'$) includes all expenses of circulation that are the institutional peculiarity of the capitalist mode of economic organization, comprehending capitals engaged in speculative activity, whether in commerce or finance, along with the bulk of what the 'orthodox' economics today identifies as 'selling costs'. As is well known, Marx took no great care in specifying operationally the boundary line between $U'$ and $W'$, a source of much confusion and disputation among later Marxists.

Finally, under $W$, we have the class of capitals engaged in the production of luxury goods, $L$, destined for support of the capitalist classes.[1] Thus the Marxian total of unproductive expenses, $U$, is defined as $U'+W$, or, $U \equiv U'+W'+L$. These are the sectors among which he distributed 'real world' lines of economic activity. Within this conceptual framework a law of increasing unproductive expense can be defined.

Turning now to this quest, we find a clue as to how Marx might have proceeded in an interesting passage in which he perceives a breaking off of the function of circulating commodities – the primary task of merchant's capital – into a specialized branch of the economy, separate from the productive sector. This breaking off follows upon the achievement of a certain scale of industrial production:

'The capitalist producer of commodities acting as an agent of circulation differs from the direct producer of commodities only in the fact that he buys and sells on a larger scale and therefore his function as such an agent assumes greater dimensions. *And if the volume of his business compels or enables him to buy [hire] circulation agents of his own to serve as wage-labourers, the nature of the case is not changed thereby* . . .

[1] Marx disagreed with Malthus that these goods could be counted as unproductive but necessary items in the social budget.

It is as though one part of the product were transformed into a machine which buys and sells the rest of the product.'[1]

He associates the growth of $U$ with increasing scales of production, an association expressed at other points in *Capital* as well.[2] However, it is of particular significance that Marx is apparently uncertain as to whether or not the enlargement of scales necessitates a growth (relative?) of $U$, or whether it merely facilitates this growth. This uncertainty, if it is that, is revealed by his use of two verbs, 'compels' and 'enables' in the passage cited. Surely the former implies a lack of entrepreneurial choice and the possible existence of some law of an expanding $U$, while the latter suggests the presence of an entrepreneurial option. Is there law? Whim? or only accident?

It is tempting to say that this extraordinary ambiguity demonstrates that Marx was at an impasse, that he was shying away from something that he knew that his theory could not explain and which therefore called for a slippery bit of semantics. It is possible that the sceptic would be right, but there is another possibility. He may have been saying, albeit in a peculiar manner, that since all scientific laws are conditional a growth of $U$ occurs only under certain conditions ('compels or enables', where 'or' is disjunctive), the most important condition being that scales of production should be increasing. He did not extrapolate and predict a growth of $U$ because this occurrence seemed unlikely at that particular juncture in the development of capitalism.[3] Let us consider the second hypothesis.

Assume that the capitalist accumulates capital, that his scale of production is increasing. At the outset of a period of reproduction (the interval required for the production of a commodity plus the time required for its circulation), the capitalist advances a total capital of $c+v$ and, at the close of the period, realizes this original capital plus a surplus product, $s$, from the sale of the product. Call the portion of his revenues deriving from the sale of the surplus product $m$ ('potential money capital'), and assume

---

[1] *ibid.*, pp. 132–3. My italics.

[2] See *ibid.*, Vol. III, p. 175, and Ch. XX, 'Historical Facts about Merchant's Capital', *passim*.

[3] This is Gillman's explanation.

that the whole of $m$ is reinvested in the second period of reproduction along with that portion of his realized capital represented by $c+v$. His total invested capital is now larger by $s$ ($= m$) than it was at the outset and thus the capitalist is 'enabled' or 'compelled' to devote some portion of the additional capital, $m$, to unproductive purposes. Since his 'scale of production' is larger than it was in the first period, it is certainly conceivable that some portion of the $m$ should go for $u$-purposes, even for those purposes other than providing luxury goods for himself which is, presumably, always the fate of some portion of $m$.[1]

We can now define a law of relatively increasing unproductive expenses that refers to successive periods of reproduction for each and all capitalists whose scales of production are increasing from one period to the next. The productive sector comprehends a certain number of producing units, enterprises, $i$, numbered 1, 2, ..., $n$. There will also be a certain number of successive reproduction periods, $j$, numbered 1, 2, ..., $n$. Then for an individual producer let:

$m_{11}$ represent the $s$ realized in the first reproduction period by producer number 1 in its form of money capital the whole of which we assume to be reinvested (the first subscript denotes the number of the producer, the second the number of the reproduction period).

$u_{11}$ represent the portion of $m_{11}$ going to unproductive expenses of all kinds ($u'+w'+l$), following upon the close of the first period of reproduction.

$m_{12}$ represent the $s$ realized by producer number one in the second period of reproduction. This is the source of his $m$ for the second period.

$u_{12}$ represent the portion of $m_{12}$ going to unproductive expenses following upon the close of the second reproduction period.

$m_1 j$ represent the $s$ realized in the last reproduction period considered reinvested, as always, en toto.

$u_1 j$ represent the portion of $m_1 j$ going for unproductive

[1] The assumption that $s = m$ and that the whole of the recovered capital is reinvested in the second and each successive reproduction period is essential in order to allow us to abstract from problems of instability and unemployment that would otherwise intrude.

purposes following upon the close of the final period of reproduction.

With this notation we can state a law of increasing (relative) $u$ for the case of the single producer, producer number 1:

$$u_{11}/m_{11} < u_{12}/m_{12} < \ldots < u_1j/m_1j \qquad \ldots (1)$$

which says that the ratio of the unproductive expenses of all kinds to the new net reinvested increments of realized money capital grows progressively larger from one reproduction period to the next. If one wishes to assert that there is a progressive growth of waste ($w$) with this growing scale of production, it must be shown that $w$ bears some fixed proportion to $u$. In any case, a relative ascendancy of $u$ is the minimal condition to be satisfied if it is to be argued that unnecessary and unproductive expenditures undergo a relative growth with the evolution of the scale of the enterprise. Equation No. 1 must first be satisfied so long as it is assumed that all unproductive labour derives its sustenance from productive labour or, in other words, that all unproductive product derives from the surplus product of productive labour.

If there is a general law of increasing relative expenses of circulation, it must apply to the economy as a whole which is simply the aggregate of the $u$'s and $m$'s of the individual producers. A law can be defined for the economy as a whole as follows. Assume that periods of reproduction are similar for all producers. Then, during period of reproduction number one, the sum of the $u$'s gives us the aggregate of unproductive expenses for all producers, that is:

$$U_1 = \underset{j-1}{\Sigma u_{i1}}, \qquad (i = 1, 2, \ldots, n) \quad \ldots (2)$$

Similarly, the aggregate of the $m$'s for the first period of reproduction will be:

$$M_1 = \underset{j-1}{\Sigma m_{i1}}, \qquad (i = 1, 2, \ldots, n) \quad \ldots (3)$$

And the ratio of $U_1$ to $M_1$, of the aggregate of unproductive expenses of circulation to the aggregate net reinvested money-capital in the first reproduction period, may be stated:

$$U_1/M_1 = \underset{j-1}{\Sigma u_{i1}}/\underset{j-1}{\Sigma m_{i1}} \qquad (i = 1, 2, \ldots, n) \quad \ldots (4)$$

For each successive period of reproduction a similar ratio can be defined, e.g. for the second period:

$$U_2/M_2 = \sum_{j-2} u_{i2} / \sum_{j-2} m_{i2} \qquad (i = 1, 2, \ldots, n) \qquad \ldots (5)$$

and so on for each period of reproduction. Hence a general law for increasing relative unproductive expenses of circulation can be stated:

$$U_1/M_1 < U_2/M_2 < \ldots < U_j/M_j, \qquad \ldots (6)$$

which asserts that growing relative unproductive expenses are a general phenomenon of capitalist development. As a statement of a law of increasing relative $U$, this appears to be consistent with Marx's assertion cited earlier:

> 'The general law is that all expenses of circulation . . . are, *from the point of view of the entire capitalist class*, a deduction from surplus value or surplus product.[1]

This is only a definitional statement within Marx's conceptual framework of a law of relatively increasing unproductive expenses. In order to say that it describes a true law, two requirements must be met. First, the statement must be derived formally from Marxian premises. Second, it must be tested with relevant evidence. So far as empirical evidence for an increasing $U$ is concerned, Gillman's study is interesting and provocative. In relation to the purely theoretical aspect of the issue, however, his work is incomplete, whatever the authenticity of his statistical observations: $U$ is unexplained in the required sense of that term.[2] The difficulties of constructing such an explanation solely

---

[1] *Loc. cit.* My italics.

[2] Gillman argues that unproductive expenses of circulation increase with the progress of capitalism because the expenses that must be assumed by capitalists in order to realize surplus value (selling costs, administrative expenses, taxes for the maintenance of supportive government, etc.) must grow ever larger. But this is no explanation. It is merely a repetition in other terms of a *definition* of unproductive labour which is classified at the outset as that labour engaged in the circulation of commodities. To argue that unproductive labour expands because the cost of realizing surplus value grows ever larger is to argue that unproductive labour increases because it increases.

of Marxian materials seem almost insurmountable. We must see now why this is the case.

## THE MARXIAN MECHANISM OF RESOURCE ALLOCATION

There is a line of reasoning within *Capital* which could lead one to anticipate a progressive reallocation of social resources in favour of unproductive activities with the maturation of capitalism. If we reconstruct this 'explanation', we will be in a position to assess properly its quality and establish the limits of its applicability.

To begin, Marx accepts the principle that returns to the scale of production may be subject to increase within the sector of the economy employing productive labour and, on occasion, within other sectors as well. He assumes that the occurrence of increasing returns to scale within one sector need not coincide in point of time with its occurrence within some other sector and this gives rise to some interesting possibilities. Indeed, he not only assumes the possibility of intersectoral and intertemporal differences in returns to scales of production, but he fixes upon these as the basis for his explanation of observed historical trends.

Historically, he argues, merchant's (unproductive) capital was first on the scene: 'merchant's capital is older than the capitalist mode of production, is, in fact, historically the oldest free state of existence of capital.'[1] Its accumulation prior to the advent of industrial capital sets the stage for the latter's appearance. It provides industrial capitalists a money fund ('potential money capital') on which they may draw, and so helps to create a market which, in scope and mores, is conducive to exchange on the scale that is required by industrial production:

'Its (merchant's capital) existence and development to a certain level are in themselves historical premises for the development of capitalist production, (1) as premises for the concentration of money wealth, and (2) because the capitalist mode of production presupposes production for trade, selling on a large scale ... All development of merchant's capital tends to give production more and more the character of

[1] *op. cit.*, Vol. III, p. 320.

production for exchange-value and to turn products more and more into commodities.'[1]

Mercantile capital sets the stage, but what is it that signals the historic entrance of the principal, industrial capital? The cue is given by the appearance of differential advantages of scale, by what Marx calls an 'increasing disproportion' between the unproductive and the productive sectors. Having stressed the necessity for large scales in industrial production, he now declares the possibility of decreasing returns to scale in the older, unproductive line and concludes that these differential returns entail the ascendancy of industrial capital. The relevant passage is worth citing:

'If every merchant had only as much capital as he himself were able to turn over by his own labour, there would be infinite fragmentation of merchant's capital. *This fragmentation would increase in the same proportion as productive capital raised production and operated with greater masses in the forward march of the capitalist mode of production. Hence an increasing disproportion between the two.* Capital in the sphere of circulation would become decentralized in the same proportion as it became centralized in the sphere of production.'[2]

Underlying his historical explanation of the rise of industrial capital is the postulate of an inverse relationship between returns to scales in the respective sectors, returns to industrial scale increasing, returns to mercantile scale decreasing. In the earlier terminology, Marx argues that the aggregate fund of net realized money capital, $M$, is funnelled in rising proportion into the exploitation of productive labour at the dawn of industrialism. This is, of course, an assertion of the precise converse of the previously defined 'law' of relatively rising unproductive expenditures. We seem to be at polar extremity from the required law.

[1] *ibid.*, pp. 321–2.
[2] *ibid.*, p. 289. My italics. Marx means by 'fragmentation' of capitals the opposite of their concentration or consolidation. Note that in Volume III he establishes the possibility of these disproportionate returns before he describes the historical relationship between the two capitals.

Yet an hypothesis is right at hand. One need only declare that these early historical relationships reverse themselves with the maturation of capitalism, so that unproductive merchant's capital comes back eventually to the position of dominance from which it all began. Accumulations of potential money capital from industry are reinvested in ever growing proportion in the unproductive mercantile sector once the differential advantages of sectoral returns to scale are again inverted. The same 'increasing disproportion between the two' may then be invoked to explain the gradual reallocation into unproductive directions. It is remarkable how close Marx came to this thesis without following through its implications.

He does see that the primacy of industrial capital comes to rest on an increasingly tenuous footing, the more developed the capitalist mode of production:

'In the pre-capitalist stages of society, commerce ruled industry. In modern society the reverse is true. Of course, commerce will have more or less of a counter-effect on the communities between which it is carried on. It will subordinate production more and more to exchange value by making luxuries and subsistence more dependent upon sale than on the immediate use of the product. Thereby it dissolves old relationships. It multiplies money circulation. It encompasses no longer merely the surplus of production, but bites deeper and deeper into the latter, and makes entire branches of production dependent upon it. Nevertheless this disintegrating effect depends very much on the nature of the producing community.'[1]

Nor is he content to make such an impressionistic statement without regard to its economic foundations. In his analysis of extended reproduction (Vol. II), where scales of production are assumed to be increasing, he contemplates the theoretical base for such a mercantile renaissance:

'The surplus-product converted into virtual money capital will grow so much more in volume, the greater was the total amount of already functioning capital whose functioning brought it into being. *With the absolute increase of the volume of the annually reproduced virtual money-capital its segmentation*

[1] *ibid.*, p. 325.

*also becomes easier, so that it is more rapidly invested in any
particular business* ... By segmentation of money–capital is
meant here that it is wholly detached from the parent stock in
order to be invested as a new money–capital in a new and
independent business.'[1]

Growing accumulations of virtual money capital out of industrial expansion stand to the revival of merchant's capital as
merchant's capital stood at an earlier juncture to the emergence
of industrial capital. The segmentation of $U$ out of $M$ becomes
easier as a consequence of the sheer magnitude of the accumulations out of industry of virtual money capital for there are
economic advantages to its promotion. With some care, Marx
settles the question of the nature of these advantages.

Since the prime source of value is always productive labour,
Marx views all expenses of circulation as a chronic drain upon
the surplus product of industrial capital. For the capitalist, there
is only the question of how this drain is to be minimized. The
quest for this minimum leads the capitalist to acquiesce in the
evolution of 'a distinct form of the social division of labour',
merchant's capital, within the maturing capitalism:

'In so far as it contributes to shortening the time of circulation, it may help indirectly to increase the surplus-value
produced by the industrial capitalists. *In so far as it helps to
expand the market and effects the division of labour between
capitals, hence enabling capital to operate on a larger scale*, its
function promotes the productivity of industrial capital, and
its accumulation. In so far as it shortens circulation time, it
raises the ratio of surplus–value to advanced capital, hence the
rate of profit.'[2]

[1] *ibid.*, Vol. II, p. 498.
[2] *ibid.*, Vol. III. Italics mine. Compare with Veblen's economic
explanation of the corrosion of values by exchange value: '. . . the
dominant price system and its commercial standards of truth and
beauty have overruled all inclinations to cultural sanity . . .' This is
because '. . . the price system gains that farther impetus and warrant
which it should come in for if the rights of ownership and investment stand over intact, and so come to enjoy the benefits of a further
improved state of the industrial arts and a further enlarged scale of
operation and enhanced rate of turnover.' *The Nature of Peace*, New
York, 1917, pp. 359–60.

As in the explanation of the emergence of industrial capitalism out of feudalism, intersectoral differences in returns to scale are invoked to explain developing patterns in the allocation of social resources between sectors employing productive and unproductive labour.

In general, an accumulation of virtual money capital within a given sector of the economy presages a resource reallocation into some other sector. The development of this new realm is provoked by the relative scale advantages that it offers which have their reflection in higher profit rates. Moreover, there is the negative incentive of falling profits in the older sector, reinforced by the recurring stimuli of economic crises which sharpen entrepreneurial perceptions of alternative opportunities.[1] Finally, the perennial 'competition among capitals' causes functioning money capital to flow always in directions where it will receive higher rewards. Altogether, these are the elements comprising the Marxian explanation of changing patterns of resource allocation within the expanding capitalist system.

This sketch of that machinery does not do justice to the detail of the argument. It does suffice to bring into view certain essential premises – to which we will shortly turn – and the extraordinary adaptability and flexibility of the apparatus. In this latter connection, recall the underlying sectoral divisions distinguished according to their productivity or unproductivity, their importance or unimportance: the realm of productive labour; $U'$, unproductive but essential labour encompassing necessary financial and commercial operations; $W'$, including many monetary and commercial operations, selling expenses, expenses for the maintenance of supportive governmental activities – all expenses which are peculiar to the capitalist mode of organization; and $L$, the realm of production of capitalist superfluities and luxuries. With Marx's theoretical apparatus, we can 'predict' the historical development of patterns of resource allocation among these lines according to the degree of their previous development. As investment 'fills up' one sector, resources begin

[1] '. . . a balance is itself an accident owing to the spontaneous nature of this production . . .' *ibid.*, Vol. II, p. 495. By 'balance' in this context Marx, of course, refers to the technical co-ordination of inputs and outputs as defined by the balance equations of input–output analysis.

to spill out and into still unexploited realms. Having witnessed productive industrial expansion historically, we can foresee the exploitation and development of each remaining realm in a sequence dictated by the interests and needs of the capitalists, and facilitated by the requisite laws of cost.

The apparatus is adaptable all right; whether or not it is sufficient, scientifically speaking, is another question. As for Marx, one can only wonder that he refrained from making such an obvious projection in more specific terms than the phraseology of causal castigation that he in fact employed. At times he comes very close to predicting a rebirth of mercantile mores from accumulating industrial capitals. He does stress the progressive subordination of all values to those of money economy and exchange value, in short, to commerce. He predicts the deification of all that will sell, and that all will be sold in the end. It is not an exaggeration to say that his theory of capital accumulation and economic development is a theory of the administration of social values, of how the institutions of capitalism press all values into one narrow and crass mould. Observing this progressive subordination of values, he notes that in the ancient world the advent of commerce always presaged slavery: 'In the ancient world the effect of commerce and the development of merchant's capital always resulted in a slave economy . . .'[1] Yet at this very point in *Capital* he stops short of a projection of social imbalance. He reverts to the subject of ancient societies and the emergence of capitalism out of feudalism.

Why? Because he was old and ill? Because he had decided to place his bet upon the instability of the system rather than its allocational eccentricities; because the former appeared to be a more imminent cause of the collapse that he so desired than the possibility that it would disintegrate through a failure to solve the problem of social balance? Possibly these were influential. It is also possible that this projection, had he made it, would have forced him to face up to the outer scientific limits of his theoretical system.

### THE VALUE OF THE MARXIAN HYPOTHESIS

All theories rest upon assumptions – in principle, an infinite

[1] *ibid.*, Vol. III, p. 326.

number of them – and our emphasis upon cost assumptions of the Marxian system is not intended to detract from the possible importance of others. In particular, the Marxian theory makes implicit assumptions concerning the distribution of effective demands (in the micro sense of the phrase) among sectors, which in turn involves assumptions about the distribution of income and the functioning of credit allocational mechanisms. It assumes that supply elasticities for factors of production among these sectors do not countervail the more general cost hypotheses with which Marx was somewhat more directly concerned.

Under the cost hypothesis head, there are two principal limits to the adequacy of the Marxian explanation of historical developments in the allocation of resources under capitalism. First is the assumption that increasing returns to scale may characterize production within a given sector of the economy over a more or less extended interval of time,[1] and that this interval can be succeeded by a period of decreasing returns. Marx postulates sectoral laws of returns to scale which are dynamic rather than static, and which assert that in general and on the average among all production units within the given sector either increasing or decreasing returns may for some time prevail. The reason that this assumption is arbitrary is quite evident. The only articulated theory of returns which we currently possess is a static theory which does not suggest that either increasing or decreasing returns are likely to prevail for any appreciable period of time, if only because it is a static theory. At best, it allows that increases will be succeeded by decreases under static conditions of technology and organizational technique. At worst, it allows that returns to scale are probably constant.[2] Under no conditions, given its present state of development, does it allow that the

---

[1] Note that the assumption does not refer simply to a given line of production where we do observe and are occasionally able to explain chronically increasing or decreasing returns. It refers rather to a whole sector comprehending many lines of production and postulates pervasive returns characteristics within it.

[2] For an introduction to many of the issues, consult E. H. Chamberlin, *Towards a More General Theory of Value*, Oxford University Press, New York, 1959, especially Ch. 9 on economics of scale, and the 'Reply to Mr McLeod and Mr Hahn', pp. 204–12, together with references cited.

phase of increasing returns of an 'envelope' curve can be converted into a decreasing phase or vice versa.

The second arbitrary assumption is that returns to scales of production between (or among) different sectors bear a temporal interrelationship to each other such that when the phase of increasing returns becomes a decreasing phase within one sector, the converse may occur within some other sector. Marx postulates also an *inter*sectoral relationship in returns, a mechanism through which dynamic revisions of cost relations are brought about, throwing the relative profit advantage from the original sector into some other. In sum, he postulates both *intra*- as well as *inter*sectoral cost relationships, and both are required in order to alter the composition of the national output as a whole.

Hence, even if we are agreed that there is an observable trend towards a relative enlargement of unproductive spheres of employment, towards what might, perhaps, be called a decomposition of the national output, this trend is not adequately explained by superimposing Marx's returns hypotheses upon the data. We need to know why and how both intrasectoral and intersectoral variations in returns to scale are brought about with the passage of time. Until we know these things, we cannot predict future variations in returns relationships, nor can we explain the past, which is merely the other side of the same coin. For instance, should we observe some tendency to imbalance, there would be no way of knowing whether or not future allocations would favour a more intensive development of productive labour, or whether they might push us further in the direction of some meta-mercantilism; or whether, even, they might simply be neutral in their impact upon aggregate allocations and output composition.

Of these two intra- and intersectoral cost assumptions, the assumption of increasing returns to scale within a sector is in a sense the more fundamental. If a theory of increasing returns is a *bête noire* of the vulgar economics, it remains an unproved postulate of the Marxian system. It is conceivable, of course, that an adequate dynamic theory of returns, one that is intrasectoral, intersectoral and intertemporal, could be developed within the Marxian framework. This has not yet been done, but there are indications that Marx, as a great economist, was aware of the problem. Let us consider this matter briefly.

A considerable portion of Vol. I of *Capital* is given over to discursive analysis of the division of social labour and reasons are offered for thinking that increasing economic efficiency may be the accompaniment to increasing scales. Assuming that this has settled the matter, Marx subsequently carries his argument forward on the shoulders of two additional propositions, first, that there is some chronic necessity for scales to expand so that progressive efficiency is in fact realized, and, second, that there are forces which carry these enlarged social inputs into those sectors whose importance is confirmed by historical study. Thus, in his analysis of simple and extended reproduction Marx argues that scales must increase because extended scales are necessary to capital accumulation and capital accumulation is characteristic of capitalism.[1]

So it is; but why is this the case? If we accept (as we must) the statement that some significant portion of 'potential money capitals' are reinvested with each successive reproduction period, this still does not prove that scales must grow larger for individual capitalists. It proves only that scales may grow larger *for the economy as a whole*. If increases in outlays of functioning money capital (invested $m$'s) are required from one period to the next, the requirement can nevertheless be met by an increase in the number of functioning capitalists ('fragmentation') as well as by growing net investments in already operating enterprises, a possibility which Marx himself admits in his account of the emergence of commercial capital out of industrial capital by fragmentation.

Orthodox theory refuses to co-operate with Marx by giving any firm reason to suppose that 'new economic space' within a growing sector must be filled with enterprises whose scales of production are steadily growing. And unless this space is filled up with enterprises of steadily growing scale, it is hard to conceive of a reason why growing cost disadvantages the result of growing unproductive outlays should ultimately force investment out of this sector and into some other. What the Marxian must accomplish, in order to salvage Marx's hypotheses from their arbitrary component, is a theoretical synthesis between the

---

[1] cf. *op. cit.*, Vol. I, Ch. XXIV, 'Conversion of Surplus-Value into Capital', pp. 579–611, and Vol. II, Pt. III, *passim*.

orthodox microtheory of returns and Marx's own theoretical system.[1] There is this juncture at which the Marxian theory has a score to settle with the orthodox if it is to stay in the game of explaining imbalance.

There appear to be two lines along which the Marxian system might be extended. One might seek to show that increases in social inputs of constant and variable capital cannot be provided by ever-increasing numbers of small and intermediate scale enterprises without causing their long run cost curves to rise *en toto* to levels that would displace investment in the required fashion. Or, one might seek to show that progressive expansion of existing enterprises, coupled with their decreasing numbers (concentration of capitals) would entail similar cost effects, so as to produce the desired results. Marx preferred the latter alternative which had the great advantage of squaring with observed facts of capitalist expansion; but the how and why of it all remains to be demonstrated at the micro level that is still relevant to the issue. A general theory of returns to scales, encompassing both macro and micro elements, is required.

Is the Marxian system sufficient as an explanation of social imbalance? The answer is no, but ... No, one cannot accept unequivocally a theory with such tenuous underpinings; but, if one ignores for a moment these foundations, the view that is offered is awesome in scope. There is an imbalance that encroaches remorselessly upon a relatively narrowing base of

[1] As a part of such a synthesis, it would help if a formal demonstration of the possibility of generally diminishing returns to scale could be produced. For example, call:

$C_t$ and $V_t$ the sector inputs of constant and variable capital in period of reproduction $t$;

$C_{t+1}$ and $V_{t+1}$ the sector inputs of the next period;

$C_{t+n}$ and $V_{t+n}$ the inputs of the $n$th period;

$M_{t+1}$ the functioning money capital of the $t+$ 1st period, realized by the sale of the surplus product, $S_t$, of the $t$th period;

$M_{t+n}$ the functioning money capital of the $t+n$th period, realized by the sale of the surplus product, $S_{t+(n+1)}$ of the $t+(n-1)$th period.

Then, assuming full employment throughout, that $S_t = M_{t+1} \ldots$ $S_{t+(n+1)} = M_{t+n}$, it is required to show that:

$$S_t/C_t + V_t \quad S_{t+1}/C_{t+1} + V_{t+1} \quad \ldots \quad S_{t+n}/C_{t+n} + V_{t+}$$

productive labour. Because the system as a whole converges to unproductive effects, 'nothing that I do entitles me to eat my fill'. Capitalist organization spills its seed upon ever more barren by-ways. The impulse to economy that conceived industrialism is corrupted by the conditions of life in which it functions, producing prodigality and ultimate degeneration.

However, theoretical foundations cannot be ignored, although their flimsiness provides small consolation for those who require it, for economics does appear to be moving towards a new synthesis. If a general theory of returns should be developed which allows for intersectoral and intertemporal alternations in returns to scale – what then? Economists who are aware that integrations or reductions of theoretical systems have a way of materializing with the progress of a science will see immediately the significance of the query.


## SELECTED BIBLIOGRAPHY

BARAN, PAUL. 'Reflections on Underconsumption' in S. Tsuru (ed.) *Has Capitalism Changed?* Tokyo: Iwanami, 1961.

BARAN, PAUL and SWEEZY, P. M. *Monopoly Capital,* An Essay on the American Economic and Social Order. New York: *Monthly Review,* 1966.

BAZELON, DAVID. *The Paper Economy.* New York: Vintage, 1963.

GILLMAN, JOSEPH. *Prosperity in Crisis.* New York: Marzani & Munsell, 1965.

# Economics of Two Worlds

*Paul A. Baran* and *Paul M. Sweezy*

THE UPSURGE of interest in mathematical economics and econometrics, and the considerable effort lately devoted to their furtherance in the socialist countries, have evoked strong reactions from both Marxist and bourgeois economists. Perhaps the most remarkable thing about the two sets of reactions is that they both tend to interpret this development in substantially the same way: the socialist camp's 'conversion' to the mathematical method in economic theory and research is looked upon as a major concession or even as a surrender of Marxian economics to its bourgeois adversary. This appraisal seems to us to be mistaken. It undialectically treats economics as a discipline apart from the rest of social science and somehow concerned with an undifferentiated and unhistorical reality. And yet, as Engels correctly observed, 'political economy is . . . essentially an *historical* science [and] cannot be the same for all countries and for all historical epochs'.[1]

I

One of the principal results of Marx's scientific labours was the demonstration that capitalism, after constituting a tremendous advance in the growth of the forces of production and in the evolution of a more rational society, turns into its own opposite and becomes an irrational and retrograde system. This transformation is a protracted and complex process. There is no one date at which the change-over can be thought of as having occurred, nor is there any particular aspect of capitalist development that can be looked upon as its unambiguous indicator.

[1] *Anti-Dühring.* Part II. Ch. 1.

Reprinted from *On Political Economy and Econometrics*: Essays in Honour of Oskar Lange. PWN – Polish Scientific Publishers (Pergamon), 1965.

Whether the historical phase has been reached in which the system begins its qualitative change can only be established by considering it as a whole, in its manifold manifestations and in its global impact. Concentration on one brief time period, or on one country or geographical region, or on one set of quantitative measurements or qualitative observations, is likely to produce misleading conclusions and distorted judgments. Such, for example, were the breakdown theories of writers like Rosa Luxemburg and Henryk Grossmann which depicted the end of capitalism not as a lengthy process involving a world-wide socio-economic order but rather as a single catastrophic event like an earthquake. And at the opposite extreme, but stemming from the same root, are the theories of capitalist stabilization recurrently put forward by Social Democratic writers who are as ready to generalize from the recent past of their own countries as they are to ignore the fact that capitalism is a global system.

It is one of the greatest strengths of Leninism that it has consistently avoided both of these errors. But this is not all. There is another fundamental tenet of Leninism which sharply differentiates it from other contemporary semi-Marxian or pseudo-Marxian currents of thought – that we, here and now, are actually living in the age of transition, the period in which capitalism is going through the process of decomposition, retreat, and displacement by a new, more rational economic and social order. The validity of this view is in no way refuted by the undoubted fact that there exist at the present time a number of capitalist countries in which the forces of production are expanding at a fairly rapid rate – for example, Germany, Italy, France and Japan. For this expansion proves nothing in itself; it must be considered in conjunction with much else: with the factors that have brought it about (the vast destruction caused by, and the exceptional circumstances following, the Second World War); with the stagnation in the most advanced capitalist countries (the United States and Great Britain); with the condition of the vast majority of the people in the capitalist world who, far from moving forward on the road to economic and social development, are sliding back, either in relation to advanced countries, as is the case nearly everywhere in the underdeveloped areas, or absolutely as in most; and, last but not least, with the crucially important fact that a large number of societies are engaged in the construction of socialism. What is decisive for the validity of the Leninist thesis is that, as a world order, capitalism has ceased to be an instrumentality of advancement and has turned instead into the principal obstacle to the development of a more rationally integrated, more productive, less misery- and disease-ridden international society.

Likewise, if we seek to determine the role played in our time by the capitalist system within any particular country, it is futile to use as a yardstick the state of individual units of production or even of entire branches of the economy. There are many components of a capitalist economy – even a very undeveloped one – which become progressively more rational, more efficient, and more productive. Many a giant corporation has grown into a scientifically organized, superbly managed, and efficiently operated centre of production; and many of the technical functions of the capitalist economy, be they in the field of finance and insurance or of retail distribution and transportation, have come to be discharged effectively and efficiently.

But just as it would be a fatal mistake to judge the state of an underdeveloped country by the quality and efficiency of its tourist hotels, gambling casinos, or sometimes even railroads, so it is impossible to infer anything about the total rationality of a system from whatever level of rationality may have been reached in its individual parts. For it is an outstanding characteristic of capitalism, indeed one of its distinguishing features, that the rationalization of its parts which it undoubtedly promotes is not accompanied by an increase in the rationality of the economic and social order as a whole. As Marx noted in a different connection, 'the capitalist order of production is generally, despite all its niggardliness, thoroughly wasteful as far as the human material is concerned, just as, conversely, owing to its method of distribution of products through commerce and its manner of competition, it is very wasteful with regard to its material means, and loses for society what it gains for the individual capitalist'.[1]

It might be objected that the very fact that Marx observed (rather than predicted) this phenomenon more than a hundred years ago shows that there is nothing new about it and that it can

[1] *Capital*, Vol. III, Ch. 5.

therefore hardly be regarded as specific to the current epoch of the general crisis of capitalism. Actually, what this fact illustrates is merely the continuity of the process which transforms capitalism and turns it from a promoter into an inhibitor of progress. This continuity exists and is important, but it should not be allowed to obscure the qualitative change which has set in during the century since Marx wrote *Capital*. When the level of development was so low that universal scarcity was still inevitable, and capitalism was, however wastefully and anarchically, creating the conditions for a mighty upsurge in the forces of production, the contrast between the partial rationality of the enterprise and the total irrationality of the system could still be treated as one of the necessary costs of progress. Compare this with the situation today when science and technology have advanced to the point that scarcity and the human suffering resulting from it could easily be done away within the lifetime of one generation – if only the roadblocks put in the way of the rational utilization of available resources and knowledge by a retrograde capitalist system could be removed. In the earlier period, when scarcity was still inevitable, the critical reaction to the discrepancy between the mode of functioning of the system as a whole and that of its parts was, and indeed could only be, a feeling of outrage at the *injustice* of capitalism. It is only in relatively recent times when plenty is within easy reach and its attainment is obviously prevented by the continued dominance of capitalism that the *irrationality* of the system moves into the forefront of critical thought.

Nor is this all. The widening gap between the rationality of the parts and the irrationality of the whole, between the senselessness or even destructiveness of the purpose to which human activity is devoted and the efficiency of that activity itself, results of necessity in a distorted development of the forces of production and in particular of the most important force of production of all: man himself. To quote Marx again: 'More than any other mode of production, [capitalism] squanders human lives, or living labour, and not only blood and flesh, but also nerve and brain. Indeed it is only through the most enormous waste of the individual development that the development of mankind is at all preserved and maintained in the epoch of history immediately preceding the conscious reorganization of society.'[1] The tremendous expansion and refinement of resources devoted to the augmentation of killing power; the direction of the highest available skills to such fields as law, advertising, salesmanship, and financial manipulation; the shunting of vast amounts of energy and talent from socially vital tasks to what happens to be profitable in a shifting market – all this bears eloquent testimony to the far-reaching smothering of partial rationality under the deadweight of total irrationality.

## II

It is against this background of ever-growing tensions – within the separate parts of the system and between them and the whole – that it is necessary to consider the development of bourgeois economics in the current epoch. Reflecting these tensions, current work in bourgeois economics can be divided into two parts. The first, often referred to nowadays as micro-economics, deals with the parts; the second, or macro-economics, deals with the whole. In both, we can see clearly how developing contradictions in the economy itself call forth corresponding contradictions in the realm of theory.

It seems safe to say that most current work in micro-economics aims at exploring the conditions for raising the efficiency and improving the performance of the capitalist enterprise. Its specific content is therefore determined by the needs of the capitalist enterprise and by the standards of efficiency and performance under which it operates. These in turn depend on the nature of the enterprise itself, which is today the giant monopolistic (or oligopolistic) corporation. These economic units have evolved everywhere in the capitalist world during the past seven or eight decades and now occupy a dominant position in all of the more advanced capitalist countries. The problems engendered by this kind of enterprise differ markedly from those associated with its predecessor in the era of competitive capitalism.

At the risk of over-simplification, these differences can be described as follows. The competitive firm was small relative to the size of the industry of which it was a member. It bought its

[1] *ibid.*

factors of production and sold its standardized product at prices over which it had no control. In these circumstances, it could strive for maximum profits only by improving its techniques or its organization – in other words, by actions which were necessarily confined to its own production process. Maximum profits and optimum methods of production thus went together.[1] The ideal competitive capitalist has therefore been traditionally conceived of as an inventor and organizer, always interested in making a better product at lower costs. In so far as he studied at all, the subjects which attracted him were technological and managerial in nature – engineering and what the Germans call *Betriebswirtschaftslehre*. He could expect little benefit from studying the outside world, except for such knowledge (very limited at the time) which it might provide him about general business fluctuations and the ups and downs in the market for his own product. Within the limitations imposed upon him by the relatively narrow scope of his operations and by the anarchy of social production as a whole, the competitive capitalist was induced to promote partial rationality both by the hope of profit and by the threat of extinction if he should fall too far behind his rivals.

When it comes to the monopolistic corporation of today, the situation is very different. The firm is large not only in terms of the industry to which it may be considered to belong,[2] but also

---

[1] Needless to say, there is no implication that the attainment of a production optimum by the individual firm means a socially optimal utilization of society's productive resources. For one thing, the firm's optimum depends on the relative prices of the various inputs, including labour. But there is no reason to suppose that wages under capitalism bear any relation to what is socially desirable – quite the contrary, especially in the earlier stages of capitalist development when forced migration from the countryside, dire poverty, and abysmal ignorance conspired to depress wages often below even a bare subsistence minimum. And, for another thing, the kinds and quantities of commodities produced depend, even under ideal competitive conditions, on the distribution of income which is affected not only by the factors just noted but also by the pattern of ownership of the means of production.

[2] Many, if not most, giant corporations form parts of different industries which are not even necessarily related.

in terms of the nation's or even the world's economy; what it produces is often strongly identified with its name so that, in the eyes of buyers, there may be no close substitutes available. Commanding a significant degree of monopoly power, the giant corporation confronts the prices at which it sells its output and buys its inputs not as objective market data but as magnitudes which depend on its own operations and on those of a small number of other similarly situated concerns. As a vast enterprise not necessarily identified with any particular group of individuals but rather thought of by its owners and managers as an everlasting entity, it seeks to maximize the flow of profits over a much longer planning horizon than the small competitive capitalist can afford to take account of. Its drive for maximum attainable profits under such circumstances no longer involves merely finding the best ways to reduce the costs of production of a given commodity or group of commodities. It has to keep under continuous review the problem of what commodities to produce – their physical attributes, their outward appearance, brand names, etc. Durability and quality have to be determined in the light of the firm's other lines of production and traditional practices, as well as of the behaviour of other suppliers of related or possibly related products. In arriving at decisions, it is necessary to weigh advertising and other marketing costs; and in fixing the quantities of the various commodities to be produced as well as the prices to be charged, the shape of all relevant demand and marginal revenue curves has to be explored and taken into account. The outside world which the competitive capitalist has to take for granted not only directly influences the monopolistic corporation's production process but is subject to deliberate manipulation on its part.

It can be readily seen that the identification of the firm's path to maximum profits when all these factors – plus many others relating to taxes, tariffs, foreign exchange rates, etc.[1] – are duly considered calls for a calculatory effort that is vastly more complex than that required by a small competitive business. The

[1] It should be noted in this connection that the most important capitalist corporations today typically operate on a world-wide scale. See the essay by the present authors, *Notes on the Theory of Imperialism*, in *Problems of Economic Dynamics and Planning. Essays in honour of Michal Kalecki.*

commonsense prescriptions of the intuitive entrepreneur of old, the time-tested devices made familiar in *Betriebswirtschaftslehre* are no longer capable of coping with the task in hand. Recourse must be had to a more powerful apparatus of what has come to be called 'decision making'; a new 'management science' using mathematical techniques able to encompass a large number of variables (and constraints) has to be developed. It is therefore by no means accidental or due solely to the immanent evolution of pure thought that advanced mathematical studies of behaviour patterns, the exploration of the properties of more complex constellations of uncertainty, the development of mathematical techniques of programming, and the perfection of techniques of statistical measurement have moved to the centre of bourgeois micro-economic thought.

It must not be thought, however, that the development of all these sophisticated and often genuinely scientific methods for guiding the behaviour of a monopolistic or oligopolistic corporation has anything in common with a search for the optimal allocation and utilization of society's productive resources, or for that matter even with the partial rationality standards which were relevant to the process of commodity production under a régime of competitive enterprise. The nature and volume of output, the technology employed, the investment undertaken, the raw materials used, the prices charged – none of these, no matter how rational the methods by which they were arrived at, can be thought of as corresponding to the needs of society as a whole or even as reflecting the growth of the forces of production in one of its component parts. It is as if a superbly skilful typist operating a perfectly faultless electric typewriter were set to work, enjoined to avoid a single typographical error because one hundred typewritten pages proof-read and free of mistakes have to be ready for delivery promptly at 4 p.m. – to the janitor for removal to the dump.

III

What applies to the parts of the system applies with equal if not greater force to the whole. There the prevailing irrationality is even more drastic and obvious than that obtaining within the confines of the individual enterprise.

At a sufficiently high level of abstraction, the conditions for a rational economic organization are almost self-evident. Given a certain input of social labour and an output of goods and services corresponding to the degree of development of the forces of production and the productivity of labour, society can either consume or accumulate what it produces. If we assume a closed system, these two categories – consumption and accumulation – obviously exhaust society's total current output. And if we abstract from the possibility of consuming what was produced in an earlier period, it is clear that society must consume and accumulate exactly what it produces, neither more nor less. Should aggregate output exceed society's combined desire to consume and accumulate, labour input must be curtailed and the amount of leisure correspondingly increased. If aggregate output falls short of society's desire to consume and to accumulate, labour input has to be increased (if this is possible), or the productivity of labour has to be raised (if this is feasible). If neither alternative is open, a diversion of resources from consumption to investment with a view to augmenting society's future productivity is the only other possible course.

Just as it is necessary to allocate productive resources (human labour, living and congealed) to the satisfaction of current consumption and accumulation needs, so it is indispensable to decide on the specific apportionment of total effort to the production of different items entering into consumption and investment respectively. Marx put the matter concisely. 'Given social production, the allocation of time naturally remains of the essence. The less time society requires to produce wheat, cattle, etc., the more time it gains for other production, material or intellectual. Just as in the case of a single individual, the all-sidedness of society's development, of its enjoyment, and of its activity depends on the saving of time. The economy of time, this is what all economy dissolves itself into – in the last analysis. Society must purposefully apportion its time to realize an output corresponding to its total needs, just as an individual must properly apportion his time to acquire knowledge in appropriate proportions or to satisfy different demands on his energy. Economy of time as well as planned allocation of working time to different branches of production thus constitutes the first economic law under conditions of social production.'[1]

To be sure, this statement of the 'first economic law' leaves open a number of important questions which need to be answered if the rationality of society's economic organization is to be assured. To mention only two: first, how are the needs and preferences of society's members for various possible combinations of goods and services (including leisure) to be ascertained? The age-old problem of the relation of the individual to society is obviously not automatically solved by the overall rationality of the social organization. The second question concerns the distribution of social income: equal shares for all? To each according to his contribution to social output? Or to each according to his needs? Although the problem will lose much of its present urgency when the development and organization of the forces of production have advanced to the point where scarcity has been overcome, and when the new society has succeeded in radically restructuring human wants, nevertheless for a considerable time to come it is bound to remain an important part of the task of rationally planning social existence. From our present point of view, the thing that needs to be stressed is that it is only when the 'first economic law' has been consciously made the organizational principle of society that the rational solution of other problems moves into the realm of the feasible. It is only at this stage that many of the now known technical devices will be able to serve their proper purposes: referenda and opinion polls, democratic elections, and genuine free choice by individuals.

Comparing the elementary principles of rational economic organization with the *modus operandi* of the capitalist system puts into sharp relief the irrationality of the latter. Under capitalism neither the total amount of labour performed nor the output produced is determined by the existing level of productivity and by society's wants and needs, nor are these variables influenced by any social scale of preferences (however arrived at) with regard to labour and leisure. It is one of the most striking aspects of the irrationality of the capitalist process that all these things, which ought to be so closely intermeshed, are in fact governed

[1] *Grundrisse der Kritik der Politischen Oekonomie* (Rohentwurf) 1857–58. Berlin, 1953, p. 89.

by the separate, disconnected, and often conflicting forces which generate both the aggregate and the composition of effective demand. Thus the distribution of income, largely determined by the pattern of ownership of means of production, accounts in the main for both aggregate demand for consumer goods and aggregate individual saving. The profit-maximization policies of monopolistic corporations decide the share of social income going into surplus. The same profit objectives call forth investment outlays the magnitude of which is unrelated to the size of the extracted surplus, the amount of individual saving, or society's need for investment. Accordingly, fluctuations in the amount of work performed (regular employment, part-time employment, overtime work) are in no way governed by changes in society's desire or need for more or less output and do not take place according to any rational scheme intended to serve the best interests of society as a whole (such as, e.g. an across-the-board lengthening or shortening of the work week, advancement or postponement of the retirement age, shortening or lengthening of the time devoted to education, and so forth). The adjustment of the aggregate amount of social labour to changes in market demand takes place rather through changes in the volume of unemployment, which affects the members of the capitalist class and other privileged strata in society hardly at all but imposes untold suffering, insecurity, and degradation on the underlying population which depends for its livelihood solely on the sale of its labour power.[1]

The irrationality of the process which determines the level of employment and the volume of output is matched by the irrationality of that which determines the composition and distribution of what is produced. This is not the place to present

[1] In at least one half of the seventeen years of unprecedented prosperity following the Second World War in the United States, government-reported unemployment was in the neighbourhood of 5 million, and according to trade-union sources at least 6 million. The corresponding loss of aggregate output during the post-war period has been estimated at a minimum of $500 billion; for the years 1958 to 1962 alone, the cumulative excess of potential over actual output has been calculated by the President's Council of Economic Advisers at $170 billion. (*The Economic Report of the President*, January 1963, p. 28.)

the amply available evidence;[1] suffice it to point out that while poverty and severe privation affect more than one-third of the population of the United States, 'in 1960, the highest five per cent of all consumer units received about 20 per cent of total disposable income, or very much more than the $15\frac{1}{2}$ per cent of income received by the lowest 40 per cent of all consumer units'.[2] At the same time, the resources at the disposal of the country's entire educational establishment (public and private) are smaller than what is spent on the sales effort (advertising, direct selling, automobile model changes, etc., etc.).

This situation is necessarily reflected in bourgeois economics. As long as the productivity of human labour was so low as to render inevitable a general state of scarcity, it was possible to treat poverty and privation on one hand and wealth and luxury on the other as Hegel's 'cunning of reason'. Necessitating hard work on the part of the poor and providing the rich with the wherewithal and incentives to invest, the existing economic and social order could be regarded as history's devious but highly successful stratagem for the attainment of general progress. The apparent irrationality of the capitalist system could be depicted as merely a façade hiding the profound rationality of the process as a whole. Under these circumstances, it was seen as the task of economics to teach the uninstructed man in the street to believe in the beneficial design of the structure hidden behind the uninviting appearance of the scaffolding.

After the First World War, and in particular in the years of and following the Great Depression, this traditional justification of the increasingly manifest irrationality of the capitalist order became less and less plausible. Most of those who continue to defend the system no longer do so on grounds of rationality but instead rely on appeals to tradition, 'human nature', religion,

[1] Some of it is assembled in our forthcoming book on American capitalism and appeared partly in *Monthly Review* (July–August 1962). Much pertinent material can be found in Michael Harrington, *The Other America: Poverty in the United States*, New York, 1962; Gabriel Kolko, *Wealth and Power in America*, New York, 1962; and numerous other monographs.

[2] Conference on Economic Progress, *Poverty and Deprivation in the United States: The Plight of Two-Fifths of a Nation*, Washington, DC 1962, p. 4.

'true' versus 'false' reason, and so on.[1] Others rest their case on the assertion that only capitalism guarantees individual freedom – defining the latter so as to make it synonymous with the preservation of existing inequality and privileges, which, in turn, are 'explained' as emanations of the God-given order of nature.[2]

Dominant economic thought, however, has taken a different course. It has accepted, however grudgingly and reluctantly, the principal tenet of the Marxian critique of the capitalist order: its anarchy and deeply rooted irrationality. At the same time, bourgeois economics refuses to draw the logical conclusions from that irrefutable finding.[3] The strategy adopted has been rather to try to steal the Marxian thunder by devising schemes to make the system work without interfering with the basic features of capitalism: private enterprise and production for maximum profits. It is this strategy that has inspired the bulk of thought and research in the area of macro-economics, and it is in the requirements of this strategy that one finds much of the reason for the emergence and development of advanced mathematical techniques of theoretical reasoning and statistical work.

The characteristic focus of this intellectual effort is the elaboration and refinement of one of Marx's favourite analytic devices: the bisectoral model of simple and expanded

[1] cf., e.g. Friedrich A. Hayek, *Individualism and Economic Order*, London, 1949; in particular the first essay, 'Individualism: True and False'.

[2] Thus Professor Milton Friedman attributes the existing distribution of wealth and income to a rule of chance such as governs a lottery, and by appeal to highly questionable eugenics supposedly responsible for differences in individual endowments. See his *Capitalism and Freedom*, Chicago, 1962, pp. 163 ff.

[3] The following two statements by Keynes are highly characteristic of this attitude: 'When the capital development of a country becomes a by-product of the activities of a casino, the job is likely to be ill-done.' And 'a somewhat comprehensive socialization of investment will prove the only means of securing an approximation to full employment; *though this need not exclude all manner of compromises and of devices by which public authority will co-operate with private initiative.*' *The General Theory of Employment Interest and Money*, New York, 1936, pp. 159, 378 (italics added).

reproduction.[1] In Marx's work, to be sure, this model had no independent standing. Its purpose was rather to illustrate the anarchy and irrationality of the capitalist mode of production. By the specification of the conditions necessary for the harmonious expansion of the economy he sought to demonstrate the stringency of the requirements that would have to be fulfilled,[2] and tried to show how small was the likelihood of such a harmony being achieved under capitalism. This, it cannot be over-emphasized, is the very opposite of the use to which Marx's model has been put by bourgeois writers who, following in the footsteps of Tugan-Baranovsky, see in it a proof of the capacity of the capitalist system to expand harmoniously *ad infinitum*.

For such harmony to prevail and for the economy to expand on the basis of a full utilization of available human and material resources, the strategic variables determining the mode of functioning of the system as a whole would have to be controlled. Since the classical and neo-classical view – that the necessary controls are efficiently, albeit indirectly, exercised by the price mechanism and the rate of interest – has been exploded, the question of the nature and availability of alternative controls within the framework of the advanced capitalist system has become the central issue facing bourgeois economics. So far, however, it has carefully avoided facing up to this issue and instead has sought to deal with the problem by assuming it away. Either the relevant magnitudes and relations (volume of investment, proportion of income consumed, rate of technological advance, etc.) are assumed to turn out correctly as a result of the working of the competitive mechanism – although the incapacity of the mechanism to produce such a result has been amply proven; or else these variables are treated as though they were

[1] It is amusing that the parentage of contemporary model building in bourgeois economics is generally treated as strictly 'classified information', with Walras (whose entire system has very little to do with the aggregative method employed) being substituted for Marx as a more respectable ancestor.

[2] In fact, as has emerged from subsequent research, the requirements formulated by Marx were not even sufficient and need to be supplemented both by disaggregation of the two sectors which underlay his model as well as by a specification of technological relations.

determined by a social plan – although the absence, and, as we believe, the impossibility, of such a plan under capitalism is one of the system's outstanding characteristics.[1] Much ingenuity has been devoted to elaborating these growth models, but in view of their failure to provide any concrete indications of the processes which determine the relevant magnitudes and functional relations, the significance of the results achieved is, to say the least, somewhat dubious.

This is not to deny that to the extent to which they contribute to the clarification of the requirements for the maintenance of correct proportions and balanced growth in *any* economy based upon division of labour and involving technological change, models of this kind are essential to the furtherance of the theory of economic planning. By leading to improved knowledge of the variables and relations that need to be controlled to assure a rational utilization of resources, they not only can help to indicate the nature of the informational material which is essential to the planning authority but also to identify the strategic leverages that can be successfully employed for the attainment of the plan's goals. Where functional relations are concerned, they may direct attention to the need to study behaviour patterns which were previously neglected. In these ways, they can enrich the toolbox needed for the rational, socialist administration of society's resources.

But the situation appears in quite a different light when these constructs are viewed as elements of a theory of capitalist reality. We have then to ask which aspects of that reality are taken into account and which are abstracted from. If, as we believe to be the case, what is abstracted from includes essential characteristics of capitalism, the models involved not only fail to advance our understanding of the working principles of the system but actually help to obscure them. For by postulating the existence of adequate direct or indirect controls over the behaviour of key variables when in fact none exist; by assuming the absence of monopoly when in fact it is ubiquitous and far-reaching in its

[1] The settlement of all the basic problems stemming from the irrationality of the capitalist process by means of suitable assumptions is well illustrated in Nicholas Kaldor and James A. Mirrlees, 'A New Model of Economic Growth', *The Review of Economic Studies*, Vol. XXIX, No. 3.

effects; by supposing full employment in the long run when in fact it is rather an exception than a rule – in all these ways, the currently fashionable models abstract not from secondary features of the process that they seek to explain but from its most essential characteristics. Thus they substitute for the capitalist economy an imaginary rational system which has nothing in common with capitalism but the name. The result, it need hardly be said, is an apologetic defence of the *status quo* – and this quite apart from the subjective intentions of the model-builders.

The apologetic role played by this type of theorizing is by no means reduced by the apparent precision attained through the use of mathematics. In fact, it is the other way around. Both mathematical language and mathematical reasoning can be particularly treacherous in that they permit the drawing of logically impeccable conclusions from inadequate premises and create the appearance of a co-ordinated and cohesive system when in reality no such system exists. Just as, in the micro-economic case, the glittering efficiency of the modern corporation covers up the meaninglessness of the purpose which it serves, so in the macro-economic case the elaborate mathematical model serves to conceal the irrationality of the economic organization which it purports to illuminate.

# IV

The tasks of Marxian political economy are different under different economic and social orders, in different countries, and in different historical periods. It is an error to believe, as some Marxist writers have, that political economy, being the science of capitalism *par excellence*, becomes superfluous under socialism.[1] While under socialism both the object and objectives of political economy undergo a profound change, its responsibilities actually increase.

On the macro level, it becomes the theoretical guardian of the rationality and socialist orientation of the system as a whole, as well as the chief instrumentality for the formulation of society's economic goals and the general strategy for attaining them.

---

[1] See, e.g. N. Bukharin, *Oekonomik der Transformationsperiode*, Hamburg, 1922, p. 2.

To the fulfilment of these tasks, only Marxian political economy brings the great intellectual tradition of socialist thought and the theoretical lessons learned from the accumulated experience of socialist construction. It alone disposes over the theoretical tools needed for the analysis of the economic institutions, scientific possibilities, and social relations that are decisive in the elaboration and carrying out of society's economic plans.

But while on the macro level, it is only Marxian political economy that can serve as a guide to a socialist society, it has no such 'comparative advantage' when it comes to the micro level, to the problems of the rationality and efficiency in the individual sectors and units of a socialist economy. Indeed, Marxian political economy has never addressed itself to the problems of optimization that arise in the separate parts of the economy, neither to the minimization of costs of production of a given output nor to the maximization of returns from a given amount of invested capital. Concerned with the totality of the capitalist process and with the developmental tendencies inherent in it, Marxian political economy has never sought to compete with *Betriebswirtschaftslehre* and its more modern variants, any more than it has attempted to develop a theory of consumer's choice or of investor's behaviour under conditions of uncertainty. It has been content to leave the exploration of the conditions for optimizing the capitalist's position within the capitalist order to bourgeois economics which quite naturally responded to *that* challenge with alacrity and ability.

As a result, on the micro level, bourgeois economics has been able to evolve a body of theoretical reasoning and techniques of empirical observation which now turns out to be of considerable value to the economic administration of a socialist society. Not that *all* the results of bourgeois micro-economics can be included in this category. For example, the (often highly subtle) analysis of the interacting strategies of oligopolistic corporations, or the analysis of the interrelations between inventory policies and market fluctuations, is obviously 'dated'. Their relevance is confined to the capitalist system. At the same time, the techniques developed in the solution of these and similar problems may well be usable for different purposes by socialist economic planners. Lenin put the essential point concisely when he wrote: 'Large banks constitute the "state apparatus" which we *need* for the realization of socialism and which *we take ready-made* from capitalism. Our task is only to *cut off* what are *capitalist perversions* of this excellent apparatus, to make it still larger, still more democratic, still more comprehensive.'[1] And a few months later, after the Revolution, he repeatedly stressed that 'if we correctly understand our tasks we must learn to build socialism from the managers and organizers of capitalist trusts'. He might have added that there is something to be learned from the capitalist economists as well.

Thus from the viewpoint of the political economy of socialism, there is everything to be said for the adoption of all the advanced, mathematical and non-mathematical, techniques of observation and analysis developed by bourgeois economics. So long as care is taken to 'cut off the capitalist perversions', much of what has been established in bourgeois economics – but constitutes under capitalism a manifestation of naïve, ahistorical rationalism and turns inevitably into apologetics for the *status quo* – can be effectively used under socialist planning. To take one example among many: the theory of consumer's behaviour conveys under capitalism the false, ideological notion that the 'autonomous' consumer is the sovereign ruler of the economy, while in fact it is the capitalist system itself that determines the nature of his wants, tastes, standards, spending habits, and so forth. The very same theory of consumer's behaviour, however, can be employed (and developed) under socialism as a powerful means for ascertaining needs and wants of consumers within an entirely different social setting. Such adoption and adaptation of elements of bourgeois economic research and theorizing to the needs of socialist planning not only do not constitute 'concessions' by Marxian political economy to bourgeois economics; they do not even bear any relation to its subject matter and its interests.

Under capitalism, in advanced and underdeveloped countries alike, Marxian political economy has a twofold task. One is to continue exploring the *modus operandi* of capitalism with a view to ascertaining the changing forms in which the irrationality of the system manifests itself, and to assessing its capacity to survive despite the fact that it has already turned into an impedi-

[1] *Can the Bolsheviks Maintain State Power?* (October 1917).

ment to the further development and progress of society. In this connection, bourgeois economics can be of some help. What it has to offer is primarily the analytical techniques for studying the short-term determinants of income and employment developed by Keynes and some of his followers. Even here, however, it is important to distinguish between those contributions which really advance our understanding of the capitalist mechanism and those which depict capitalism as an essentially rational system which needs only a few reforms to make it viable and beneficent.

The second task of Marxian political economy was aptly defined by Engels: 'The task of economic science is to demonstrate the newly emerging ills in society as the necessary consequences of the existing mode of production, but also as indications of its impending dissolution, and to uncover within the dissolving economic structure the elements of the future, new organization of production and distribution under which those ills will be abolished.'[1] For obvious reasons, bourgeois economics is no help here. In fact, far from being interested in showing the relation between prevailing social ills and the underlying mode of production, it can be said that present-day bourgeois economics devotes all its ingenuity to obscuring this connection.

It is not that the existence of these ills can be denied. They are too obvious and have even inspired an extensive popular literature of the Vance Packard type.[2] Nor can they be brushed off as of no importance: there has probably never been a period in United States history when the responsible leaders of ruling-class opinion have been so outspokenly alarmed about the state of the nation's morals and manners. What they cannot admit, however, is that these conditions are the direct outcome of the capitalist social order itself. They must be attributed to some external or universal malaise – to the weaknesses of 'human nature', to the deadening effect of 'industrialization', to the unchecked propensity of people to procreate – to anything but the profoundly irrational and anti-human nature of an economic system based on private property and exploitation. And the

[1] *Anti-Dühring*, Part II, Section 1.
[2] Packard's books are as follows: *The Hidden Persuaders* (1957); *The Status Seekers* (1959); *The Waste Makers* (1960).

elaborate apparatus of modern economic theorizing is placed unreservedly at the service of these hard-pressed defenders of the *status quo.*

The leading economists of the English neo-classical school – from John Stuart Mill through Marshall and Pigou to Keynes – were all outspoken, even if relatively moderate, reformers. They knew that many grave social ills such as extreme poverty, maldistribution of wealth and income, and unemployment were directly caused by the working principle of the economic system, and they did not hesitate to advocate remedial reforms. There is hardly a trace of this honourable tradition in bourgeois economics of today: even the most 'radical' wing, represented by Galbraith's works on *American Capitalism* and *The Affluent Society*, turns out on careful inspection to be the most enthusiastic apologist for a society dominated by *big* business. And if the neo-classical concern for reform has been jettisoned, how much more complete has been the abandonment of the older classical economists' passion to discover in the present the shape of the future, and to single out for intensive analysis whatever forces seemed to hold promise of new and better times to come. Anti-historical to the core, present-day bourgeois economics scorns any effort to investigate the nature of the changes that are taking place or where they are leading. The great question *Quo vadis?* which occupied not only Adam Smith and David Ricardo and John Stuart Mill but also in our time Joseph Schumpeter has simply disappeared from the agenda of bourgeois economics, yielding its place of honour to a species of what has come to be called 'operations research' – the quest for appropriate means to achieve predetermined ends, regardless of the nature or the historical significance of the ends in view. Thus economics in the age of monopoly capitalism becomes a kind of scientifically refined tool for the manipulation of society and its members by the dominant interests. And, ironically, it is precisely this scientific refinement which so successfully obscures the all-important fact that thereby reason is being put into the service of unreason. If, before the advent of capitalism, science to gain recognition had to pose as magic, nowadays magic can only achieve acceptance by posing as science.

As against this development in bourgeois economics, Marxian political economy must maintain its traditional critical position.

It must indefatigably confront the society of monopoly capitalism and its ideological embellishments with the mirror of
unadorned reality. It must abide by its age-old commitment to
treat society as a whole and to lay bare the connection between
the misery prevailing in different aspects of human existence
under capitalism and the irrationality of the entire system, an
irrationality which cannot be assumed away but rather must
occupy a central place in all genuinely scientific endeavour.
Taking from the bourgeois sciences everything that can be useful
to the construction of a new society, it must combat everything
that is being used for the preservation of the old. As a variant of
Marx's last thesis on Feuerbach might state: At the present time
science is creating the conditions for changing the world; what
matters, however, is the *nature* of the change for which it is used.

## SELECTED BIBLIOGRAPHY

BUKHARIN, N. *The Economic Theory of the Leisure Class*. London:
Martin Lawrence, 1927.

JOHANSEN, L. 'Marxism and Mathematical Economics', *Monthly
Review*. January 1963.

LANGE, OSKAR. *Political Economy*: Vol. 1. Pergamon, 1963.

MEEK, R. L. *Economics and Ideology*. London: Chapman & Hall,
1967.

ROBINSON, J. *Economic Philosophy*. Penguin, 1964.

# 4. Neo-Marxism

# A Crucial Difference Between Capitalism and Socialism

*Paul M. Sweezy*

THE ORIGINAL draft of this article was submitted to five economists for comment. Each had criticisms; and, except for a few that were based on misunderstanding, all the criticisms made good sense. Some I have tried to meet by changes in formulation. But the more important ones, it seemed to me, could be satisfactorily dealt with only within the framework of a different and much longer article. Since it would undoubtedly be prudent to assume that the same or similar criticisms will occur to other readers, I would like to explain in advance that this is *not* an attempt to expound a theory of industrialization. Rather, it is an attempt to throw light on what happens *after* a process of basic industrialization has been completed. In other words, what I have to say about the process of industrialization itself is by way of setting up a problem, not solving one. With regard to the main thesis of the article, my conviction both that it is valid and merits attention has been strengthened by the comments of those who read the first draft.

Every economically advanced society must go through a phase, which will be measured in decades rather than years, of *industrialization,* that is to say, the building of its basic industrial equipment from the ground up. This phase, to be sure, has no precise beginning and no precise ending, but it has a very real existence and importance all the same.

We can perhaps best appreciate this if we imagine ourselves in the position of central planners in a backward country whose task it is to develop an advanced industrial economy. They will first think of all the basic industries, using the term in its widest sense, that must be built up. They will realize that during this

Reprinted from *The Present as History*. New York: Monthly Review Press, 1953.

build-up period a very large part of production will have to be, as it were, ploughed back and that the rate of expansion of consumption will be severely limited. And they will make at least rough estimates of when the build-up period will be over and the harvest can be reaped in the form of rapidly expanding consumption.

All this is clear enough if we think in terms of a planned economy. But most economists seem to have overlooked it in their theories of the unplanned economy, perhaps precisely because it harbours no one whose point of view corresponds to that of the central planner. At all events, I believe that the facts alluded to are important and that by explicitly taking them into account we can gain significant insights into the functioning of both unplanned (capitalist) and planned (socialist) economies.

I

Let us begin by dividing the economy into two departments. Department I produces all producers' goods, Department II all consumers' goods. The dividing line between the two departments is not clearly defined, but the distinction itself is perfectly clear and usable.[1] In order to avoid getting entangled in the problems of technological change, let us assume that we are dealing with an economically underdeveloped country which can draw on the known techniques of more advanced countries. To begin with, this country has a very small Department I, most of its economy being concentrated in Department II. We will suppose that there are no relevant shortages of natural resources or labour power. Under these conditions, the economy can expand all around, in both departments at the same time. 'Saving' or, more accurately, accumulation of capital does not involve cutting down on current consumption but rather

[1] This departmental schema, of course, originated with Marx and has been extensively used by later Marxian economists. See my *Theory of Capitalist Development*, especially Chapters 5, 10, and 11. But it is not incompatible with most non-Marxian theories and does not imply acceptance of such specifically Marxian doctrines as the labour theory of value or the theory of surplus value. See Ragnar Nurkse, 'The Schematic Representation of the Structure of Production', *Review of Economic Studies*, June 1935.

proceeds *pari passu* with an increase in consumption. This increase in consumption, in turn, can be broken down into a component due to the growth of the labour force and a component due to rising real incomes.

If we assume, as we should, that workers on the average consume the whole of their incomes, then the remainder of the demand for the output of Department II will depend on two factors: (1) the division of income between workers and capitalists, (2) the rate of capitalists' accumulation.[1]

Generally speaking, the demand for the output of Department I is made up of what we can call replacement and expansion demands of the capitalists of both departments. Let us make the simplest possible assumption about replacement demand, that is, that a given proportion of capital requires to be and is replaced each year. Then the replacement demand of each department will vary directly with the size of the department. This brings us to the key question: What determines the expansion demand of the two departments?

As to Department II, a sensible assumption would seem to be that capitalists base their investment decisions on the actually observed and experienced trend of consumption. If consumption is growing slowly, the expansion demand of Department II will be small; and conversely if consumption is growing rapidly, the expansion demand of Department II will be large.

Finally, then, there is the expansion demand of Department I for the products of Department I. This, it should be noted at once, lies at the very heart of the question of industrialization. A large expansion demand from Department I is equivalent to rapid industrialization, a small expansion demand to slow industrialization.

Let us pause to note that it is not wholly obvious why there should be such an expansion demand in Department I. It could be reasoned that both departments, after all, have to be geared

[1] Each of these factors, of course, is extremely complicated. For example, the inflationary creation of bank credit can expand the capitalists' share of total income and at the same time raise the capitalists' rate of accumulation. I am not trying to exclude such processes, which indeed have played a crucial role in the development of all capitalist countries, but merely to subsume them under shorthand formulas.

to the output of consumption goods; that the expansion demand of Department II therefore measures the primary requirement for more means of production; and that expansion demand in Department I could consequently be expected to be limited to what would be needed to meet slowly rising replacement demands. Such a case is certainly conceivable, but it is completely unrealistic. In practice, Department I cannot expand slowly and continuously in the wake of rising consumption. Whole industries, transport networks, communication systems, and so on, that will be absolutely essential when consumption has reached a certain level, simply do not exist at the outset, and they cannot be brought into existence bit by bit. For a long time the growth of Department I must anticipate and be largely independent of the growth of consumption. This anticipatory and independent expansion of Department I is precisely what we mean by industrialization.[1]

During this phase of development, the only limit to the size of the expansion demand of Department I – or, to put it otherwise, the only limit to the speed of industrialization – would seem to lie in the capitalists' capacity to accumulate. This, of course, is the obverse of their demand for consumers' goods and is determined by the same two factors, namely, the division of income between workers and capitalists and the capitalists' rate of accumulation.

Our main conclusions to this point can be expressed in two brief propositions. (1) The economic development of a backward society implies a period of industrialization during which the demand for the products of Department I comes to a considerable extent from Department I itself. (2) The higher the rate of profit and the stronger the capitalists' urge to accumulate, the

---

[1] The point can be illustrated by the growth of the American railroad system. Mileage expanded at an extremely rapid rate from the middle of the nineteenth century to about 1910, after which further expansion tapered off nearly as suddenly as it had begun. During the whole period of rapid expansion, building was ahead, and sometimes way ahead, of demand for railroad services. After the basic network had been completed, further investment (in double-tracking and the like) followed and was closely geared to traffic requirements. This is an extreme case, but the phenomenon it illustrates is typical not only of individual industries but of Department I as a whole.

slower the growth of consumption and the more rapid the rate of industrialization.[1]

Let us now analyse what happens as the period of industrialization approaches an end. Basic industries have been created, a railroad network is in existence, and so on. Department I, in other words, has been built up to the point where it can meet all the replacement and expansion demands of Department II. Leaving aside the question of new industries (which we shall touch upon later), Department I will no longer present a substantial expansion demand for its own products. Such expansion demand as does arise within Department I will be derived from the gradually rising replacement demands of Department II and to a much smaller extent of Department I itself. In other words, as the period of industrialization approaches an end, most of the expansion demand of Department I simply vanishes. Note that this does not imply any earlier slowing down, still less cessation, in the growth of either consumption or the expansion demand of Department II. It results from the simple fact that Department I has been built up to a point where it can handle existing and prospective requirements for its output, and that to go on adding to it at the established rate would simply be to pile up excess capacity.

The question now arises as to whether there is anything in the mechanism of the capitalist economy which will tend to produce an offset to this falling off in the expansion demand of Department I. (We can assume that it occurs gradually, so as not to introduce the problem of sudden dislocations or immediate adjustments.) Classical and neo-classical theorists would for the most part have answered this question in the affirmative. They would have argued that the price mechanism would operate to bring about a falling rate of profit (or interest) which, in turn, would check accumulation and stimulate consumption. This would happen in one or both of two ways. First, the fall in the rate of profit might be sharp enough to lower the relative share

[1] Note that if the rate of growth of consumption were faster, the rate of industrialization would be cut down on two separate counts: first, because the rate of accumulation would be lower, and second, because a higher proportion of accumulation would have to go into Department II.

of capitalists, or, in other words, to involve a transfer of income from accumulators to consumers. Second, the decline in the rate of profit would in any case induce capitalists to accumulate less and consume more. In terms of our two-department schema, the result would be that the gap in total demand created by the disappearance of expansion demand in Department I would be made up by an increase in consumption demand on the one hand and an increase in expansion demand in Department II on the other.[1]

But it is certainly impossible today to maintain that the capitalist price system works this way. Relative shares have been shown to be remarkably resistant to change under the most diverse conditions, and very few would still argue that there is a significant relation between the mere rate of profit and capitalists' attitudes towards accumulation and consumption. In other words, there is no reason to suppose that the approach of the end of the period of industrialization would set in motion a mechanism accelerating the growth of consumption at the expense of accumulation and thus taking up the slack which the disappearance of expansion demand in Department I would otherwise cause. Other things being equal, in a capitalist system the fruits of industrialization, instead of being enjoyed in the form of rapidly increasing consumption, are dissipated in unemployment and depression.

Of course, other things do not remain equal, and new factors may intervene to take up the slack. For example, new industries

[1] At first sight, it might appear that even so there would be trouble in Department I, since the increased expansion demand from Department II would not be enough by itself to compensate for the diminished expansion demand from Department I. But to reason in this way is to conceive the departmental schema too rigidly. Actually, a considerable part of the resources employed in Department I can be quickly shifted to Department II, and, with a changing pattern of demand such as the older theorists envisaged, this would certainly happen. For example, firms that had been constructing new factories would turn to constructing new houses, truck plants would shift to passenger cars, and so on. In other words, a smooth transition at the end of the period of industrialization – if it were possible – would involve some immediate expansion of Department II at the expense of Department I.

generally produce an effect akin to that of industrialization, and if they are sufficiently numerous and important they may keep the system going at or near full capacity.[1] But in each case the effects are bound to wear off sooner or later. The *tendency* to collapse is always there in an industrialized capitalist society; depression or stagnation or whatever we choose to call it must be regarded as its normal condition, in precisely the same sense that the classical and neo-classical economists regarded full-employment equilibrium as the normal condition of capitalist economies at every stage of their development.

II

Let us now turn to the case of a centrally planned socialist economy. Here, unlike in the capitalist case, the allocation of resources to the various departments and industries is decided upon by a central planning board; and prices and income flows are to a large extent adjusted (also by the planning board) with the object of enabling the allocation decided upon to work itself out smoothly and efficiently.[2]

We assume a planned economy in the same position we earlier assumed a capitalist economy to be in, in other words, at the beginning of the process of industrialization and handicapped by no shortages of natural resources or manpower.

---

[1] New or improved methods of producing existing commodities present a more complicated problem. They may take the place of, and in an economic sense destroy, means of production already in use. To this extent, their effect is similar to that of new industries. But they may also be introduced as part of the process of replacing worn-out capital, and to this extent they do not create any expansion demand at all. If innovations of this kind are introduced by new firms, they are more likely to have the former effect; if by existing firms, the latter effect. The problem is therefore not only one of technology but also of industrial organization.

[2] Naturally this statement is subject to all sorts of qualifications, but it stresses what is important from our present point of view, namely, that socialist central planning deals fundamentally with production and relegates the price system (using the term in the broadest sense) to an essentially auxiliary role.

We also divide the economy into the same two departments.[1]

The question of how fast to industrialize – or, to put it the other way round, how much to brake the growth of consumption in the interests of accumulation – will be determined not by the distribution of income and the desire of one class in the community to increase its wealth, but by a deliberate decision of the planning authority. This basic decision will guide the allocation of resources to the two departments. In order to ensure that money demands correspond to the chosen pattern of resource allocation, the planning board will have to establish a level of consumers' goods prices in relation to workers' incomes which will leave the workers just enough real purchasing power to absorb the planned output of Department II. The more rapid the industrialization decided upon, the higher will be the level of consumers' goods prices, and vice versa. The revenue accruing to the state from this price mark-up can be looked upon as profit, or it can take the form of a turnover tax, or some combination of these approaches can be used. For the sake of simplicity, and to facilitate comparison with the capitalist case, we will refer to it as profit. But it is important to bear in mind that profit in the socialist society is not a crucial factor in the operation of the economy in the sense that it is in the capitalist case; it merely measures what is being withheld from current consumption for purposes of accumulation.[2]

Now, during the period of industrialization, Department I, in the socialist as in the capitalist case, exercises an expansion demand for its own products which is the stronger the more rapid the rate of industrialization. And, likewise in both cases, as the period of industrialization approaches an end, this expansion demand quickly shrinks to an insignificant fraction of its former size. The question is whether this circumstance should be a source of difficulty for the socialist economy, as we have seen it to be for the capitalist economy.

---

[1] The departmental schema, it need hardly be emphasized, is descriptive of the physical process of production, not of its social organization. It can therefore be employed in the analysis of both capitalist and socialist economies.

[2] And other public purposes too, of course, but we are abstracting from this aspect of the problem.

The answer is surely that there is not the slightest reason why it should be. The planning board, seeing that the basic build-up of the country's industrial equipment is nearly accomplished, will shift resources to Department II as rapidly as they become available and will channel the greater part of fresh accumulation into further expanding Department II. In other words, the board will plan for a much more rapid expansion in the output of consumers' goods. And in order to ensure that this flood of consumers' goods finds a market the board need only progressively lower their prices. True, this will involve a continuous fall in the profit accruing to the state, but this will be merely a technical detail which it would never occur to anyone in a socialist society to worry about. Under socialism, in other words, the end of the period of industrialization ushers in, not a period of continuous depression (actual or potential), but rather a period of genuine fulfilment.

### III

The reason for the difference between capitalism and socialism disclosed by the foregoing analysis is an extremely interesting and important problem, not of pure economic theory but of what may be called economic sociology. Basically, as we have hinted, this reason lies in the wholly different character and role of profit in the two forms of society. Under capitalism, profit is the form in which the economically dominant class gets its income. It is, so to speak, the economic foundation of the very existence of this class. The vested interest which this class has in the maintenance of profit as such, as well as in the maintenance of a large volume of profit – the two are not really distinct problems in the minds of the capitalists – is by far the most powerful and passionately defended vested interest in capitalist society. Every conceivable kind of support and protection – economic, institutional, legal and ideological[1] – is built up around

---

[1] What is often called the degree of monopoly (in the economy as a whole) is little more than a reflection of capitalists' success in putting up economic, institutional, and legal fences around their profits. Ideological supports are of the most varied description, ranging all the way from the glorification of private enterprise through the reviling of the price-cutter to the ostracizing of the radical.

profit. As near as anything can be, profit is the be-all and end-all of capitalist society. It follows that when the economic functioning of capitalism calls for a drastic and steady decline in profit and/or a use of profit which runs directly counter to the will of the capitalists, then the system is caught in a very real contradiction.[1]

Capitalism may be temporarily rescued from the contradiction by new industries; it may seek, with more or less success, an escape through imperialism and militarism; it may even undertake, again with more or less success and certainly against the growing resistance of the capitalists themselves, to modify the functioning of the system through taxation and government spending. But one thing is certain: as long as it remains capitalism, it can never *abolish* the contradiction.

And this is precisely what socialism does do. Under socialism, profit is not a form of income at all. No one has a vested interest in its maintenance either as an economic category or as an economic magnitude. Whatever the smooth functioning of the system requires to be done to profit, can be done with no resistance and no fuss.

This is certainly only one of many differences between capitalism and socialism. But it is just as certainly, in my judgment, one of the most important and far-reaching in its implications.

[1] Compare the remark in Schumpeter's forthcoming *History of Economic Analysis:* 'If a system or model that correctly expresses fundamental features of the capitalist society contains contradictory equations, this would be proof of inherent hitches in the capitalist system – proof of real, instead of imaginary, "contradictions of capitalism".' (Part IV, Chapter 7, Section 3, Note 17.) Needless to say, the reality of the contradictions does not depend upon their taking an equational form. The reason economists have generally failed to recognize the contradiction we have been discussing is simply that they have misunderstood or ignored the role of profit in capitalist society as a whole. There could be no other way of explaining, for example, Keynes' famous passage about the 'euthanasia of the rentier'. (*General Theory*, pp. 375–6.)

## SELECTED BIBLIOGRAPHY

DOMAR, EVSEY. 'The Problem of Capital Accumulation', *Essays in Economic Growth*. Oxford University Press, 1957.

MURAD, ANATOL. 'Net Investment and Industrial Progress', in K. Kurihara (ed.) *Post-Keynesian Economics*. Rutgers, 1954.

SWEEZY, P. M. 'A Reply to Critics', *The Present as History*. New York: Monthly Review, 1953.

# The Concept of the Economic Surplus

*Paul A. Baran*

THE CONCEPT of economic surplus is undoubtedly somewhat tricky, and in clarifying and employing it for the understanding of the process of economic development neither simple definitions nor refined measurements can be substituted for analytical effort and rational judgment. Yet it would certainly seem desirable to break with the time-honoured tradition of academic economics of sacrificing the relevance of subject matter to the elegance of analytical method; it is better to deal imperfectly with what is important than to attain virtuoso skill in the treatment of what does not matter.

In order to facilitate the discussion as much as possible, I shall be speaking now in terms of 'comparative statics': that is, I shall ignore the paths of transition from one economic situation to another, and shall consider these situations, as it were, *ex post*. Proceeding in this way, we can distinguish three variants of the concept of economic surplus.

*Actual* economic surplus, i.e. the difference between society's *actual* current output and its *actual* current consumption.[1] It is thus identical with current saving or accumulation, and finds its embodiment in assets of various kinds added to society's wealth during the period in question: productive facilities and equipment, inventories, foreign balances, and gold hoards. It would seem to be merely a matter of definition whether durable consumer goods (residential dwellings, automobiles, etc.) should be

---

[1] It comprises obviously a lesser share of total output than that encompassed by Marx's notion of surplus value. The latter, it will be recalled, consists of the entire difference between aggregate net output and the real income of labour. The 'actual economic surplus' as defined above is merely that part of surplus value that is being *accumulated*; it does not include, in other words, the consumption of the capitalist class, the government's spending on administration, military establishment, and the like.

---

Originally appeared as Chapter II of *The Political Economy Growth*. New York: Monthly Review Press, 1957.

treated as representing saving rather than consumption, and it is undoubtedly quite arbitrary to treat houses as investment while treating, say, grand pianos as consumption. If the length of useful life be the criterion, where should one place the bench-mark? In actual fact, it is essential for the comprehension of the economic process to make the distinction *not* on the basis of the physical properties of the assets involved, but in the light of their economic function, i.e., depending on whether they enter consumption as 'final goods' or serve as means of production contributing thus to an increase of output in the subsequent period. Hence an automobile purchased for pleasure is an object of consumption, while an identical car added to a taxi-fleet is an investment good.[1]

Actual economic surplus has been generated in all socio-economic formations, and while its size and structure have markedly differed from one phase of development to another, its existence has characterized nearly all of recorded history. The magnitude of the actual economic surplus – saving or capital formation – is at least conceptually readily established, and today is regularly estimated by statistical agencies in most countries. Such difficulties as are encountered in its measurement are technical, and caused by the absence or inadequacy of statistical information.

*Potential* economic surplus, i.e., the difference between the output that *could* be produced in a given natural and techno-logical environment with the help of employable productive resources, and what might be regarded as essential consumption.[2]

[1] While it need not detain us at this point, it is worth bearing in mind that from the standpoint of economic development it is most important whether the actual economic surplus assumes the form of capital goods increasing productivity, or appears as additions to inventories or gold hoards only tenuously, if at all, related to the 'strengthening of society's technical arm'.

[2] This also refers to a different quantity of output than what would represent surplus value in Marx's sense. On one hand, it *excludes* such elements of surplus value as what was called above *essential* consumption of capitalists, what could be considered *essential* out-lays on government administration and the like; on the other hand, it comprises what is not covered by the concept of surplus value – the output lost in view of under-employment or misemployment of productive resources.

Its realization presupposes a more or less drastic reorganization of the production and distribution of social output, and implies far-reaching changes in the structure of society. It appears under four headings. *One* is society's excess consumption (predominantly on the part of the upper income groups, but in some countries such as the United States also on the part of the so-called middle classes), the *second* is the output lost to society through the existence of unproductive workers, the *third* is the output lost because of the irrational and wasteful organization of the existing productive apparatus, and the *fourth* is the output foregone owing to the existence of unemployment caused primarily by the anarchy of capitalist production and the deficiency of effective demand.

The identification and measurement of these four forms of the potential economic surplus runs into some obstacles. These are essentially reducible to the fact that the category of the potential economic surplus itself transcends the horizon of the existing social order, relating as it does not merely to the easily observable performance of the given socio-economic organization, but also to the less readily visualized image of a more rationally ordered society.

## II

This requires a short digression. Indeed, if looked at from the vantage point of feudalism, essential, productive, and rational was all that was compatible with and conducive to the continuity and stability of the feudal system. Non-essential, unproductive, and wasteful was all that interfered with or was unnecessary for the preservation and the normal functioning of the prevailing social order. Accordingly Malthus staunchly defended the excess consumption of the landed aristocracy, pointing to the employment-stimulating effects of such outlays. On the other hand, the economists of the rising bourgeoisie had no compunctions about castigating the *ancien régime* for the wastefulness of its socio-economic organization, and about pointing out the parasitic character of many of its most cherished functionaries and institutions.[1]

[1] 'The labour of some of the most respectable orders in the society, is like that of menial servants, unproductive of any value. . . . The

But as soon as the critique of pre-capitalist society lost its urgency, and the agenda of economics became dominated by the task of rationalizing and justifying the victorious capitalist order, the mere question as to the productivity or essentiality of any type of activity taking place in capitalist society was ruled out of court. By elevating the dictum of the market to the role of the sole criterion of rationality and efficiency, economics denies even all 'respectability' to the distinction between essential and non-essential consumption, between productive and unproductive labour, between actual and potential surplus. Non-essential consumption is justified as providing indispensable incentives, unproductive labour is glorified as indirectly contributing to production, depressions and unemployment are defended as the costs of progress, and waste is condoned as a prerequisite of freedom. In the words of Marx, 'as the dominion of capital extended, and in fact even those spheres of production not directly related to the production of material wealth became more and more dependent on it, and especially the positive sciences (natural sciences) were subordinated to it as means towards material production – second rate sycophants of political economy thought it their duty to glorify and justify every sphere of activity by demonstrating that it was "linked" with the production of material wealth, that it was a means towards it; and they honoured everyone by making him a "productive worker" in the "narrowest" sense – that is a worker who works

---

sovereign, for example, with all the officers both of justice and war who serve under him, the whole army and navy, are unproductive labourers. They are the servants of the public, and are maintained by a part of the annual produce of the industry of other people. . . . In the same class must be ranked . . . churchmen, lawyers, physicians, men of letters of all kinds: players, musicians, opera singers, opera dancers, etc. . . .' Adam Smith, *Wealth of Nations* (Modern Library ed.), p. 295.

'When the annual productions of a country more than replace its annual consumption, it is said to increase its capital; when its annual consumption is not at least replaced by its annual production, it is said to diminish its capital. Capital may, therefore, be increased by an increased production or by a diminished unproductive consumption.' Ricardo, *Principles of Political Economy and Taxation* (Everyman's Library ed.), p. 150.

in the service of capital, is useful in one way or another to its increase.'[1]

Yet 'capitalism creates a critical frame of mind which after having destroyed the moral authority of so many other institutions, in the end turns against its own: the bourgeois finds to his amazement that the rationalist attitude does not stop at the credentials of kings and popes but goes on to attack private property and the whole system of bourgeois values'.[2] Thus from a standpoint located outside and beyond the capitalist frame of reference, from the standpoint of a socialist society, much of what appears to be essential, productive, rational to bourgeois economic and social thought turns out to be non-essential, unproductive, and wasteful. It may be said in general that it is only the standpoint which is intellectually outside the prevailing social order, which is unencumbered by its 'values', its 'practical intelligence', and its 'self-evident truths', that permits critical insight into that social order's contradictions and hidden potentialities. The exercise of self-criticism is just as onerous to a ruling class as it is to a single individual.

As can be readily seen, the decision on what constitutes potential economic surplus, on the nature of non-essential consumption, waste, and unproductive labour, relates to the very foundations of bourgeois economics and in particular to what has come to be called the economics of welfare. Indeed, the purpose of this – perhaps most ideological and apologetic – branch of economic theorizing is to organize our knowledge of the conditions that determine the economic welfare of people. Needless to say, the first and foremost prerequisite for such an effort to be meaningful is a clear notion of what is meant by economic welfare and of the criteria by which states of economic welfare may be distinguished. The welfare economists meet the issue (or, rather, believe they meet it) by referring to the utility or satisfaction experienced by individuals. The individual himself, with his habits, tastes and preferences, is taken as given. Yet it should be obvious that such a view of the individual is altogether metaphysical, in fact misses the most essential aspect

[1] Marx, *Theories of Surplus Value* (London, 1951), p. 177.
[2] J. A. Schumpeter, *Capitalism, Socialism and Democracy* (3rd Edn. New York, 1950), p. 143.

of human history. As Marx remarked in a passage devoted to Bentham: 'To know what is useful for a dog, we must study dog nature. This nature itself is not to be deduced from the principle of utility. Applying this to man, he that would criticize all human acts, movements, relations, etc., by the principle of utility, must first deal with human nature in general, and then with human nature as modified in each historical epoch. Bentham makes short work of it. With the driest *naïveté* he takes the modern shopkeeper, especially the English shopkeeper, as the normal man. What is useful to this queer normal man and to his world is absolutely useful. This yard-measure then he applies to past, present and future.'[1]

Indeed, in the course of history, the individual with his physical and psychic requirements, with his values and his aspirations, has been changing with the society of which he is a part. Changes in the structure of society have changed him, changes in his nature have changed society. How are we then to employ the utility or satisfaction accruing to an individual at any given time as a criterion by which the conduciveness to welfare of economic institutions and relationships is to be judged? If we refer to the observable behaviour of an individual, we are obviously moving in a circle. His behaviour is determined by the social order in which he lives, in which he was brought up, which has moulded and determined his character structure, his categories of thought, his hopes and his fears. In fact, it is this ability of a social constellation to produce the mechanism of such personality-moulding, to provide the material and psychic framework for a specific type of human existence, that makes this social constellation a social *order*.

Economists, nevertheless, try to appraise that social order, its so-called efficiency, its contribution to human welfare, by criteria that it has itself evolved.[2] What would we think of judging the welfare contribution of homicide by the code of

---

[1] *Capital* (Kerr ed.), Vol. I, p. 668.

[2] 'The function of economic institutions is to organize economic life in conformity with the community's wishes ... the efficiency of economic organization will ... be judged by its conformity to the community's preferences.' T. Scitovsky, *Welfare and Competition* (Chicago, 1951), p. 5.

behaviour established in a cannibalistic society? The best that
can be attained in that way is a judgment on the *consistency* of
the cannibals' behaviour with their own cannibalistic rules and
regulations. This kind of inquiry may be useful to an effort to
devise arrangements needed for the preservation and better
functioning of the cannibalistic society – but what is there to be
deduced from such an investigation in terms of human welfare?
Assuming, indeed, that the life of the cannibals fully conforms
to the precepts of their society, that their headman gets exactly
as many scalps a year as are called for by his wealth, his status,
and his connections, and that all the other cannibals consume
exactly the number of foreigners that corresponds to their
marginal productivity and never in any other way but through
a free purchase in a free market: do we then have a state of an
optimum, can we then say that the cannibals' welfare is well
looked after? It should be obvious that nothing of the sort follows. All we have established is that the practice of the cannibalistic society corresponds more or less fully to the principles
evolved by that society. We have said nothing at all about the
validity or rationality of those principles themselves or about
their relation to human welfare.

Thus welfare economics engages in what comes very close to
compulsive brooding on the extent to which the existing
economic organization satisfies the rules of the game laid down
by the existing economic organization, on the degree to which
the productive apparatus of a capitalist society is 'efficiently'
organized for the production of an output the size and composition of which are determined by the structure of that productive apparatus. Furthermore, it laboriously inquires into the
degree to which the existing socio-economic organization allo-
cates resources in such a manner as to correspond to consumers'
demand which in turn is determined by the distribution of
wealth and income, by the tastes and values of people which are
themselves shaped by the existing socio-economic organization.
All this has absolutely nothing to do with the exploration of the
conditions that are conducive to welfare or with the study of
the measure to which the economic and social institutions and
relationships of capitalist society further or impede the well-
being of people.

But a conventional practitioner of welfare economics will

stop us here, and ask what other criteria of welfare do we have.[1]
If the actual, observable performance of the individual in the
market is not to be accepted as the ultimate test of what constitutes his welfare, what other test are we to use?

The mere fact that this question is raised indicates how far we
have travelled along the road to irrationality and obscurantism
since the days of classical philosophy and classical economics.
In truth, the answer to this question is simpler than one may
think – at once simpler and more complicated. The answer is
that the sole criterion by which it is possible to judge the nature
of a socio-economic organization, its ability to contribute to
the general unfolding and growth of human potentialities, is
*objective reason*. It was objective reason that underlay the criticism of the then existing society undertaken by men like Machia-
velli and Hobbes, and it was objective reason that inspired
Smith and Ricardo to call feudal lords, courtiers, and the established clergy of their time parasites because they not only did
not contribute to the advancement of their societies, but drained
them of all possibilities of growth.

Not that the substance of objective reason is fixed immutably
in time and space. On the contrary, objective reason itself is
embedded in the never-resting flow of history, and its contours
and contents are no less subject to the dynamics of the historical
process than nature and society in general. 'One cannot step
twice into the same stream', and what is objective reason on one
historical stage is unreason, reaction on another. This dialectic
of objective reason has nothing in common with the relativistic
cynicism of pragmatism or with the opportunistic indetermi-
nateness of the sundry philosophies of the *élan vital*; it is firmly
anchored in man's expanding and deepening scientific understanding of both nature and society, in the concrete exploration

[1] For instance Professor Scitovsky – one of the most authoritative
writers in the field – observes: '. . . if we begin questioning the consumer's ability to decide what is good for him, we embark on a road
on which it is difficult to stop, and we may end up by throwing over-
board the whole concept of consumers' sovereignty.' *op. cit.*, p. 184.
In actual fact, what is at issue is not the 'concept of consumers'
sovereignty' but merely the unhistorical, apologetic version of that
concept that underlies bourgeois economics.

and practical exploitation of the natural and social conditions of progress.

The historically shifting and ambivalent attitude towards progress and objective reason that has been characteristic of bourgeois thought ever since the bourgeoisie began to be continuously torn between opposition to feudalism and fear of nascent socialism accounts for the fact that the socialist critique of prevailing social and economic institutions used occasionally to find a relatively sympathetic reception on the part of bourgeois economics as long as it was directed at the residues of the feudal order. The squandering of wealth by the landlords in backward countries was no less an admissible target of attack than their prodigality under the *ancien régime* in the more advanced countries. There has always been much less tolerance when it came to the critique of capitalist institutions *sensu stricto*. And at the present imperialist stage of capitalist development, to emphasize for instance the sociopolitical structure of backward countries as the main obstacle to their progress is considered almost as suspect as to insist on the role of imperialism in the advanced capitalist countries in retarding development at home and in perpetuating stagnation in underdeveloped areas.

Similarly economists socially and mentally anchored in the competitive, petty-bourgeois phase (and stratum) of capitalist society have developed a certain degree of clairvoyance with respect to the irrationality, wastefulness, and cultural consequences of monopoly capitalism. Oblivious of the fact that it is liberal, competitive capitalism that inescapably breeds monopoly, they recognize some of the economic, social, and human costs of capitalism's monopolistic phase, discern some of the most obvious manifestations of excess consumption, unproductive activities, the irrationality and brutality of 'economic royalism'. At the same time the writers who have either liberated themselves from the shackles of an earlier age, or who have grown directly into the 'new era', are at times impressively perspicacious when debunking the competitive order of the past – the sacrosanct virtues of capitalism's competitive adolescence.

While this tension within bourgeois thought accords a certain amount of insight (and information) that permits at least a proximate assessment of the nature (and magnitude) of potential economic surplus, the always latent and sporadically erupting conflict between the interests of the capitalist class as a whole and those of its individual members offers another opportunity for the comprehension of the issues involved. Thus in times of war, when victory becomes the dominant interest of the dominant class, what under the circumstances constitutes objective reason is permitted to ride roughshod over particular interests and subjective utilities. Whether it is compulsory service in the armed forces, war economic controls, or requisition and confiscation of necessary supplies, objective needs become recognized as fully ascertainable and are assigned a significance vastly superior to that of individual preferences revealed by market behaviour. Yet as soon as the emergency passes, and further admission of the existence and identifiability of objective reason threatens to become a source of dangerous social criticism, bourgeois thought hastily retreats from whatever advanced positions it may have temporarily reached and lapses once more into its customary state of agnosticism and 'practical intelligence'.

What constitutes 'excess consumption' in a society could be readily established if this question received but a fraction of the attention that is accorded to problems as urgent and as important as for instance the measurability of marginal utility. With regard not only to underdeveloped countries but to advanced ones as well, what represents 'essential consumption' is far from being a mystery. Where living standards are in general low, and the basket of goods available to people little variegated, essential consumption can be circumscribed in terms of calories, other nutrients, quantities of clothing, fuel, dwelling space, and the like. Even where the level of consumption is relatively high, and involves a large variety of consumer goods and services, a judgment on the amount and composition of real income necessary for what is socially considered to be 'decent livelihood' can be made.[1]

[1] The Bureau of Labor Statistics of the United States Department of Labor works with some notion of 'essential consumption' in compiling its cost of living index. The Heller Committee for Research in Social Economics at the University of California employs similar concepts. Food, housing, and medical requirements for various countries have been studied by the United Nations, by the Food and Agriculture Organization and other agencies, and represent

As mentioned before, this is precisely what has been done in all countries in emergency situations such as war, post-war distress, and the like. What an agnostic apologist of the *status quo* and the worshipper of 'consumers' sovereignty' treat as an insurmountable obstacle, or as a manifestation of reprehensible arbitrariness, is wholly accessible to scientific inquiry and to rational judgment.

### III

More complicated and quantitatively less easily encompassed is the identification of unproductive workers. As pointed out earlier, the mere distinction between productive and unproductive labour encounters a determined opposition on the part of bourgeois economics. From the experience of its own youth it knows this distinction to be a powerful tool of social critique, easily turned against the capitalist order itself. Attempting to do away with it altogether, it seeks to quench the entire issue by judging the productivity, essentiality, usefulness of any performance in terms of its ability to fetch a price in the market. In this way, indeed, all differences between various types of labour disappear – all except one: the magnitude of the remuneration that any given activity commands. As long as a performance rates *any* monetary reward, it is treated as useful and productive *by definition.*[1]

---

a most important field for further investigations. cf. Food and Agriculture Organization, F A O Nutritional Studies No. 5, *Caloric Requirements* (Washington, June 1950); National Research Council, Reprint and Circular Series, *Recommended Dietary Allowances* (Washington, 1948); United Nations, *Housing and Town and Country Planning* (1949–50), as well as the material referred to in these sources.

[1] It may be interesting to note that this drive to glorify the capitalist order by eliminating the distinction between productive and unproductive labour has seriously contributed to the self-emasculation of modern economics. Committing its protagonists to treat as productive *all* activities in capitalist society that earn a monetary reward, the criterion of market approval and market valuation that might have at least a claim to consistency under conditions of *pure* capitalism becomes a source of serious troubles when what has

From the preceding discussion it should be clear, however, that market valuation cannot be considered a rational test for the appraisal of the 'adequacy' or 'efficiency' of a socio-economic organization. Indeed, as stressed above, the acceptance of this test would involve circular reasoning: judging a given socio-economic structure by a yardstick that itself represents an important aspect of that very socio-economic structure. Thus what is productive and what is unproductive labour in a capitalist society cannot be decided by reference to the daily practice of capitalism. Here, again, the decision has to be made concretely, from the standpoint of the requirements and potentialities of the historical process, in the light of objective reason.

Considered in this way a not insignificant part of the output of goods and services marketed and therefore accounted for in the national income statistics of capitalist countries represents unproductive labour. To be clear about it: all of it is altogether productive or useful *within the framework of the capitalist order*, indeed may be indispensable for its existence. And needless to say, the individuals engaged in this type of labour may be, and in most cases are, 'upstanding citizens', hard-working, conscientious men doing a day's work for a day's wage. Therefore their classification as 'unproductive labourers' involves neither moral opprobrium nor any other stigmatization. As very frequently, men of good will may not only not achieve what they strive to achieve but may accomplish its very opposite if constrained to live and to work within a system the direction of movement of which is beyond their control.

As can be easily seen, the isolation and measurement of this unproductive share of a nation's total economic effort cannot be undertaken by the application of a simple formula. *Most*

---

to be dealt with is a society permeated with feudal remnants. Adherence to the market valuation principle under such circumstances forces economists either into the somewhat ludicrous position of having to criticize the existing state of affairs from the unhistorical and unrealistic standpoint of Mises, Hayek, Knight and others of that school, or into the uncomfortable necessity to twist and bend the 'principle' by claiming usefulness and essentiality for various non-marketed activities in view of their 'indirect' contribution to marketable output or in view of their essentiality for the preservation and functioning of the capitalist system as a whole.

*generally speaking, it consists of all labour resulting in the output of goods and services the demand for which is attributable to the specific conditions and relationships of the capitalist system, and which would be absent in a rationally ordered society.* Thus a good many of these unproductive workers are engaged in manufacturing armaments, luxury articles of all kinds, objects of conspicuous display and marks of social distinction. Others are government officials, members of the military establishment, clergymen, lawyers, tax evasion specialists, public relations experts, and so forth. Still further groups of unproductive workers are advertising agents, brokers, merchants, speculators, and the like. A particularly good example is given by Schumpeter – one of the very few contemporary economists who was not content to dwell on the level of 'practical intelligence' but attempted to rise to some understanding of the historical process:

> A considerable part of the total work done by lawyers goes into the struggle of business with the state and its organs . . . in socialist society there would be neither need nor room for this art of legal activity. The resulting saving is not satisfactorily measured by the fees of the lawyers who are thus engaged. That is inconsiderable. But not inconsiderable is the social loss from such unproductive employment of many of the best brains. Considering how terribly rare good brains are, their shifting to other employment might be of more than infinitesimal importance.[1]

What is crucial to remember is that unproductive labour as just defined is not directly related to the process of essential production and is maintained by a part of society's economic surplus. This characteristic it shares, however, with another group of workers that would not fall under our definition of unproductive labour. Scientists, physicians, artists, teachers and similarly occupied people live off the economic surplus but engage in labour the demand for which in a rationally ordered society, far from disappearing, would become multiplied and intensified to an unprecedented degree. Thus while it is perfectly appropriate from the standpoint of the measurement of the *total*

[1] J. A. Schumpeter, *Capitalism, Socialism and Democracy* op. cit., p. 198.

surplus currently generated by society to include these workers in the class of individuals supported by the economic surplus, it would seem advisable to treat them separately if what is at issue is the assessment of the magnitude of the surplus *potentially* available for rational utilization. 'Labour may be necessary without being productive.'[1]

This distinction becomes particularly useful when not only the possibilities of economic growth but also the transition from capitalism to socialism is considered. For what is defined above as unproductive labour is bound gradually to disappear as a socialist society advances in the direction of communism. In fact, certain classes of unproductive workers are immediately eliminated with the introduction of a planned economy, while others remain for considerable periods of time in systems transitional from capitalism to communism such as, for instance, the USSR. It may well be said that the degree to which unproductive labour in our definition has been abolished, and institutions such as the army, the church, and the like have been dispensed with, and the human and material resources thus freed have been directed to the advancement of human welfare, represents the most important single index of a socialist society's progress towards communism.

The group of workers, on the other hand, that is supported by the economic surplus and that is *not* covered by our definition of unproductive labour expands greatly with the development of a socialist society. As Marx predicted, the part of the total product '... which is destined for the communal satisfaction of needs such as schools, health services, etc. ... is ... from the outset ... considerably increased in comparison with present-day society and it increases in proportion as the new society develops ... [while] the general costs of administration not belonging to production ... will from the outset, be very considerably restricted in comparison with present-day society and it diminishes in proportion as the new society develops.'[2] Thus the resources used for the maintenance of the individuals who

[1] Marx, *Grundrisse der Kritik der Politischen Ökonomie* (Rohentwurf) (Berlin, 1953), p. 432.

[2] Marx, *Critique of the Gotha Program*, in Marx and Engels, *Selected Works* (Moscow, 1949–50), Vol. II, pp. 20 ff.

draw on society's economic surplus, but are not included in unproductive labour as I defined it, cannot be considered to represent a fund potentially available for purposes of economic growth.

Once more: regardless of the difficulties that may be encountered in attempting to gauge accurately the volume of unproductive work performed in a capitalist economy, in times of emergency the nature of *this* task is no less clear than the need for curtailment, if not elimination, of non-essential consumption. Unproductive workers are drafted into the army while productive workers are deferred. Labour exchanges try to move people from unproductive to productive employment. Rationing boards issue different ration cards to individuals in different occupations, with productive workers receiving preferential treatment.

Conceptually no more complex, although perhaps still more difficult to measure, is the *third* form in which potential economic surplus is hidden in the capitalist economy. The waste and irrationality in the productive organization that fall under this category can be observed in a great number of instances, and result in a reduction of output markedly below what could be obtained with the same input of human and material resources. There is first the existence (and continuous reproduction) of excess capacity unproductively absorbing a significant share of current investment. We do not refer here to manpower, plant and equipment that are reduced to idleness in times of depressions. To that we shall come later. What we have in mind now is the physical capacity that remains unused even in years of prosperity, and not merely in declining but also in expanding industries.[1]

An investigation of excess capacity in the United States in 1925–29 was made by the Brookings Institution.[2] 'Capacity' of

---

[1] Incidentally, in a rationally planned economy there is no need for excess capacity to exist for any length of time even in declining industries, that is, in industries facing a shrinkage of demand for their products. Timely conversions of such capacities to the production of other outputs could reduce such excess capacity to a minimum.

[2] *America's Capacity to Produce and America's Capacity to Consume* (Washington, 1934). For an excellent summary of this study,

an industry is there defined as the output which it would turn out with the length of the working day and number of shifts ordinarily in use in the industry, and with a proper standard of plant maintenance (i.e. taking account of necessary shutdowns for repairs, etc.). Plants which are shut down have been excluded, so that they do not count as excess capacity. The capacity so (conservatively) defined is thus lower than the 'rated capacity' usually given by trade statistics and based on technical estimates. The Brookings Institution found that 'in general . . . in the years from 1925 to 1929 available plant was used between 80 and 83 per cent of capacity'.[1] The study cautions that 'probably not all the additional productivity indicated as possible by the above figures could have been realized, for there were striking differences in the potential capacity of the different branches of industry, and if each industry would run to its full capacity, huge surpluses of some goods would no doubt soon pile up'.[2] Yet as the authors of the study realize, 'if new productive effort were directed towards co-ordinating the various industries', this disproportionality could be markedly reduced, if not altogether eliminated. They do not estimate the volume of output that could have been produced given such co-ordination. Even in its absence, however, 'an output of 19 per cent greater than was realized would have been possible. Stated in terms of money, this increased productivity would have approximated 15 billion dollars' – i.e. nearly 20 per cent of the national income in 1929.

No excess capacity studies of a similar scope have been undertaken during the post-war period. From such scattered data as are available it would seem, however, that even in the unprecedentedly prosperous years following the end of the Second World War excess capacity in American industry assumed tremendous proportions. Calculations by one investigator suggest that merely 55 per cent of capacity (conservatively

---

cf. J. Steindl, *Maturity and Stagnation in American Capitalism* (Oxford, 1952), pp. 4 ff., from which some sentences in the text above have been borrowed.

[1] *America's Capacity to Produce and America's Capacity to Consume* (Washington, 1943), p. 31.

[2] *ibid.*

estimated) was in use in the boom year 1952.[1] This does not include the prodigious quantities of food, the production of which is prevented by various control schemes, or which is allowed to spoil, to be destroyed, or fed to animals.

All estimates of capacity (and excess capacity) are highly tenuous. Apart from suffering from the inadequacy of the underlying statistical information they depend on what definition of capacity is adopted, on the degree of utilization that is assumed as 'normal', and on the extent to which market, demand, and profit considerations are taken into account in deciding on the magnitude of the excess. Yet difficulties encountered in the measurement of a phenomenon should not be permitted to obscure the existence of the phenomenon itself; in any case, they do not matter in the present context where our purpose is not to assess the magnitude of the potential economic surplus in any particular country at any particular time, but merely to outline the forms in which it exists.

Equally clearly discernible is the waste of resources caused by various aspects of monopoly and monopolistic competition. The potential economic surplus under this heading has never been analysed in its entirety, although its components have been frequently referred to in the literature. There is first and probably foremost the output foregone in view of underutilization of economies of scale stemming from irrational product differentiation. No one, to my knowledge, has undertaken to calculate the aggregate saving that would be realized if a great number of purely nominally different articles were to be standardized, and if their production were concentrated in technically the most efficient and economic plants. Whether we look at automobiles and other consumers' durable goods such as refrigerators, stoves, electrical appliances, and the like, or whether we think of products such as soaps, toothpastes, textiles, shoes, or breakfast foods, there can be little doubt that standardization and mass production could appreciably lower the unit costs of output. To be sure, instances can be found where even under monopolistic conditions firms are operating technologically optimal-size plants, where, in other words, no further economies of

---

[1] Lewis H. Robb, 'Industrial Capacity and Its Utilization', *Science and Society* (Fall 1953), pp. 318–25.

scale can be realized in the present state of technology. There is ample reason to believe, however, that such cases are relatively rare, and that limitations of the market for individual trademarks, and of capital available to individual firms, account for plant sizes that are less (and frequently considerably less) than what would be rational. The continuous existence and proliferation of small, inefficient, and redundant firms – not merely in industry but in particular in agriculture, distribution, and service trades – result in an amount of waste of human and material resources the magnitude of which can hardly be fully assessed.[1]

The multiplication of facilities and the squandering of resources called forth by irrational smallness of enterprises have their counterpart in the waste on the part of monopolistic giants who, shielded by their monopolistic positions, need not bother with minimizing costs or with maximizing efficiency. We have to consider in this connection the large so-called overhead costs of corporate business with their skyrocketing expense accounts, their exorbitant salaries paid to executives making no contribution to the firms' output but drawing revenues on the strength of their financial connections, personal influence, or character traits making them particularly adapted to corporate politics.

Nor should one overlook the imponderable but perhaps most valuable potential asset that is being systematically despoiled by monopolistic business: the human material ground up in the degrading, corrupting, and stultifying mill of vast corporate empires, and the ordinary man and woman whose entire upbringing and development are being warped and crippled by continuous exposure to the output, the propaganda, and the sales efforts of big business.[2]

---

[1] While even under emergency conditions only a relatively small part of this type of potential economic surplus is actually tapped, what has been accomplished on occasions suffices to indicate at least the dimensions of the problem involved. The wartime increase in output that resulted merely from concentration of production in large-scale plants, from the elimination of the most flagrant cases of duplication, cross-hauling, and inefficiency, was most impressive in the United States as well as in Great Britain and Germany.

[2] Not that Babbitt – the fittest participant in the 'rugged' competitive struggle for survival – who is idolized by some liberal economists and some old-fashioned Chambers of Commerce is a more

Even more elusive is the benefit to society that could be derived from scientific research if its conduct and exploitation were not subject to profit-oriented business control or armaments-oriented government control.[1]

This kind of support and administration of scientific work heavily influences its general outlook, its choice of subjects, and the methods that it employs. Demoralizing and disorienting scientists, depriving them of genuine stimuli for creative work, it hampers and distorts the development of science. Determining at the same time the mode of utilization of scientific achievements, it limits severely the benefits resulting from scientific progress. Whether in reference to atomic energy and to public

---

attractive human specimen than the 'modern' man described in David Riesman's *The Lonely Crowd*, in C. Wright Mills' *White Collar: The American Middle Classes*, in T. K. Quinn's *Giant Business*. There indeed would be little room for confidence in the future of the human race if these two types were the only ones to choose from.

[1] 'We know that under international cartel agreements, patents frequently served not as an incentive to investment but rather as a device for limiting production, establishing restricted market areas, limiting the rate of technical advancement, fixing prices, etc. We know that the pre-war Standard Oil–I G Farben marriage seriously retarded the development of a synthetic rubber industry in the United States. We know that Standard's concessions to Farben were, in large part, motivated by a desire to suppress the synthetic gasoline patents outside of Germany. We know that Du Pont's arrangements with I C I resulted in a division of world markets rather than a dynamic, competitive development of these markets. ... Investigations revealed ... that when Du Pont developed a pigment which could be utilized either in paints or as a textile dye, the director of one of its research laboratories wrote: "Further work may be necessary on adding contaminants to 'Monastral' colours to make them unsatisfactory on textiles but satisfactory for paints." The investigations described the Rohm & Haas research effort to discover a contaminant which would make methyl methacrylate suitable for use as a commercial moulding powder but unfit as an ingredient for dentures. The investigations told of the heroic effort by the General Electric research organization to shorten the life of flashlight batteries, etc.' (Walter Adams, *American Economic Review* (May 1954), p. 191.)

utilities, to substitutions among materials or to manufacturing processes, evidence abounds that the productive employment of technical possibilities is frequently and seriously stymied by the interests of the sponsors of technological research.

This myriad of more or less readily identifiable forms in which the potential economic surplus hides in the complex spiderweb of the capitalist economy has never been subjected to a systematic investigation, let alone a statistical assessment. Not that economists have not in the past attempted to expose the waste and irrationality permeating the capitalist order. They treated them, however, as imperfections and frictions of the system that could be overcome by suitable reforms, or as anachronistic residues from pre-capitalist times that could be expected to disappear in the course of capitalist development. Lately, as it has grown increasingly obvious that waste and irrationality, far from being fortuitous blemishes of capitalism, relate to its very essence, it has become fashionable to minimize the importance of the entire problem, to refer to it as a 'minor matter' which is of no concern to our age of plenty.[1]

The last but by no means least important is the *fourth* heading in our catalogue of the forms in which potential economic surplus is hidden in the capitalist economy. This is the output lost to society through unemployment of human and material resources caused partly by the inadequacy of co-ordination of productive facilities, but mainly by insufficiency of effective demand. Although it is very difficult, if not impossible, to disentangle those two causes of unemployment, imputing to each the share for which it is responsible, it is most useful for analytical purposes to keep them clearly apart. The former, usually referred to in economics as 'frictional' unemployment, was alluded to above. It appears as displacement of workers occasioned either by shifts in the composition of market demand or by the introduction of labour-saving devices of various kinds, accompanied by discarding of productive plant and equipment. While both the manpower and the facilities involved are capable

[1] This approach, suggested originally by Schumpeter, has been given wide currency by J. K. Galbraith's *American Capitalism* (Boston, 1952), where we read: '... the social inefficiency of a wealthy community grows with the growth of wealth that goes far to make this inefficiency inconsequential' (p. 103).

of being converted to useful employment and thus of being reintegrated into the productive process, in the capitalist economy such conversion, if it takes place at all, proceeds even under the most favourable circumstances with a great deal of delay and waste. Under conditions of rational planning such losses may not be entirely avoidable; they could, however, be greatly reduced.

More important still, in fact next to military spending the most important single cause for the continuous existence of a large gap between potential and actual surplus, is the unemployment resulting from insufficiency of effective demand. It affects both fully employable manpower and fully usable productive facilities, and, while varying in intensity from period to period, immobilizes a large proportion of the available human and material resources. The impact of this continuously present unemployment of productive potentialities is not adequately gauged by assessing and aggregating the differences between output in times of prosperity and times of depression. This procedure overlooks in the first place that even in most periods of so-called full employment there is not inconsiderable unemployment of labour and productive capacity, and secondly that even boom outputs are lower than what they could be if businesses were not constrained to reckon with bad years as well as with good years and to adjust accordingly their plans for production and investment. Thus calculations based merely on comparisons between outputs in different phases of the business cycle necessarily understate the volume of output lost through fluctuations in the level of employment.

Yet even such calculations, conservative as they are, present a picture sufficiently illustrative of the volume of potential economic surplus attributable to mass unemployment. For instance, Isador Lubin, then Commissioner of Labor Statistics, United States Department of Labor, stated in his testimony at the Hearings of the Temporary National Economic Committee (December 1, 1938): 'Assuming a working population of the size of 1929, you will note that if you add the employment lost in '30, '31, '32, up to 1938, the total number of man-years lost during that period of time was 43,435,000. Or, to put it in other words, if everybody who had worked in 1929 continued their employment during the past 9 years, all of us who were working could take a vacation for a year and 2 months and the loss in national income would be no greater than it has actually been.'[1] In terms of national income valued in 1929 prices the total loss amounted to $133 billion (as compared with the national income in 1929 of $81 billion).[2] This unemployment of man-power was accompanied by surplus capacity of productive facilities amounting in the aggregate to about 20 per cent 'at the peak', that is, in 1929, and to 'more than a third' at the time of the hearings, that is, in 1938.[3]

It should be remembered that Lubin's calculations were based on the assumptions that the working population remained con-stant from 1929 to 1938 and that its productivity also stayed un-changed during the entire period. In actual fact, as he himself realized, the working population had grown by 6 million, and output per capita would have grown at usual rates given more or less prosperous economic conditions. Taking this increase of employable manpower into account, and considering the rates of growth of productivity that were observed in the 1920s and that could have been expected to prevail in the 1930s, 'Dr L. H. Bean of the Department of Agriculture has estimated that the loss in national income has been $293 billion since 1929'.[4]

These calculations were carried to 1938 because that was the time the hearings were held. The conditions of underemploy-ment there depicted prevailed until the outbreak of the Second World War. The war mobilization demonstrated even more convincingly than all statistical computations how large a pro-ductive potential had been dormant in the American economy. As is well known, in the years of the war the United States was not merely able to raise a military establishment comprising over 12 million people, to produce a prodigious quantity of armaments, to supply its allies with large quantities of food and other goods, but to *increase* simultaneously the consumption of its civilian population. The entire war, in other words – the largest and most costly war in its history – was supported by the

[1] TNEC Investigation of Concentration of Economic Power, Hearings, Part 1 (Washington, 1939), p. 12.
[2] *ibid.*, p. 16.
[3] *ibid.*, p. 77.
[4] *ibid.*, testimony of Leon Henderson, p. 159.

United States by the mobilization of a *part* of its potential economic surplus.

It hardly needs stressing that the waste resulting from unemployment is neither an exclusively American phenomenon nor of merely historical interest. It can be readily observed at the present time, and it has been characteristic of the entire history of capitalism everywhere. While its magnitude has been different in different countries at different times, it always depressed total output considerably below what it could have been in a rationally organized society. Nor is the impact of unemployment adequately expressed in any measure of output foregone. No one can estimate the benefits to society that might have been realized, if the energy, the ability to work, the creative genius of the millions of unemployed had been harnessed for productive ends.

IV

If the potential economic surplus is a category of considerable scientific interest for the understanding of the irrationality of the capitalist order, and of major practical significance to a capitalist society under emergency conditions or facing the necessity of economic development, the *planned* economic surplus is relevant only to comprehensive economic planning under socialism. It is the difference between society's 'optimum' output attainable in an historically given natural and technological environment under conditions of planned 'optimal' utilization of all available productive resources, and some chosen 'optimal' volume of consumption. The meaning and contents of the 'optimum' involved are essentially different from those attached to this notion in bourgeois economics. They do not reflect a configuration of production and consumption determined by profit considerations of individual firms, by the income distribution, tastes, and social pressures of a capitalist order; they represent a considered judgment of a socialist community guided by reason and science. Thus as far as resource utilization is concerned, it implies a far-reaching rationalization of society's productive apparatus (liquidation of inefficient units of production, maximal economies of scale, etc.), elimination of redundant product differentiation, abolition of unproductive labour (as previously defined), a scientific policy of conservation of human and natural resources, and the like.

Nor does this 'optimum' presuppose the maximization of output that might be attainable in a country at any given time. It may well be associated with a less than maximum output in view of a voluntarily shortened labour day, of an increase in the amount of time devoted to education, or of conscious discarding of certain noxious types of production (coal-mining, for example). What is crucial is that the volume of output would not be determined by the fortuitous outcome of a number of unco-ordinated decisions on the part of individual businessmen and corporations, but by a rational plan expressing what society would wish to produce, to consume, to save, and to invest at any given time.[1]

Furthermore the 'optimum' husbandry of resources in a socialist economy does not call by any means for reduction of consumption to merely what is essential. It can and will go together with a level of consumption that is considerably higher than what the criterion of essentiality might suggest. Again, what is decisive is that the level of consumption and therefore also the volume of the actually generated surplus would not be

---

[1] That a planned economy could easily dispose of the most striking irrationality of the capitalist system – unemployment caused by insufficient demand – is most succinctly shown by M. Kalecki: 'It is useful to consider what the effect of a reduction in investment in a socialist system would be. The workers released from the production of investment goods would be employed in consumption goods industries. The increased supply of these goods would be absorbed by means of a reduction in their prices. Since profits of the socialist industries would be equal to investment, prices would have to be reduced to the point where the decline in profits would be equal to the fall in the value of investment. In other words, full employment would be maintained through the reduction of prices in relation to costs. In the capitalist system, however, the price–cost relationship ... is maintained and profits fall by the same amount as investment plus capitalists' consumption through the reduction in output and employment. It is indeed paradoxical that, while the apologists of capitalism usually consider the "price mechanism" to be the great advantage of the capitalist system, price flexibility proves to be a characteristic feature of the socialist economy.' (*Theory of Economic Dynamics* (London, 1954), pp. 62 ff.)

determined by the mechanism of profit maximization but by a rational plan reflecting the society's preference as to current consumption versus future consumption. Therefore the economic surplus under socialism may be smaller or larger than the actual economic surplus under capitalism, or may even be equal to zero if society should choose to refrain from net investment. It would depend on the stage that has been reached in the historical process, on the degree of development of productive resources, on the structure and growth of human needs.

## SELECTED BIBLIOGRAPHY

BARAN, PAUL. 'Economic Progress and Economic Surplus', *Science and Society*: Vol. XVII, No. 4, 1953.

BARAN, PAUL, and SWEEZY, P. M. *Monopoly Capital*. New York: *Monthly Review*, 1966.

HOROWITZ, DAVID. 'Analysing the Surplus', *Monthly Review*. January 1967.

MANDAL, ERNEST. 'The Labor Theory of Value and "Monopoly Capital"' *International Socialist Review*. July–August 1967.

O'CONNOR, James. 'Monopoly Capital', *New Left Review*. November–December 1966.

# Index

# Index of Authorities and Publications

Subject Index

# MONTHLY REVIEW

## an independent socialist magazine
## edited by Paul M. Sweezy and Harry Magdoff

*Business Week:* ". . . a brand of socialism that is thorough-going and tough-minded, drastic enough to provide the sharp break with the past that many left-wingers in the underdeveloped countries see as essential. At the same time they maintain a sturdy independence of both Moscow and Peking that appeals to neutralists. And their skill in manipulating the abstruse concepts of modern economics impresses would-be intellectuals. . . . Their analysis of the troubles of capitalism is just plausible enough to be disturbing."

*Bertrand Russell:* "Your journal has been of the greatest interest to me over a period of time. I am not a Marxist by any means as I have sought to show in critiques published in several books, but I recognize the power of much of your own analysis and where I disagree I find your journal valuable and of stimulating importance. I want to thank you for your work and to tell you of my appreciation of it."

*The Wellesley Department of Economics:* " . . . the leading Marxist intellectual (not Communist) economic journal published anywhere in the world, and is on our subscription list at the College library for good reasons."

*Albert Einstein:* "Clarity about the aims and problems of socialism is of greatest significance in our age of transition. . . . I consider the founding of this magazine to be an important public service." (In his article, "Why Socialism" in Vol. I, No. 1.)

DOMESTIC: $11 for one year, $20 for two years, $9 for one-year student subscription.

FOREIGN: $13 for one year, $23 for two years, $10 for one-year student subscription. (Subscription rates subject to change.)

62 West 14th Street, New York, New York 10011

## Modern Reader Paperbacks